MOMISM

MOMISM

The Silent Disease
of America

Hans Sebald

Nelson Hall nh *Chicago*

Library of Congress Cataloging in Publication Data

Sebald, Hans.
    Momism : the silent disease of America.

    Includes bibliographical references and indexes.
    1. Mothers. 2. Mother and child. 3. Children
in the United States. I. Title.
    HQ759.S42   301.42'7   75-45223
    ISBN 0-88229-275-7

Manufactured in the United States of America

To Betty Friedan and Philip Wylie

who described the same
phantom, one from the
inside and the other
from the outside.

Contents

Preface   ix

1. Introduction: The Contours of Momism   1
2. The Rise of Momism   19
3. The Middle Class: Breeding Ground for Momism   41
4. The Vulnerability of the Boy   85
5. Types and Techniques of Moms   123
6. The Consequences of Momism   169
7. Prevention, Cure—and Other Optimisms   239
   Epilogue: Children Learn What They Live   289
   Notes   291
   Name Index   305
   Subject Index   309

Preface

This preface has three purposes: to say a word about
the style and structure of the book, to expose the perils of
writing about the subject at hand, and to express gratitude.

I visualize the audience of the book as primarily the
so-called *layman* and not, particularly, the small academic circle of sociologists, psychologists, anthropologists, and their students. Hence an effort was made to
keep the style of communicating the vital processes of the
problem clear and free from undue technical jargon. Although this book is perfectly suitable for adoption in college courses of a wide variety—especially psychology,
sociology, anthropology, home economics, family life, and
education—it is hoped that people who are not involved
in academia will find it interesting and helpful.

Hopefully, the arrangement of the chapters will help
the reader recognize the systematic investigation that is
attempted here. The work tries, step by step, to build a
perspective on the issue of Momism—a type of motherhood that is immensely detrimental to the well-being of

the child. It begins with a general statement of what Momism is and does, continues with a discussion of its historical roots, examines the conducive setting of middle-class America, emphasizes the greater vulnerability of the boy vis-à-vis the girl, delves into the details of the sly techniques employed by the destructive mother, surveys the range of problems incurred by the victim of Momism, and, finally, suggests preventive measures.

The perils involved in writing about Momism are many. With some degree of arbitrariness, they can be classified into two areas. Because this book is the first attempt to present Momism in a systematic and integrated manner, it is an exploratory effort, and "pioneer" efforts tend to reflect shortcomings that are characteristic of first attempts and usually become noticeable only later, when more evidence concerning the subject matter has accrued. The first peril is therefore a certain degree of simplification, which appears unavoidable if the goal is the ordering and overall understanding of the otherwise utterly unintegrated material.

Second, writing about American motherhood has a way of stirring up controversy. After all, motherhood—or, as Betty Friedan and others put it, the Motherhood Myth—is still protected by the cultural taboo against criticism and negative depiction. Although this book in no way tries to debunk motherhood in general, and instead chooses to focus selectively on a particular type of mothering, it may nevertheless find itself under the wrath of American mothers who interpret it as an attack on their hallowed institution.

I am indebted to a number of colleagues, friends, and students who, through encouragement and/or critical examination of the first drafts of these chapters, have added clarification and insight. It goes especially to the credit of some of my students that I started writing the manuscript. Knowing from my lectures and previous writing that I have interest in the problem, they encouraged me to write a book about it. To them I pay special thanks because they helped me overcome the hedonistic inertia that is opposed to the hard work of writing. In this context, I gratefully mention Marina Ynez Martinez, Michelle Zelkovitz, Theresa A. McCabe, Carolyn Sue Lindsey and Kenneth Einbinder.

I am particularly indebted to Professor Richard H. Nagasawa, to my assistant Andrew J. Kwiatkowski, Jr., and to Alan R. Austin for their critical evaluations of the first drafts of the chapters. To Patti Delano goes my appreciation for competently typing the manuscript.

I am further indebted to a number of my students (who shall understandably remain anonymous) who came to me with very personal reports about their intimate experiences with the Momistic curse. For most of them, becoming acquainted with the concept of Momism was an eye-opening revelation: for the first time in their lives, they clearly recognized the hitherto vague and hidden symptoms of the malaise in their own personalities. The Silent Disease was suddenly revealed! The discovery gave them the courage to speak to me about their problems, anxieties, and unhappiness. They, in turn, gave me permission to share their stories with the readers of this book, and their case histories are found throughout Chapters 5 and 6.

I hope that these young adults, suffering from the crippling aftermath of their exposure to a stifling Mom, have benefited from opening their hearts to me. I also hope that their sharing will be of benefit to the unknown many who suffer equally, and happen to come across this book. May they derive insight and comfort from these pages.

H. S.

Chapter 1

*It is short-sighted view indeed to consider
the immature wife, dominating mother, or
interfering mother-in-law as a less serious
problem to the larger society than the male
homosexual, psychoneurotic soldier, or
ineffectual worker, for it is the failure of the
mother which perpetuates the cycle from one
generation to the next.*—Alice S. Rossi

Introduction: The Contours of Momism

The "star" of this book is the type of mother who is
an expert in personality assassination. Her art of ambush
resides and specializes in playing the "good" mother, and
she goes about her stealthy business with impunity and,
indeed, social reward. Her name is Mom, and her in-
trigues are called Momism.

From the very beginning, we must make clear that
the word Momism is not name calling but is a definite
concept referring to the situation where a child incurs
emotional pathologies because of exposure to a mother
who is afflicted with a particular type of neurosis. The
situation will leave the child with immature and undeveloped emotions. This will happen, in most instances,
without the handicap's becoming apparent to the casual
observer. It resembles an insidious disease whose masked
symptoms do not reveal themselves until a later age.

1

This book is an exposé of Momism. It is *not* a polemic that tries to degrade the time-honored institution of motherhood, but a systematic investigation of a revered institution that is rapidly going defunct. We have had enough tirades, attacks, and other emotional prose lashing out at American motherhood over the past years. Enough temperamental punches like Philip Wylie's *Generation of Vipers* and Philip Roth's *Portnoy's Complaint*[1] have been delivered. It is time for a cool and clear examination of all the vipers and the complaints. No attempt will be made to dazzle the reader with either academic or grandiloquent style; rather, we present a straightforward discussion not only of scattered clinical cases of sick motherhood but what looks like an epidemic of perverted motherliness.

The terrible harm that this type of mother is able to wreak needs attention and exposure. One can only speculate on the reasons why the problem has not received more objective attention until now. Perhaps one reason is that we are dealing with a sacrosanct institution and that criticism of it violates a long-standing American cultural taboo. The very fact that this is a book about the American mother may in itself raise a fundamental objection: although it seems acceptable to give advice to mothers, a severe, searching analysis of motherhood is something else. Many perceive it as unkind, unwise, and un-American. In short, it constitutes a threat. While maligning a father begets indifference, maligning a mother begets outrage.

Another reason is the dramatic flair with which the typical Mom often covers her ulterior motives. In fact, she covers them so well that even she is hardly aware of what she is *really* doing, which can be frightening. What she sees, when she looks at herself, is an immaculate image of a "good mother." Moreover, her maternal pursuits are gullibly supported by the community, which encourages and rewards her "motherly" endeavors. This is a welcome reinforcement and incentive for Mother to carry on. In fact, Mother's appetite is whetted by the promise of praise and laurels for a "well raised" child. In pursuit of this goal, she rapaciously devours the budding self-confidence and self-worth of her helpless offspring.

Still another reason why investigation of maternal corruption has been tardy has to do with the seeming harmlessness of Mom's style of child raising. It seems to be all the more harmless because the victim usually manifests the pathetic consequences later in life, when he is removed from his Mom. Before that time, the symptoms often lie deep but unrecognized. This is why we have chosen to call it the Silent Disease. This is also the reason why we so often observe the puzzling, paradoxical spectacle in which the "best" mothers produce some of the "worst" children.

This book, then, should be read by anyone who is interested in better understanding the intricate connections between a woman's ambitions and her child's failures. Perhaps more importantly, it scrutinizes the social and psychological conditions which create mothers who, against their will, make psychological wrecks of their own children—*particularly boys*. It is only when these dangerous conditions are understood that they can be changed, and that thousands of young boys and their mothers can be freed to grow into healthy, mature citizens.

Let us now delve into a thorough examination of the problem—a problem held so surprisingly secret in our society that it almost appears as if American culture had stamped it "Classified Information"! The aim of this work is to declassify it. In overall terms, the book starts out by designing a systematic framework within which the causes of the malaise can be understood—in Chapters 1 through 4. Then the work takes a more descriptive and

colorful turn and presents numerous case histories—
throughout Chapters 5 and 6. Finally, suggestions—
sometimes bordering on bold optimisms—concerning prevention and cure of the Silent Disease are made in Chapter 7. Readers who are interested in innovative social policy may find this concluding chapter particularly challenging.

Neuroses in Sequence

What is a neurosis? A neurosis emerges in a situation where unresolved conflict or deep-rooted uncertainty
(especially if it is about one's own self) causes considerable anxiety, tension, and unhappiness. As a consequence,
the person engages in excessive defense tactics. It is important to realize that these tactics have the potential of
severely hurting and curtailing the happiness of others—
particularly if those others, for some reason, come to depend upon the neurotic individual. The outcome of this
type of situation may well show that the dependent person has likewise acquired a neurosis, although it may
appear quite different from that of the relied-upon person.

This definition of the neurotic situation all too often
applies to the mother-child relationship. It can be called
a Momistic situation. Such a mother, for reasons discussed later, tends to suffer profound conflict and discontent concerning her place in life. Her relentless search
for self-meaning causes her to have doubts about whether
the wife-mother role and the daily activities associated
with it are really meant for her. Often she suffers deep
disappointments and frustrations about being limited to
the wife-mother role. It is important to understand that
these emotional dynamics are not on the mother's awareness level; rather, they are *unconscious* processes.

Because of these doubts and frustrations, the mother
seeks compensation through trying to become a "perfect"

mother, and in the process *uses* her child as an indication of her *success*. The child, in turn, acquires deep anxieties and uncertainties about his basic self-worth, and his mental health is undermined. Commonly understood standards of mental health include a person's ability to care for himself and others and to engage in productive work —which implies, and requires, the ability to make decisions that a mature person should not expect others to make for him. And this is the most characteristic defect of the Momistically impaired person: he is incapable of making his own decisions and becomes extremely dependent. As a consequence, he tends to engage in irresponsible behavior, because the "gyroscope" of judgment and guidance is not within him but outside him, making him an easy prey of persuasion and indoctrination. If these forces of influence are irresponsible, the emotionally undeveloped individual will follow suit and act irresponsibly, perhaps even cruelly, and without thought for the consequences.

This dependency neurosis of the mother is as powerful as an addiction, making the child's loyalty and obedience the substance of her craving. In turn, the mother succeeds in getting the child addicted to her. Some psychologists want this to be understood as more than a metaphor; they don't mean to say that this dependency is *like* an addiction, but that it *is* an addiction.[2] Such sick dependency exhibits all the symptoms of drug addiction: the need for the regular "fix," the tolerance level, the withdrawal symptoms, the immaturity growing out of exclusively and compulsively adhering to the one avenue of seeking ways to overcome problems and satisfy security needs.

All mothers are powerful agents who occupy, even under normal circumstances, psychological power positions vis-à-vis their children that are rarely equaled by any other position or attempt at influence. Therefore a

critical approach to motherhood, with intent to examine
those aspects that can result in immense harm and crippling effects, is more than justified; indeed, it is overdue.
(This should, of course, in no way obscure the fact that
the influence of a mother, when exerted through normal
and healthy maternal care, is of utmost benefit to the individual child and the total society.) It is surprising that
social scientists have neglected to fully explore and, above
all, meaningfully *integrate* those aspects of motherhood
which are of such extreme detriment to the unfortunate
offspring. Hence the major contribution of this book is
to gather these separate, unintegrated ideas and observations and to present a coherent picture of a most vital issue of modern American life.

It must be reiterated that, typically, a child bears the
effects of Momism in a latent and rather invisible way.
At the core of the Momistically induced pathology lies the
child's—and later (and more obviously) the adult's—
inability to achieve a normal degree of self-reliance, make
his own decisions, form independent opinions, acquire
self-confidence, and engage in responsible behavior. These
traits are generally recognized as normal adult characteristics, and their absence in a child is, of course, usually
not noticed—*precisely because the normally expected
childlike behavior in our society does not require manifestation of such "grown up" traits.* In fact, we expect
the behavior of a child to reflect a low degree of self-
reliance and self-confidence; and we prefer to make
most, if not all, important decisions for him.

Momistically caused emotional deficiencies can conceal themselves perfectly behind childlike behavior patterns. It may indeed be this type of emotionally crippled
child who has the appearance of a well-behaved and pliable youngster. It is not until he grows older, and adult
demands are leveled at him, that the pathological condi-

tion reveals itself. *The young adult has retained the emotions, attitudes, and behavior patterns of the child.* And *this* is the core effect of the Momistic situation. Under the facade of good and compliant behavior, childlike immaturity has persisted; now, however, it no longer appears childlike—it has become childish, immature, and irresponsible. Often, profound anxiety accompanies this immaturity, and a consuming preoccupation develops to be accepted and "loved" by others.

In sum, then, "neuroses in sequence" refers to the situation where a deeply troubled mother—showing enough personality turmoil to justify the label *neurotic*—imposes her problems on the child and attempts to obtain compensation and alleviation through him. Thus, in the course of raising him, she instills enough anxiety and complexes to create—ironically—another neurosis.

Mom as a Social Problem

One could raise the question why the negative aspects of motherhood have not yet been thoroughly examined and exposed. The answer would have to consider that motherhood has been a hallowed and sacred tradition in American life, safeguarded by taboo against attack. Like an age-old fetishism, motherhood has always been regarded as something that cannot possibly go awry. This traditional view has delayed the investigation of the status of mother and her psychological transactions. Another reason is very simple. It has been only recently—if one or two generations may be called recent in American history—that the phenomenon of Momism has started to spread and become a noticeable problem.

The early attention to the problem can hardly be classified as scientific. The traditional American perception of motherhood, ever so Utopian, was initially shaken by playwrights, polemists, and feminists who tried to shatter the naive and unrealistic monument that had been erected for the American mother. Probably the earliest publicity given to Mom, with the Momistic connotation as used today, came from Sidney C. Howard in the form of a play, a comedy-satire called *The Silver Cord.*[3] In her 1928 work, the playwright depicted the mother as a possessive and manipulative Mom who wants to live through her child, although her intention is subtly and unwittingly concealed under the guise of "sacrificing" herself for the child.

Far wider publicity for Mom (actually *against* Mom) was secured by Philip Wylie's controversial *Generation of Vipers* (1942). This represented (unfortunately in somewhat hyperbolic form) a cynical debunking of a traditional optimism by trying to expose what the author felt was the psychological bankruptcy of motherhood in urban-industrial society. Wylie insisted that American motherhood had become a social problem. He felt that during preceding generations the American mother had been so preoccupied with raising a large family and running a cumbersome household that "she was rarely a problem to her family or to her equally busy friends, and never one to herself." It was Wylie who, by and large, became known as the discoverer of Momism: who named it, focused attention on it, and encouraged examination of the issue in a more scientific vein.[4]

Another writer who examined the mystique of motherhood is Betty Friedan. In her scathing but honest and forthright book *The Feminine Mystique,* her exposé included not only the feminine myth but also the Motherhood Myth.[5] In her opinion, the Motherhood Myth reflects a pathological, overcompensatory attitude.

It is interesting to note that this myth flourished at a time in American history when many mothers entered the first phases of emancipation, the struggle for freedom and equality. But the visions of the ideal were sadly curbed by an inert social structure that had a tendency to trap them, in spite of "higher" aspirations, in the conventional wife-mother role. To compensate for being caught in an undesirable arrangement, they developed the need to see something mystical in being a mother. This need was profound because it stemmed from the basic craving to establish self-worth. Thus the Motherhood Myth evolved as a compensatory myth to counteract the frustrations that came with the dawn of women's emancipation.

It was this type of attack, as illustrated by Howard, Wylie, and Friedan, that heralded the demise of the image of motherhood as an infallible source of kindness and benefit. As has happened so often in the history of the social sciences—as probably in all sciences—image-shattering accusations preceded the more objective, cooler analysis of a problem. This heated iconoclasm is particularly noticeable if the problem deals with an honored position, a human relationship protected since time immemorial, which suddenly shows signs of malfunction.

Mom and Her Tactics

The central technique that a mother, hereafter defined as Mom, employs throughout her child-rearing activities consists of *conditional love*. This means she tries to manipulate the child by extending acceptance and love on a conditional basis. It is important to understand that this manipulation of love and acceptance pertains to the child as a *total person*, not just to the specific act of behavior that is under consideration. Thus a typical Mom would not say "I don't like (or love) *what* you are doing" but, instead, "Mother won't love *you* if you do that." One immediately recognizes that this approach provides a most powerful and usually very successful *lever* to make the child obedient and malleable to the wishes and demands of the parent.

This technique works, of course, only when the child is first made to believe that mother's love *is* the most important thing in his life, without which he would be lost and unhappy. The typical Mom is skillful in instilling this belief in the child. So profoundly can a child be conditioned by this emotional premise that he will look upon his mother's love as the ultimate source of security. In the process, mother's love and mother's authority become virtually synonymous. This means that the way Mom extends her love is really her way of exerting authority. And, most likely, she will be singularly successful: the child will be manipulated toward greater manageability and dependence through this method than through physical force or punishment. In fact, once the psychological mechanism that makes Momism possible is installed in the mind of the child, manipulative efforts become easy, routine, and their results quite predictable.

Rarely, however, does a mother who preys on her child come straight out and say, "If you don't please me, I won't love you." Rather, she disguises the trick of putting conditional love to work under a variety of diabolically colorful stratagems. Direct and open application of the conditional love technique would expose her true motives; and the unmasking of her "motherliness" is one thing she can neither endure nor afford. Her goal, which is the total subjugation of the child, is something she wants to hide from herself as well as others. She clings to a "good mother" image, and hence carries out her dismal transactions without being aware that they are so detrimental to the child.

Moms have been using a fascinating array of masking styles. The "overprotective," "martyr," "star," and "child worshiping" Moms are particularly intriguing examples. They can occur anywhere in our society, but their favorite spawning grounds seem to be in the middle class.

All this is not to say that Momism is strictly an American disease; studies have also found the malaise in other countries. For example, many Mexican mothers, particularly in the urban middle class, succeed in tying their children to their apron strings by combining the "martyr" and "overprotective" styles.[6] Japanese mothers have been known for their remarkable skill in being "martyrs to motherhood," and in the process create a guilt-ridden slave: a son who is apt to do almost anything to be delivered from his profound guilt feelings.[7]

This book, however, is primarily an examination of the American scene and focuses on the American Mom and her cunning styles of disguising a gruesome strategy behind the facade of "good mothering."

Momism and Its Consequences
Probably the most serious and lasting effect of Momism in later life is the victim's tendency to crave external authority as the ultimate instance of guidance whenever he is confronted with questions, decision-making, and tasks of any significance. He is absolutely unequipped for making personal decisions and, in essence, looks for surrogate Moms to tell him what to do. This type of man is inclined to marry a woman who will exploit his overdependence and make decisions for him. In other words, his wife becomes a substitute Mom—a horrifying prospect indeed.

Not only does he have a dire need to be guided, he has an even more extreme need to be approved when he makes a decision or completes a job. He craves the reassurance of being acceptable and "loved." The extent to which Momistically impaired persons go in trying to achieve a feeling of belonging, being approved of, being "loved"—in short, feeling secure—is truly fascinating. It is not only the degree of extremity to which the afflicted person resorts to assure himself of a margin of security which fascinates the investigator, but also the rich variety of attempts to achieve this goal. Chapters 5 and 6 will sample the spectrum and present numerous examples and case studies: drug addiction, homosexuality, mental disorders, suicide, and even the True Believer, whose Mom has been metamorphosed into a radical movement or ideology which he endorses with fanatic and unquestioning loyalty.

The dynamics of this process, including Mom's manipulation and the child's attitude formation, proceed largely on an unconscious level. The long-range psychological effects, especially the induced pathologies, are likely the unintended consequences of a child-rearing technique that was efficient and expedient at the time. One could rarely accuse a Mom of *willfully* trying to harm her child. Chances are that a mother who qualifies as a Mom would probably not only be very astonished but unbelieving if one could point out to her that her style of child raising inflicts severe psychological damage on the child. She might, in fact, use her very own product and point to her child, who reflects an unswerving obedience syndrome, to defend her style and technique of child rearing. She might point out, with considerable pride, that he is doing quite well in school, "stays out of trouble," and "loves" his mother. It might be very difficult to convince such a Mom that the malignant consequences of her conditional love technique will appear later in life —consequences that can take manifold expressions and stubbornly resist change and therapy attempts.

Observations, many of them purely spinoffs from other research, have shown that the major pathogenic figure behind many drug addicts, homosexuals, and True Believers is Mom, albeit functioning unconsciously so. This conclusion has been drawn by a number of psychiatric experts diagnosing patients, sociologists carrying out surveys, social workers preparing case studies, clergymen trying to save souls, and law-enforcement personnel trying to curb crime. In its earlier historical stage, this conclusion might have been more properly described as a suspicion, a sort of educated guess not yet worthy of full credence. Gradually, however, the guessing game was replaced by more substantial findings and insights. A more trustworthy identification of the underlying cause of confused, anxiety-ridden, overly dependent, and potentially unhappy human beings has been achieved and has brought the Utopian image of motherhood under attack and more careful scientific examination.

The Role of the Father

In the process of preparing this book, consideration was given to an alternative approach to Momism. It was thought that a *direct* criticism of Momistic practices, a "frontal attack," would give rise to acute defensiveness on the part of mothers who read these pages—mothers who are not necessarily Moms. These mothers might feel that this treatment is just another criticism of their difficult job of raising their children. Thought was therefore given to avoid outraging the mothers' sensibilities and approach the subject through the role of the father. (Momistic practices have a chance to develop *only* if the father does not share the responsibilities and daily chores of helping the child to grow up.) Since Momism works only if the father is remote or removed from the socialization process *and* if the mother starts out with pertinent neurotic inclinations, it would be possible to broach the question of Momism by focusing on the mother's activity *or* the father's inactivity. In the latter case, we would introduce the issue in a roundabout way, through a sort of side door. The outcomes—recognizing and describing the emotional impairment of the child—would probably be identical. Hence shifting the focus of inquiry to the father would be a logical alternative to analyzing and understanding the issue of Momism.

But the idea to opt for the circuitous route was abandoned. This decision, besides being a matter of the author's temperament, is rationally justified insofar as the mother-child relationship is the *immediate* problem and the father-child relationship, or its desired modification, constitutes the *solution* to the problem. We believe greater fruitfulness and clarity of analysis can be gained by first describing the problem, then tracing the causes, and finally suggesting a remedy or preventive.

Focus: The Mother-Son Relationship

Momism is a selective process, and it makes a difference whether the child is a girl or a boy. From all available evidence, it appears that *a boy is much more vulnerable to the effects of Momism than a girl.* While the girl can identify with Mom—and ultimately become a Mom herself—the boy may not identify with the authority figure. He learns that he may not use mother as a model, that he is to grow into a different type of person. Since he believes that it is generally taboo to imitate mother, he comes to include power-wielding in the not-to-be-imitated category. In other words, the boy associates the wielding of power over people with the female gender.

Mom represents an absolute authority and guiding principle to which he must surrender, without holding the slightest prospect that he may one day assume this type of authority himself. The roles he is expected to play in life are introduced to him primarily through female authority. His identity formation proceeds not, as in the case of his sister, through imitation and *direct* identification but through an infinitely more abstract and *indirect* learning process. He is severely limited in *actually* seeing what he is supposed to be or become; he is *told* what to be. His exposure to absolute authority, without the opportunity to share in it, renders the boy helpless and wide open to the indoctrination process at hand. Although the most plausible assumption concerning the outcome of a Momistically exposed female child is that she will imitate her mother and become a Mom herself, the alternative possiblility should be examined briefly. (A rough estimate would be that the ratio of a Mom's victims is about one girl to fifty boys; therefore most illustrations deal with boys—but there is an interesting exception in Chapter 5.) If Mom *should* succeed in having a suppressive and stifling impact on the girl, the personality damage would hardly show up as a problem. The effects, later in life, would be found to be in line with feminine submissiveness and dependence. Unlike the judgment the public renders on the stifled personality of the boy, the stifled personality of the girl can travel under the flag of femininity. Her personality style would not be interpreted as abnormal or immature, since her subservient, compliant, and nondecisive manner would fit perfectly into the traditional and expected role of a woman. Hence it would not be defined as a pathology.

In sum, then, we are better equipped to substantiate the claim that Momism cripples the emotions of the boy more frequently and to a greater degree than those of the girl. The pronoun "he," when referring to the child throughout this book, is therefore in line with this focus.

Understanding Momism

This book, which reconnoiters the process and dynamics of the Momistic situation, does not present a specific research, as a research monograph would do, but an integrated and systematic approach that will convey a basic understanding of the Momistic malaise and determine the common dimensions and characteristics of the process. The value of this book may be seen in its attempt to *integrate* and *interpret* knowledge and research findings, rather than as another isolated, specific, and narrow study. To accomplish this purpose, an array of hopefully pertinent ideas, observations, and studies is presented, whose sources are psychiatrists, psychologists, sociologists, social workers, medical doctors, educators, clergymen, law-enforcement officers, court documents, and numerous case histories of Moms' victims.

The statistical incidence of Momism among American mothers is at best an intelligent guess, but the suspicion seems justified that it is increasing in rate and number—most probably in direct correlation with the further rise and development of urban-industrial conditions. (A discussion of these conditions is presented in Chapter 2.) More and more case studies reveal that the genesis of neurotic problems can be traced to the neurotic problems of the mother. In turn, investigations have discovered that the causes of the neurotic problems of these mothers are intricately tied to the conditions of urban-industrial living and our emancipated and egalitarian culture. The grim logic of the argument, therefore, is that the further evolving of certain urban-industrial conditions will create greater numbers of neurotic mothers, who, consequently, will create increasing numbers of neurotic offspring. This societal process has been going on for at least one or two generations.

The incidence of Momism is therefore not only a *psychological* problem, dealing with the individual, but also a *sociological* problem, involving the conditions of society. Indeed, it is a very specific sociological issue, since its occurrence is not randomly distributed throughout society but depends largely on membership in certain social classes. It appears mainly in the American middle class, where urban-industrial factors combine to prepare the ground for Momism. A number of social and psychological factors, and a peculiar interrelationship among them, prevail in the middle-class setting, which makes it easy for Momism to flourish.

These conditions include the psychological peculiarity of the halfway-emancipated mother, the remoteness of the father from the child-raising process, the existence of only one child in the family (or, at most, two children), the "educated" and objectified approach to the mother-child relationship, parents' excessive sensitivity to community standards, parental endorsement of competition as a method for raising a "successful" child, the frequency of the situation in which the mother is a divorcee, and the absence of a "rite of passage" for the growing offspring that could promote his self-definition and independence at and above a certain age. (The middle-class situation and these conditions will be discussed in detail in Chapter 3.)

If these social-psychological circumstances are the prime movers in the rise of Momism, it follows that societies that acquire these characteristics will also acquire Momism. This logic is especially relevant to the advancing urban-industrial societies, because they are rapidly acquiring and adopting the conditions and life-styles of urban-industrial living that are now commonplace in the United States.

Let us now turn to the next chapter and examine the roots of Momism and trace the various dimensions of its growth.

Chapter 2

*As we see it, the American father either
abdicated or was pushed out of his position
as head of the family during the process of
female emancipation. In a sense, he was
kicked upstairs, as they say in industry, and
was made chairman of the board. As such he
did not lose all of his power—he still had to
be consulted on important decisions—but his
wife emerged as the executive director or
manager of the enterprise which is called
the family.*—E. E. LeMasters

The Rise of Momism

Although Momism is a relatively new phenomenon
on the American scene, the contours of its historical evolution and gradually emerging in the wake of present-day
turbulence and are clarifying the myopic conditions imposed by its immediacy and closeness in time. Enough
years have passed to allow us to recognize the social and
psychological circumstances that have encouraged this
distinct style of motherhood. As with many other societal
processes, no definite point in time can be identified as
the birth year of Momism. It is safe, however, to think
of its development as having stretched over the past two
generations. To make certain that the initial develop-
ments of the Momistic evolution are covered, we will look
at the American family of several generations ago, when

19

it was largely free from "practicing Moms." Then we will trace the sociocultural changes that have brought about the Momistic style of child raising.

Motherhood before the Rise of "Moms"

The traditional role of the mother used to be rather narrowly confined to the nurturing functions of the home. This confinement was born of the necessity for a mother to render time-consuming services, many of which are today taken over either by nonfamilial institutions or advanced technological appliances. For example, only a small portion of the modern family's food supply is grown, preserved, and readied for "instant" consumption by the housewife herself. "Instantness oriented" American industry takes care of such steps.

Family sociologist William J. Goode reminds us, however, that these new techniques should not be equated with a reduction of the overall time investment a modern housewife makes in homemaking.[1] While some appliances may reduce the time needed to do a *specific* chore, the modern homemaker feels compelled to accomplish many more chores than her grandmother. Standards for cleanliness, hygiene, repair, and comfort have increased to the point where it takes a formidable array of appliances to meet the raised expectations. So more jobs, with speedier appliances, appear to add up to the same time investment as the former fewer chores that needed more time for their completion. Furthermore, past generations of homemakers availed themselves of more domestic help and lower-class labor for a number of chores, such as laundry and sewing, than today's typical housewife.

Most importantly, the modern housewife devotes herself to a deliberate style of child raising, and tries to "spend time" with the child. Likewise, she tries to "spend time" on social and civic activities—considerably expanding the domain of the traditional homemaker. Also, the objects in the home have become so numerous that the middle-class housewife must spend appreciable time in ministering to them. Many of these objects, though designed to save her time, have turned out to require so much care, cleaning, and repair that they consume as much time as they promised to save. A vacuum cleaner, for example, may help keep the house cleaner, but it really hasn't shortened the working hours.

In short, higher standards of living, especially in respect to cleanliness, luxury, child rearing, and civic activities, probably keep the modern homemaker as busy as her grandmother—in spite of the modern labor-saving devices. She now turns her attention to an impressive range of "domestic production"—including "production" of the child's "proper" personality.

When reference is made to the traditional family, the focus is primarily on rural living. For example, in 1800 more than 90 percent of the United States population was rural. This proportion consistently declined, to 85 percent in 1850 and 60 percent in 1900. In the 1920s, the United States Bureau of the Census started to distinguish between the rural-farm and the rural-nonfarm population and found that only 30 percent of the nation's population were farm people. The proportion decreased further: to 23 percent in 1940, 15 percent in 1950, 9 percent in 1960, and 6 percent in 1965.[2]

Membership in the traditional household was not limited to "nuclear" members (parents and their offspring) but tended to include grandparents, uncles, aunts, and cousins. A child who grew up within the large family group was in close association with a number of blood relatives who included adults as well as children. In addition, there often were nonrelatives, such as maids and farmhands, who were looked upon as members of the family. But the larger size of the early family was primarily due to parents' having more children. In all, it made for a considerably larger family unit than the typical modern nuclear family. This is reflected in family statistics, which show that the average number of persons per family household was nearly six in 1850, declined to about five in 1900, and dwindled to a little over three in the 1960s.[3]

Due to the size of the household and the work load of the adults, parents found little opportunity to take time out to consciously and individually counsel and exert influence over their offspring. Instead, the major interaction and process of growing up occurred among the children themselves—which again reminds us that the number of children born into a family can play a critical role with respect to the style of child raising. Siblings were important sources of fundamental education for each other. This did not rule out the role of adults as models; they were clearly visible in their daily life and work, and could be emulated—or, sometimes, rejected with near impunity, since selectivity was possible among a large number of men and women.

Conditions of the Nuclear Family

In the small family of today the situation is quite different. A child has no selectivity in models on which he can pattern his attitudes and, ultimately, his role identity; he has only one member of each sex for use as a role model. If the model or role teacher is unacceptable to the child—and this may happen for myriad reasons—it is just too bad for the child. He is "trapped" in a small and relatively isolated family unit and has limited possibilities to look elsewhere for a consistent adult image. Some of the possibilities include teachers (from an extremely limited male supply during grade school!), ministers, distant (geographically) relatives, or images on the television screen. The latter, however, may prove to be more of a curse than a blessing; all too often they are unrealis-

tic images that serve as false models and lead to immature thinking and behaving.

As a rule, the young child in the modern family is
almost exclusively exposed to the influence of his parents'
emotions—mature or immature as they may be. David
Cooper, in his telling book *The Death of the Family*, offers a poignant description of the situation.[4] He sees the
modern family as consisting of individuals who relate to
each other on the basis of extemely demanding emotions.
This reflects psychological incompleteness on the part of
each of them and creates the tendency to be "glued" to
someone else in order to function and feel alive: the
mother needs her son, the husband his wife (or, in many
cases, as compensation for an unsatisfactory marital relationship, his career and the associates who come with
it). The unfortunate outcome is that people live according to sterile roles, with stifled creativity and rigid, un-
adaptive personalities rather than as free and autonomous beings.

Anthropologist Margaret Mead, long an observer of
the family scene, recognized this trend several decades
ago when she warned of the increasing "isolation" of the
American family. She described the small modern family
as living in a community where they do not know anyone
closely, lack relatives, and have no close person to depend
upon to care for their child in the evenings, except an impersonal baby-sitter. The alienation and anonymity in the
community may be so strong that they can't even be sure
the sitter is not a psychopath.[5] Mead found in the social
innovation of "the sitter" an expression of remoteness
from those family ties which once provided the service
of baby-sitting—besides numerous other services now
equally defunct. She pointed out that, in effect, we call
upon the nuclear family to accomplish what a whole clan
used to do. These demands are made on the few members
of today's individualistic family, and we inflict feelings

of inadequacy on them if they fall short of discharging those duties.

The nuclear family, with its confining social structure and psychological isolation, has been held responsible for the rebellious expression of modern adolescents. Sociologist Barrington Moore has offered one of the most vitriolic views on this matter, announcing that the nuclear family is anachronistic and dysfunctional, and is doing more harm than good—in short, is obsolete. In "Thoughts on the Future of the Family" he accused the modern family of being replete with outmoded and barbaric features, especially with the resentment-encouraging obligation to give affection as a duty, and obedience as an unquestioned expectation, to a particular set of persons for no other reason than that they happen to be one's progenitors.[6] The "accident of birth," Moore felt, does not legitimize the exploitation of socially sanctioned and protected demands for gratitude, especially when the situation no longer generates a genuine feeling of relatedness and respect. If, under such adverse conditions, parents make a claim to authority merely on the basis of occupying the *position* of parent—in one or another way saying, in effect, "I tell you so because I am your *parent*" —their children will rebel and reject the demands and commands as being based on irrational authority.

Rational authority, on the other hand, would be understood as the type that relies on personal knowledge, experience, and expertise, and not merely on the incumbency of a position. The point is that if the number and variety of persons who lay claim to a certain authority are small, the possibility increases that a dependent will confront *unacceptable* authority. On the other hand, the dependent can adjust to authority more easily if the number of authority figures is large enough that he can equate an *acceptable* person with the authority position. Moore believed that the opportunity for such selectivity is sadly lacking among children and adolescents in the small modern family.

For example, if suburban Johnny experiences a chronic personality clash with his father, he is out of luck. There is probably no other adult male in the household whom he can admire and associate with. If rural-farm Johnny of a few decades ago experienced a similar clash with his father, the chances were good that he could turn to another grown man and observe, admire, and be guided by him. Generally, the large traditional family was conducive to the establishment of such alternative bonds. Child raising was considered a family or kin activity and not an exclusive person-to-person (mother-child or father-child) relationship.

The protracted job of converting the youngster into a competent and normal member of the community was not a studied project and hardly reached the specific awareness level of the adult. If it did, it was usually for disciplinary action. In other words, the more conscious and deliberate moments of the child-raising process occurred in negative situations, when it was felt necessary to correct or punish the child. Most of the positive activities consisted of more or less routine imitation of parental or other adult behavior. There was little emphasis on formal training; and there was little or no concern about such present-day preoccupations as "attitude formation," "emotional development," or whether the child's psyche acquired its "self-actualization."

The structure and atmosphere of the family have changed, and today the vast majority of Americans live in the confined family of the urban-industrial environment. Industrial technology has profoundly affected family life and has freed parents—especially mothers—from the interminable, exhausting tasks of daily reassuring the survival of the family. Now, thanks to modern appliances and thousands of technological innovations in and outside the family, they can replace cumbersome hours of producing, preserving, and preparing food by a few minutes at the nearest supermarket. Instead of fetching wood or coal to start a fire in the proverbial hearth, the turn of a knob allows electricity or gas to do the job. A meal can be prepared in a fraction of the time it took a few generations ago. And, of course, now there are fewer family members who have to be fed, clothed, and looked after.

Other changes deal with the cultural orientation of the family. Family life patterns have changed from familism, where the needs and goals of the family as a unit supersede those of the individual member, to individualism, where the goals and aspirations of the individual dominate his decisions and actions. A gradual deterioration of the family as a religious, economic, and cultural unit has been accomplished.

As mothers acquired more freedom from the age-old treadmill of basic menial tasks and raised their expectations in all sectors of life, they came to look at having and raising children in a new light. They pondered the *meaning* of child raising, and experienced an awakening! No longer need all their thinking and energy be concentrated on canning, cooking, making and mending their children's and husband's clothes, keeping a home clean and warm, and—above all—frequently being pregnant, giving birth, and nursing babies. With liberation from the traditional drudgery came the freedom and urge to achieve something new. Comparable to a law of physics, the vacuum created within family life by the withering away of old functions had to be refilled.

A greater awareness of the role of mother—not just wife-mother, housekeeper, or homemaker, but *Mother*—became prominent. No longer was she solely an auxiliary to the father. The gradual accentuation of this new status culminated in a myth, an almost cultic devotion to the new "specialized career" of motherhood. Apparently, a profound need had been at work to replenish with meaningfulness the void created by the dwindling away of the daily survival chores mothers had tended to for ages. The Myth was the answer to the Need. Young mothers became mother-entrepreneurs.

But they suffered certain frustrations in the process. Being energetic, well read in child care, and extremely concerned, they felt an increasing urge to experience tangible results and to produce products. But modern technology made it nearly impossible to experience tangibility and completeness in modern family life, because it—the near-omnipotent technology—did the completing and producing for the housewives. Their work, which became less and less concerned with production, compelled them to waste a vast amount of time on repetitious and uninteresting tasks. The creation of tangible results was reduced to a minimum. (By "tangibility" we mean the visible results of work and effort, through which we derive a feeling of task completion.) These psychological rewards became rare in the modern household. The process of completing almost everything that was tangible—animal husbandry, gardening, canning, tailoring clothes, etc.—was removed from the family and taken over by specialized agencies and institutions. In most cases, a visit to the supermarket took care of all these needs and processes. We commenced to buy the finished product, neatly wrapped and with a tag that gives us the necessary directions for use.

Where did this leave a modern housewife in relation to the feeling of completing and producing something? If she retained such a need—and there appear to be ubiquitous indications that normal individuals have the need for completion experience—she may have felt frustration within (and because of) the confines of the modern household. As an attempt to assuage this frustration, she may have selected motherhood as a means to regain a modicum of the sense of production completion. Hence many mothers, resembling so many determined entrepreneurs, set out to see the production process of their child's personality through to the end.

Women's Liberation and Motherhood

In the preceding passages we described the convergence of a number of significant dimensions that profoundly influence the style of child raising and the mother-child relationship. They dealt with industrialization and technological innovations, which create more freedom and time to focus on child raising; with raised standards of competence and luxury; with the frustrating intangibility concerning creativity and productivity in modern marriages and families; and with the ensuing attempt to substitute a sense of the concrete and the complete through "producing" the personality of the child.

Now, a most important dimension must be added to these conditions: the development of women's liberation.

The newly evolved liberation demanded its price from its followers. Although certain old needs were being satisfied, new needs began to proliferate. These needs dealt directly with the woman's sense of self-worth. She needed to prove herself, to test her capability for successfully carrying out a career. Experiencing a touch of liberation without living up to it would have been tantamount to a demonstration of defeat—to an admission that the traditional male chauvinism had a rationale and justification; namely, that the woman's most fulfilling role *is* the role of the traditional homemaker. Defeat in the face of new opportunities would have been a psychological blow from which recovery might have been very difficult.

Hence American women tried their utmost to take full advantage of the enticing promises and liberalized conditions.

But were the conditions really that liberalized? As it turned out, the vast majority of women experienced a discrepancy between the initial visions of liberation and equality, on one side, and the implementation of them in actual life, on the other. This discrepancy created tensions—psychological as well as social. Women found themselves in dire need of compensation. Compensation always deals with something that is less than ideal—that means making do with the available, putting up with compromises, and tolerating the limitations of one's situation.

This was precisely what happened. Most young American mothers, in spite of more liberated visions, were still incarcerated by the structural legacy of the social order, which always tends to lag behind ideas and dreams. Formal as well as informal social arrangements continued to maintain and reinforce the traditional male and female roles. In other words, whether they liked it or not, women found that they continued to be mothers and wives with limited opportunities. Whatever improvements appeared to be possible had to be obtained largely *within* the old structural setup. And this is where the Myth of Motherhood, as a presumably blissful-creative-productive career, helped to dull the edge of disappointment and frustration. The myth served as *rationalization* and *solace* at the same time.

Betty Rollin has made one of the most descriptive indictments of the myth's artificiality. She felt that mothers "wallowed in the aesthetics of it all—natural childbirth and nursing became maternal musts. Like heavy-bellied ostriches, they grounded their heads in the sands of motherhood, only coming up for air to say how utterly happy and fulfilled they were."[7] But Ms. Rollin, and a host of other writers—most prominently Ms. Friedan—had no doubt that mothers were unhappy. Yet the myth has survived, and even gained momentum, though having babies has long since changed from an asset to a liability for the individual family as well as society. Writers found it remarkable that the Motherhood Myth persisted in the face of tremendous maternal unhappiness and incompetence. Still, the cultist devotion has continued, and is still being practiced.

Once an apparently inevitable and mostly routine experience, having children and raising them evolved gradually into a self-conscious and rational experience: it became a *project*. (A project is a planned intellectual endeavor, which includes goal definition and correct procedure.) The goal for the mother became the achievement of a worthy *product*: a well-behaved child who reflects successful child raising. And this project became the *specialization* of increasing numbers of American mothers, whose all-encompassing home-maintenance and family-survival duties gradually lost their stringency, allowing preoccupation with a specialized project. Today's ubiquitous acceptance—even recommendation—that child raising should be a specialization makes it difficult for many readers to realize that such specialization is *new*.

For previous generations of mothers, child rearing was only one of their many functions, and was normally overshadowed by other tasks, such as keeping a home together and assuring the physical survival of the family members. Raising children was *not* a specialization. In fact, there was no specialization at all, since there were *too many vital* functions to be taken care of. For example, food was not merely to be prepared but also produced. Additional examples are the making and mending of clothes, administering folk medicine, observing religion in the home, etc. Traditional mothers, compared to their grand- and great-granddaughters of today, were slaves to menial work—to an everyday, routine struggle of keeping a household intact and running.

New Family Orientation: The "Personality Function"
While the difference between the roles of a traditional and a modern urban mother appears stark and spectacular from the perspective of history, it must be remembered that the actual process was slow and almost imperceptible for the persons directly involved. It therefore had little practical impact when a number of family sociologists anticipated and predicted changes. For example, the transference of many, if not most, traditional family functions was forecast in the 1930s by Pitirim Sorokin, who viewed the contemporary urban-industrial life-style as hostile to family life and felt that the "sociocultural functions of the family will further decrease until the family becomes a mere incidental cohabitation of male and female while the home will become a mere overnight parking place mainly for sex relationships."[8] The opinion that American society is well on its way to achieving such a liberal and flexible family life-style was strikingly reiterated, almost four decades later, by Alvin Toffler in *Future Shock*.[9]

Although most, if not all, social scientists concur that the family has lost a number of previously well-grounded functions, they may differ in their assessment of the pace of deactivation and the number of functions involved. There is general agreement that the economic, protective, recreational, educational, and religious functions are being, or already have been, transferred to other, specialized institutions. What have been retained as an important function is emotional involvement and dependence, conceptualized by Talcott Parsons as the "personality function,"[10] whereby a husband and wife attempt to derive emotional nurture and security through marriage and the family.

This emotional demand is a relatively new burden on the institution of marriage and the family. It appears that this intense attachment and weighty investment reflect the frantic attempt of late-twentieth-century American men and women to extract a sense of identity from their intimate involvements, and the singular intensity of this craving has to be understood in light of the decline of a vital function of culture. Throughout the ages, one of culture's foremost purposes has been to help and guide the members of society in the formulation of their identity. This cultural function was accomplished all the more forcefully when the given culture extended strong and unequivocally clear standards that could anchor the various thoughts and emotions of the people within a meaningful framework. The dilemma in modern American society, however, is that its cultural dimensions, with its component norms and values, have become relatively nonspecific, and fraught with confusion and conflict. American culture—traditionally serving as a strong mainspring of personal identity—has become too indecisive and too full of conflict to continue its vital role in the development of personal identity.

Like a number of other social scientists, Max Lerner, in his book *America as a Civilization,* observed that modern Americans are engaged in a desperate search for models and a stable identity. He called the symptoms of this groping the "neurosis of the ego" and believed that this type of mass neurosis is a relatively new mental problem of the Western world, varying significantly from previous mass neuroses.[11] This ego crisis deals with the inability to *know* where we are, what we are, and where we are going. It is a problem of basic *orientation and definition.* (Previous historical epochs have accentuated other human questions of fundamental significance, for example, the interrelated questions of *morality* [the struggle of the "superego"] and *repression* [the struggle of the "id"].)

The frenetic search for alternative media from which a modicum of identity could be derived has led Americans to think of marriage and the family as the most hospitable setting for answering the question, "Who am I?" This, naturally, is an enormous demand, and has placed a gigantic burden on family life. Perhaps most marital partners turn out to be unprepared to cope with or accept the limitations of their relationship in respect to this demand. Many of them suffer profound frustrations and unhappiness, ultimately leading to the dissolution of the relationship. However, because they cannot visualize an alternative structure for obtaining the psychological rewards, they are prone to remarry and try anew with a different partner.

Not surprisingly, our insistence on identity, "self-fulfillment," and "self-actualization" is probably one of the major reasons for our high divorce rate. As alarming as the rate of marital disintegration appears, it has not necessarily indicated the doom of the family institution; rather, it may reflect the deep needs of contemporary Americans (perhaps contemporary Western people in general) and their determination to meet their needs, regardless of obstacles and initial or even repeated failure. If the need for "self-actualization" is not met in a particular setting and with a particular partner, the setting and the partner are changed. It is interesting to note, however, that—by and large—the same conventional institutions—marriage and the family—are used, reused, and upheld.

The new emotional strain introduced by the family's "personality function" has greatly affected—and changed—the parent-child relationship. In the new context, the child has acquired a unique value. He has become an emotionally important figure, a different creature from the child of generations past. Then, he had usually been considered unavoidable—a socialization task undertaken almost coincidentally by blood-related peers and adults—and assessed as a usable force in the family's division of labor. Now he has become an end in himself, a self-contained entity, a product soon to be sent on his own way—presumably without hindrance on the part of the parents.

Mom's Needs Arise

But, alas, the end can be perverted. If the end is an object (a son!) and if the producer of the object is beset by deep frustrations and anxieties, the temptation to use the object for alleviation of these frustrations can become irresistible. In other words, the child is the product which becomes the means to attaining a solution to the anxieties that stem from unfulfilled needs, or from unsuccessful attempts at meeting such needs.

Mom's core need is to establish a stable identity. The unfortunate person who has to depend on such an anxious individual easily incurs his share of the pathology; that is, he will suffer pathological consequences himself. What may have begun as an idealistic enterprise, with the intention of treating the child as an individual whose growth and maturity were to be safeguarded, ends unhappily with "career mothering," because this seems to be the only way for the mother to rescue a faltering sense of meaningfulness and identity. In sum, the child becomes an irreplaceable figure, who is needed by the mother so that she can deduce her identity as *Mother*—which is capitalized to denote the central meaning that this status and activity have for her identity and self-definition.

It is important to understand that for the identity to stick, the chosen activity has to be pursued with almost stubborn seriousness in order to produce the impact on one's self-definition that is necessary to keep creeping doubt, conflict, and anxiety from interfering. Above all, it has to be made public for all to see. Public recognition and commitment have a way of reinforcing one's self-image.

Since the child was thought of as the end product, many mothers came to prefer a small family, with only one or two children, thereby creating a situation that facilitated their focusing on the "manufacture" of personality. The "manufacturing process" included such features as exclusive supervision, "scientific" approach, and psychological manipulation (in preference to the "barbaric" physical approach of spanking or slapping the child). Since many young mothers were convinced that child raising was the only major function left in their marriage and family life, and that—at least for the time being—it was the only alternative to an outside career, they entered the project of child raising with zeal and determination, and set about to produce "quality."

What they defined as quality dealt with the *development of the child's abilities so as to ensure him success in an industrial and commercial world.* Hence guidance, reasoning, and encouragement were substituted for the "unscientific" corporal punishment of previous generations.[12] It is again interesting to note that these traits are needed or desirable for professionals, managers, and owners and that, therefore, they were more emphasized among the American middle class than among any other segment of the population.

"My Child"—The Project

It was during this phase of the changing philosophy of child raising that a host of eminent authors spoke out in favor of an "objective" and "scientific" approach to parenthood. This occurred simultaneously and as a largely independent trend from Momism, though unintentionally supporting it. The intent of these educators was to render a service to young mothers and assist them in their task of manufacturing achieving and successful human beings. Notice that the *success principle* has entered child raising! In essence it said: "If you want a successful child, you first have to be a successful mother, and vice versa."

Such an evaluation established an intense reciprocity between the two parties, and created an overly interdependent twosome. To the mother this process came to mean—largely unconsciously—that her value as mother depended entirely on the quality of the child. Moreover, her *total human self-worth* became contingent on the outcome of her parenthood, as if her self-definition were restricted to motherhood—or, perhaps, Momhood. A mother who perceived her self-worth in such a manner would energetically pursue what, to her, appeared only logical: to make sure that the "quality child" would establish and enhance *her* value. (In subsequent chapters we will go into the techniques she applies to exert "quality control.")

The psychological intensity and interdependence in the contemporary mother-child enclave have become a most suitable site on which a variey of writers could unload their philosophy of child raising and educating. Some of the earliest remarks have become classics. For example, John B. Watson wrote: "There is a sensible way of treating children. Treat them as though they are young adults. . . . Let your behavior be objective."[13] Arnold Gesell suggested that parents should respect the child's different phases of maturation, should not interfere with them, should allow self-regulation, and mothers should make the baby "with all its inborn wisdom a working partner."[14]

The stage was set during the 1950s and '60s for a number of follow-up writers, most prominently Dr. Benjamin Spock, to provide America's mothers with a dazzling array of scientific and not-so-scientific suggestions on how to successfully raise their babies. ("Successful" was understood as meaning "lovable.") Another well-known figure among the child-care theorists, who until his death in 1973 commanded a large forum, was Dr. Haim Ginott, who functioned as the "resident psychologist" on the National Broadcasting Company's "Today Show." He also wrote a syndicated column, "Between Us," that was published weekly in about 100 newspapers, and was a traveling lecturer here and abroad. His principal concern was teaching mothers how to relate to their children through a language of compassion and understanding. In his books, he emphasized that a loving and forgiving approach will create loving and caring human beings.[15]

The pervasive tenor of this type of widely read literature on child raising was the almost obsessive desire to have the child turn out "lovable," "nice," "agreeable." For example, Dr. Spock stated that the most vital element of child raising is the parents' desire to see the child "turn out well," and that through parental love "he's nice to people a majority of the time simply because he likes people (there's more agreeableness than disagreeableness in him)."[16]

In sum, the bulk of child-raising literature supported, encouraged, and enhanced an overintellectualized approach to a situation that, for the sake of mental health, should include reliance on personal, creative emotions.

Why is it so difficult to find adequate, creative emotions? While many people would expect that they come as a "natural experience," which does not have to be learned, psychiatrist Helen De Rosis reminds us that "parenthood is not a natural state."[17] A mother does not instinctively know how to rear her child, how to love it, and, least of all, how to let it grow in such a way as to permit it to develop the essential independence from her at a proper pace.

On the other hand, childhood is a natural state. While children do not have to learn to be children—they just are, without trying—parenthood is imposed on top of everything else a person is by the time he or she achieves that status.

A healthy experience of motherhood, then, is monitored neither by an innate program nor by a foolproof theory, but by a balance of sound emotions and intelligent insight. Off-balance situations will result in less than creative or wholesome experiences—for the mother as well as the child.

The Child as "Conspicuous Consumption"

Our modern age, then, has witnessed the rise of mothers who visualized that in an era of large-scale organization the ability to get along with people is more important than technical skills, and that to instill and develop this ability in their children is of utmost importance. *The child's proficiency in congeniality has become the fervent goal of a mother's effort.* This means that he is to be "cooperative," "participating" (in the "right" activities and groups), and "acceptable" (to the people who "count"). To ensure the successful outcome of the "manufacturing process," "scientific" manipulation was applied.

But, actually, it was not so much the manufacture of a product as its *consumption*, because the child's personality and behavior patterns were *used* to point up success on the part of the mother. And thus it was not essentially different from other consumption techniques, for example, flaunting a Cadillac, owning a modern town house, or taking a vacation in Acapulco. So child raising was added to the long list of items in the overall success-and-conspicuous-consumption syndrome of post–World

War II. Momistically inclined mothers could now proceed unopposed—in fact with social encouragement and laudation—to embrace motherhood as *the* success test.

Once the basic success principle was internalized, it turned out that many young mothers found themselves lacking a reasonable number of alternatives for testing their craving and capacity for success. The dynamics of this socially instilled and reinforced drive were powerful and compelling because they were perfectly in line with the Protestant ethic of hard work and demonstrable success, which underlies the sociocultural norms in virtually all sectors of American life. (There are, however, indications that the younger generation is modifying this tradition.) If a young woman found herself in a situation that was limited to only one talent—namely, the demonstration of the talent for motherhood—she would almost predictably work unstintingly on it. In effect, the American woman—once the nurturing family functions were radically reduced and her access to equal rights and opportunities was eased—was entering the same psychological arena in which males have battled and battered each other since time immemorial. As a consequence, she has been undergoing similar mental gyrations and manifesting the same stress and anxiety symptoms that are familiar to us from the male domain, and she is driven by the same work-and-success ethos.

Freedom and independence are a heavy burden. It is a difficult and often dismaying responsibility to make decisions for oneself and to determine what is right or wrong, mature or immature, important or trivial. The modifications of the traditional female role demand their price. Sometimes the price is exorbitant and claims psychological and physical fatalities.

Maybe this role change is the main explanation for the chilling suicide statistics, which indicate a phenomenal rise in female suicides. Both male and female rates have increased over the past decade; but while the rates for males under twenty years of age jumped from 3 to 10 per 100,000 population (roughly tripled), the rate for females under age twenty skyrocketed from 0.4 to 8 (a twentyfold increase). Similarly, while the rate for males between twenty and thirty years of age increased from 18 to 41 (more than doubled), the rate for females of the same age increased from 6 to 26 (more than fourfold).[18]

American females, particularly mothers, have apparently come to insist—understandably from their viewpoint as equal persons—on trying to partake of the "glories" of successful work, no matter what the cost. Most likely, the more pronounced their sense of equality, the greater their desire for "self-realization" and "self-actualization." For many, this was achieved by "producing" a child. The emphasis here is not on the biological process but on the psychological dynamics. Females wanted to *create* and *achieve* "like everybody else," and many females invested this drive in child raising. The child became an *object*, the main ingredient of the psychological concoction such a mother was going to brew, and through which she would try to establish herself as an *achiever*. Such an endeavor satisfied her newly acquired success drive, and ultimately provided her with a sense of identity.

This, then, is the road Momism has traveled. The mother who pursues this specialty is called Mom. The personality damage that is suffered by the child we shall call Momistic impairment.

With this historical sketch we have set the stage for further investigation of the problem we have attempted to define. We will move directly to the present-day scene. The next chapter will narrow our search for the more specific conditions on which Momism thrives and will focus on a number of important factors that prevail in the American middle class.

Chapter 3

And far from the least of the Mom causes,
because it is the fertile soil in which the
seeds of Momism grow, is our social system
and our way of life. Pretty much everything
we do—socially, politically, educationally—
glorifies Mom and praises her
"self-sacrifice" and her "giving her life for
her children."—Edward Strecker

The Middle Class: Breeding Ground for Momism

As stated earlier, the middle class is the most fertile breeding ground for the growth of Momism. To expand on this assumption, two interrelated questions must be examined. First, what do we mean by the middle class? Second, what are the peculiar circumstances that foster Momistic child raising in this segment of the American population?

Sociologists seem to have difficulty in coming up with a clear set of criteria defining a socioeconomic class. The best we can do here, without going into lengthy theoretical wanderings, is indicate a number of major factors that appear to be helpful in distinguishing different social classes. These factors can be divided into *life-style* and *value orientation.*

Life-style includes such variables as type of home, neighborhood, occupation and education of the head of the household, and financial resources. In middle-class families, the homes generally meet rather demanding standards of comfort, technical appliances, hygiene, and esthetics, and the image of the three- or four-bedroom house in suburbia is not out of place. Certainly, the middle-class family is rarely found in the run-down, crime-ridden inner city.

In most cases, middle-class parents have had at least some college education, and virtually always have a high school diploma. The occupational opportunities are aligned accordingly; they fall primarily into the category of white-collar jobs, including business, management, skilled professions, academic careers, etc. Their incomes range from fairly comfortable to very comfortable, though one can rarely speak of "rich" families. A common indicator of their financial standing is the fact that wives do *not* have to go to work out of economic necessity and therefore can, if they wish, entirely devote their time and energy to motherhood.

The most important characteristic of a socioeconomic class deals with the more intangible value orientation. The middle class is characterized by its enforcement of the traditional American norms and values, including adherence to the Protestant ethic, which values work, investment, and reinvestment and believes in deferring gratification until its "proper" time. Time is highly valued, and is thought of as deserving "proper" usage. Unlike the typical lower-class attitude, it considers time a valuable resource. Other middle-class attitudes include high esteem for education and science, including the "objective" approach to child raising.

By contrast, lower-class families have a different life-style and exhibit a different value orientation. Anthropologist Walter B. Miller describes the lower-class ethos as including preoccupation with "staying out of trouble," being "tough," being "smart," seeking excitement, believing in "fate," being anti-intellectual, and reflecting authoritarianism.[1] Education enjoys little esteem, and the expression "eggheaded" indicates the scorn felt for the academic process. Time is not considered a sparse resource but, rather, is taken for granted or largely ignored. In this context, child raising takes on a quality quite different from that of the middle class.

The middle class is the mainstay of the values of American society; it is the perpetuator of our major traditions. How is it that the "backbone" of American culture offers the strange conditions that facilitate the practice of Momism? It is argued that the very conditions described above, when taken together as a constellation, create a formidable breeding ground for Moms and allow their stifling influence over their children. Let us portray this constellation and scrutinize its most salient features.

In this chapter we shall examine seven features of the middle-class family which set the stage for the development of Momism. The extreme effects of Momism are most likely to be found when all seven conditions coincide, but it is entirely possible to find lesser (although severe) cases of Momism where only a few of these conditions exist. The seven main features are as follows.

1. The role of the *incompletely emancipated woman.* We shall try to understand why this type of woman is so strongly tempted to adopt Momistic practices.

2. The *remoteness of the father* from the child-raising process, which is a typical condition of middle-class careers.

3. The circumstance that middle-class families often include *only one child,* which allows the mother fuller reign over the child-raising process.

4. The prevalent *intellectualized approach* to child raising.

5. Extreme *sensitivity to community standards,* which generates emotional motivation in mothers to use their children as success symbols.

6. The regrettable, unfortunate fact that young children witness the divorce of their parents and then are often exposed to manipulation by their *divorcee-mother.*

7. Finally, the failure of American society to provide a *rite of passage,* a publicly recognized breakpoint between childhood and adulthood, which would amount to a surrender of the last bastion against the inroads of Momism.

These, then, are the typical conditions that can be held responsible for the Momistic problems that arise in increasing number in the middle-class families of the United States. They will be discussed in detail throughout this chapter.

The Halfway-Emancipated Mother

It would be illusory to assume that there are many *fully* emancipated women in America today. A more accurate assessment would reveal that, by and large, American women are only partly emancipated. It is important to understand this qualification, for it has decisive relevance to the Momistic tendency displayed by large numbers of American middle-class mothers. American middle-class women who are not completely emancipated are more inclined to seek self-expression and career satisfaction within the family. This incompleteness is not caused entirely by the legacy of legal and occupational inequities that keep American women from seeking self-actualization and career satisfaction outside of the family structure but, rather, by their psychological self-incarceration. They have failed to liberate their psyches from the traditional role definitions of Western civilization.

The situation can be compared to the hesitancy with which a long-incarcerated prisoner steps toward a gate that suddenly is opened, not knowing what to do with the unaccustomed freedom. There would be absolutely nothing wrong in making the choice for the domestic career *if* it were chosen freely and consciously—as is likely in the case of a fully emancipated female. But the halfway-emancipated woman makes the choice grudgingly and with the feeling that she is settling for a *secondary* career. And this is precisely the consequence of being partly liberated. She feels uncertain whether or not she really wants to settle for it.

This is the curse of the unfree mind. It leads to psychic self-incarceration. Such a woman is continuously uncertain of her motives—never sure whether her decisions are based upon her own desire or are a mere outgrowth of her status. Only a completely free spirit is assured the conviction that the choice is actually a choice, not merely resignation.

In any case, the crescendo of the emancipation drive (alias "women's liberation," "feminist revolution," or any other label descriptive of modern women's struggle for equality) has been reached in the American middle class. Hence it is in this segment of the population that we find the majority of the partly liberated females. Many, if not most of them, are mothers—exclusively so; that is, exclusive of careers outside the home. Yet they have begun to acquire a new perception of themselves; they visualize new vistas of role possibilities, new goals, and the means to achieve them. The former, all-important wife-mother role is no longer seen as the absolute and unalterable destiny of womankind. Instead, from the vantage point of their new personhood, women are beginning to recognize alternative roles, among which the conventional wife-mother role is considered just one possibility—and one that smacks slightly of inferior standing.

The irony of this movement is that women are experiencing their liberation more on the ideal than on the real level. They have visions and anticipations of liberation and role freedom, but they are held back—captives of the family setup. In other words, the conventional family structure enforces domesticity and locks many women into the motherhood role. This confinement causes severe conflicts in them, and raises self-doubt and confusion. On the other hand, the further-emancipated women of tomorrow, who might manage a closer approximation of the ideal and the real, would escape such conflicts and frustrations. This reflects an historical process, whereby the earlier emancipation movement is more apt to frustrate women than the later movement. One might speculate that the truly emancipated woman of the future will feel no role conflict because she will be free to choose what she wants. She will feel more at ease with the world and with herself—displaying a more relaxed child-raising method in which she, as the mother, will no longer feel the need to live vicariously through her child.

The halfway-emancipated woman is therefore inclined to practice Momistic child raising. It is she—having experienced an incomplete liberation—who suffers the most severe conflicts and who is most likely to clamorously demand freedom. Freedom appears to be in the offing; but there is evidence that it is levying a heavy price in feelings of anxiety, insecurity, and frequent anguished pondering as to whether she has made an adequate decision on the choice of role. If she occupies the wife-mother position, she may wonder whether she should have chosen a different and more fruitful avenue, for which she feels she is equally, if not better, equipped. The suspicion that she may have made an inferior choice and thrown away the chance of achieving a more significant— that is, "equalitarian"— position leaves her with an uneasy sense of conflict and defensiveness.

This is the point where the need for compensatory activity arises. The "new personhood" demands to be applied and tested—and if there is no "higher" cause or purpose, *even the old-fashioned wife-mother role will do.* This role is then converted into a "career." Once engulfed in it, the mother will try to function with the same efficiency and expediency she would apply to any other career.

Of course, the fact that she is already a mother when these nagging doubts emerge gives her compensatory needs a natural and almost unavoidable direction. Unlike a disappointing marriage, disappointing motherhood cannot be resolved by divorce. Hence, out of necessity she comforts herself, as Betty Rollin puts it so well, that "motherhood affords instant identity. First through wifehood, you are somebody's wife; then you are somebody's mother. Both give not only identity and activity, but status and stardom of a kind."[2] The solution, then, is to first serve a husband and then to serve one's son.

There is reason to believe another important factor is responsible for the continuous adherence to the motherhood career and the slowdown in the push for full liberation. It has something to do with the silent realization of many women that the world of male jobs is not necessarily more pleasant, creative, and adventuresome than their traditional homemaking chores. After all, there is every bit as much monotony in driving trucks, laying bricks, mining coal, paving streets, and selling insurance as in creating a comfortable home. Perhaps many men have realized that what tradition has doled out to them as male-appropriate work is not worth defending much after all, and perhaps they are more willing to share their labor with women than is commonly thought. And this may be true not only of blue-collar work but also white-collar work. Interestingly, more men consistently approve the women's liberation movement than women themselves.

This finding emerged from reliable research on cross-sections of the national population eighteen years old and over. In 1972, 54 percent of the men and 44 percent of the women supported the movement, and in 1973 the figures were 58 and 51 percent.[3] These statistics fuel the suspicion that many women *reject* the new freedom that is now available. Many women admit this, or suspect it of others. For example, survey data indicate that a majority of women who have achieved success and prestige in traditionally male-occupied careers blame women for their own failures and frustrations.[4] They do not believe that serious discrimination stands in the way of success if a woman *seriously* wants to try her hand or head at a career. In fact, these successful professional women display a strong countermilitant and antifeminist orientation, believing that indecision, insincerity, and irrational frustrations are hiding behind the shrill voices of many militant liberationists. Perhaps the women in the study who "made it" in the man's world are trying to speak for a large but silent segment of their sisters who either do not feel discriminated against or prefer to follow traditional paths.

Could it be that a realistic glimpse through the gates of liberation has had a muting effect upon the initial rejoicing? It was easy and tempting to exaggerate the advantages of the unknown and unattainable—one could not really lose anything in the process—and it was a convenient outlet for gripes and frustrations. The situation changed radically, however, when the gates suddenly opened and real encouragement was given to step ahead and materialize the desires so vociferously voiced. Reality entered the scene! All of a sudden, what was previously perceived as a concrete deprivation didn't look so underdoggish any more. How else are we to interpret some most surprising statistics? Over the past few decades, public opinion has been polled repeatedly on the value women ascribe to work outside the home—and these polls used national samples, carefully chosen to mirror the overall mood of the nation. A 1970 poll found that 68 percent of the women felt that "taking care of a home and raising a family" is more interesting than having a job. Surprisingly, perhaps, this home orientation has *increased* since 1946, when only 50 percent felt that "running a home" was more interesting.[5]

What such research may very well tell us is that many of today's modern mothers have chosen the "motherhood career" not only because they are *halfway emancipated*, and therefore are still experiencing limitations in career development, but because they have become aware of the unpleasantness of the struggle and drudgery in the world of traditionally male jobs and actually *perfer* to stay where they are: in the home. For many of them, it may appear like choosing between two evils, and they have grudgingly settled for motherhood.

The women who are motivated by either condition often opt for motherhood as a solution to conflicts and dissatisfactions. But it presents only a pseudosolution. However glamorous the facade of motherhood, agitated considerations and reconsiderations about her role in life continue under the surface. It is difficult, if not impossible, to shirk the responsibilities of motherhood, once this condition is established. The woman locks into the limiting family role, retains unresolved conflicts and discomforts, and unwittingly projects them onto the child.

Psychiatrists have found that a vast majority of disturbed children had mothers who suffered from serious conflicts about their roles as women and their attitudes toward men.[6] Eric H. Erikson, probably the most eminent scholar and analyst of the phenomenon of Momism, observes that Mom is not a happy person because of her failure to obtain the gratifications she sought in her style of child rearing. She is as much a victim of her troubled disposition, conflicts, and obsessions as the offspring she tries to manipulate. She is not certain of her feelings as a woman and mother, and not even her ostentatious over-concern for her child gives her this assurance. "Mom . . . is not happy; . . . she is ridden by anxiety that her life is a waste. She knows that her children do not genuinely love her, despite Mother's Day offerings."[7]

It does not necessarily follow, however, that the traditional mother, in contrast, was a blissful person who enjoyed motherhood and reveled in the love of her off-spring. Many such mothers were, or still are, no happier than the Mom type. But their trouble and unhappiness were of a different nature, for their problems were directly related to the mundane difficulties of daily existence. Most likely, they experienced frustrations and worries based on the encounter with everyday survival contingencies. But unlike the modern Mom's mental trouble, such experiences did not precipitate deep and lasting conflicts. Part of the old-fashioned mother's immunity against deep-seated psychological trouble stemmed from being spared the feelings of "relative deprivation," whereby she compared her fate with "ideal" conditions that she would like to attain but could not achieve. Hence the traditional mother had no need to wrestle with her frustrations and disappointments and try to compensate for them by living through her children. A *mother*, in contrast to a *Mom*, sees no need, or only a very peripheral need, to employ the technique of conditional love.

Is Momism unique to the American middle class? Although, generally, the answer to this question tends to be affirmative, a number of qualifications should be introduced:

1. It must be understood that this answer is a broad *generalization.* This implies that its validity is statistical and that we must allow for the exceptions where middle-class families are free from Momistic elements and where families with other than a middle-class background show the symptoms of Momism.

2. While we can make reliable statements about Momism in the middle class, we are largely at a loss as to what to say about the upper socioeconomic class. It may be that these families have the means to conceal Momistic practices from the general public as well as from the social scientist.

3. It should also be noted that the women's liberation movement is not limited to the middle class. This means that incomplete emancipation in settings other than the middle class can likewise imbue a mother with conflict and discontent and the resultant need to compensate by "successful" child raising.

4. This is not to say that an incompletely emancipated woman, *ipso facto*, engages in Momism when she assumes motherhood. It is more correct to say that the emotional price for participating in the emancipation process may *possibly* entail the conflicts and complexes that so stealthily lead to the practice of Momism.

5. Finally, Momism can also be observed in the middle classes of other societies. Of course, the setting in other societies introduces variables that do not exist in our society, and it does not replicate Momism in the exact form we know it, but it yields its own brand of destructive motherhood. This point deserves exploration, and the next few paragraphs will elaborate on it.

A fascinating cross-cultural comparison focuses on Mexico, which in some major aspects parallels the development we have seen, and still are witnessing, in the

United States.[8] It strikes the observer as an instance of *déjà vu*—the rise of motherhood with all the trimmings of Momism. The main features are, again, the middle-class setting and partly emancipated womanhood, as urban Mexico slowly evolves a middle class in which women have achieved a substantial degree of freedom.

But the benefits of the liberation of many urban women are more tangible during the time they are single— when women are engaged in the labor market and *before* they get married. With marriage comes a fierce shock and nagging frustration.

For modern Mexican women, marriage suddenly reduces their equality and emancipated behavior patterns. They are asked to adjust to the traditional and highly restrictive life of the Mexican wife's role. In response, discontented Mexican wives try to compensate for conflict and disappointment by having and raising children —to regain a sense of importance and reestablish a meaningful activity. In short, the denial of an outside career is compensated for by the establishment of an inside-the-family career.

The investigators observed that these *madres* almost literally tried to take possession of their children by conditioning their thinking, feeling, and behaving and by making certain that they would stay "faithful" to the mother. The mothers used affection—its conditional offering or withholding—as the major means of conditioning and controlling. This is the Mexican equivalent of the American mother's "conditional love" technique. The researchers concluded that, much like the American middle-class Mom, her Mexican counterpart aspires to "successful" motherhood because she feels she forfeited a meaningful career outside the home.

A qualification should be added, however. The Mexican version of Momism may be associated with additional or slightly different motivations. For example, overcompensation by means of motherhood is probably spurred by *machismo* (an overbearing display of masculinity), which is prevalent among a majority of Mexican men. When behaving in accordance with *machismo*, especially in a group of men, the male feels obliged to express a mixture of aggression and condescension toward women, including his wife—but his mother is exempt from this aggressive and patronizing attitude. Mother is an object of reverence, a royal personage whose wishes must be gratified.[9]

In reaction, the Mexican wife may use Momistic practices not merely as compensation for outside-role deprivation but also as a way of countering male dominance in the family situation, and quite possibly as a way of revenging herself against what she perceives as male tyranny.

Remote Father Involvement

An additional Momism-facilitating condition, which is prevalent in the middle class, is the father's involvement in a career whose working hours do not stop at 5 p.m. His career activities reach into what otherwise would be his free time. If he is a salesman, this is more time with which to make calls, "contacts," and trips. If he is a young executive, he may arrive home with a briefcase full of work. This may also be the case for teachers and many other professionals. There are obligations to colleagues, customers, and business or professional partners; and many of them require the sacrifice of extra time—time when other fathers, such as those in the working class, can "afford" to be home with their wife and children.

The dilemma of the young American executive has been of long-standing interest to social scientists. The best-known treatment of this subject was offered by William H. Whyte, Jr., in his 1956 classic *The Organization Man*, where he describes the servitude the middle-class career person owes the Organization or Corporation.[10] Organizational "belongingness" and "togetherness" were sentiments the Organization cultivated for its own goals and purposes, and expected the white-collar employee to endorse, thereby competing with the young executive's emotional attachment to his family. This human-relations doctrine came perilously close to demanding that the individual sacrifice his private attachments so that he might "belong." Worse than that, the individual was expected to surrender his beliefs so that he might "belong and be successful."

A more recent study (1973) by the American Management Association reexamined the middle-class executive's bondage to the Organization and found that Whyte's observations are still valid.[11] In fact, some of the trends sketched by Whyte appear to have *increased* for the executive. The middle-class father is "hooked" as securely as before. His career still depends upon the degree to which he conforms to the ideal executive—the Organization Man. The Organization—and his career—force him to compromise personal principles, and his work filters into his family life. His time belongs not to the family but to the Organization.

The 1973 survey of nearly 3,000 businessmen found even greater stress and discontent than Whyte had suspected in 1956. For example, more than half of the middle-class career men felt that the pressure for organizational conformity has been increasing. Over 70 percent reported that they have been expected to compromise personal principles to conform to norms established by their bosses, and 30 percent claimed that their careers had adversely affected their health (mainly through stress and pressures on the job). The majority felt that "dynamic personality" and the "ability to sell yourself and your ideas" were more valued by the corporation than honesty and moral conviction. The respondents also felt that "know-who" ranked far above "know-how" as a criterion for success.

Whatever form one chooses to describe the career peculiarities of the middle-class father, the effect on his family life is the same: career demands force him to transfer his parental commitment to his wife, and child rearing becomes a mother-dominated process. The children have only superficial contact with their father. Although a father may occasionally—perhaps even on a regular schedule—play with them and chat with them, they rarely see him in action *as an adult* from whom responsibility and maturity are demanded or as one who demands these qualities from others. Actually, the playfulness with which such a father interacts with his children may give them the wrong idea—that, at best, he is just one of the kids, a buddy who sometimes plays with them.

The serious bulk of the socialization process takes place during the hours when the father is not around. Then, mother wields the authority, makes the decisions, displays impressive abilities in homemaking skill, and, in general, gives the impression of being a real adult. Mother manages the children many more hours than her husband does, which is a heavy burden on her—as on any person. How can she master the task? It is made doubly difficult by her belief that she has to accomplish two things simultaneously: maintain discipline and sustain the children's love for her. The former task is born partially of basic management necessity and partially of the aspiration to create a socially acceptable and superior child. The latter task is largely born of the mother's immature preoccupation with being "loved" and "accepted" by her children. A mother's normal and neurotic concerns pivot on the *degree* of preoccupation with securing that "love" and the *lengths* she goes to to get her children to demonstrate it.

Perhaps calling such preoccupation "immature" is somewhat harsh, since her need for "love" may be synonymous with the understandable need for recognition—recognition which, at the time, is not available from outside work or a career. Thus her craving for a demonstration of "love" on the part of her children may reflect the degree of her commitment to the "motherhood career."

It must be added that, up to a point, such concern is entirely natural; mothers should both desire and enjoy having the love and loyalty of their children. It is only when a certain point is surpassed that the concern becomes both pathological and pathetic. It is then that a mother turns into a Mom, by resorting to damaging manipulation of the child's psyche. (In a later chapter we shall discuss in detail the psychological means a Mom selects to achieve pseudogratification for neurotic discontent. It is *pseudo* because, ultimately it will not dispel her discontent.)

The irony of such fervent mothering and its hope to be rewarded with the child's love and devotion is the unpleasant fact that the outcome is frequently just the opposite: the child will accumulate deeply negative feelings toward his mother. Because of the manipulative disciplinarian she is, the child comes to fear her more than to love her—despite her assurances of dedication, love, and affection. This is reminiscent of the observations made by anthropologist Bronislaw Malinowski among the Trobriand islanders, where the strict disciplinarian was neither the mother nor father but the maternal uncle, who functioned in a way we would expect of a father in American society.[12] Boys in the Trobriand society directed their antagonistic feelings toward this uncle, while they established congenial and relaxed relationships with their mother, and particularly with their father. The fathers would play with them, give them presents, and generally relate to them on a playful and friendly basis.

(This observation, among other theoretical impacts, called into question the orthodox Freudian theory of a boy's Oedipus complex, in which the father assumes the role of a rival. A modified and more elastic image of this complex was henceforth encouraged.)

Far-fetched as the comparison between our complex urban-industrial society and the simple tribal society of the Trobriands might sound, there are some striking similarities. The Trobriand boy's relationship with his father is very much the same as that of the American middle-class boy, and his relationship with his *uncle* resembles the American middle-class boy's relationship with his *mother*. In both instances the father's remoteness from the disciplinary process makes him a more amiable and congenial figure.

It should be noted that it is not always the professional activity of the middle-class father that keeps him from participating more fully in the child-raising process. There may be various reasons. Some men work "regular" hours, and have the time and opportunity to be with their children, but simply choose not to take part in the child-rearing process, prefer to have their wife do the job, and feel that "keeping the kids in line" is her responsibility. Such disinterest is often couched in a traditionally acceptable evasion, such as the father who plunks down in front of the television and is virtually glued there for the duration of the children's waking hours.

Other reasons may include divorce, separation, the death or military duty of the father, etc. Divorce is a phenomenon experienced by thousands of children each year in the United States; and it is usually the father who, in this situation, recedes from consistent contact with the child. Even in an age of presumably enlightened legislation, custody of children is granted to the mother almost automatically. The death of the father is more common than the death of the mother because of superior female longevity. Military duty, especially in time of war or international turmoil, also decreases a father's availability.

Whatever the reason for the father's unavailability —whether partially through occupational responsibilities, divorce, or military duty or totally through death— its effects have been noted especially with respect to the male child's personality development. A number of studies have tied a father's remoteness to incomplete or pathological personality traits in the boy, and one of the most frequently found consequences deals with the drastically reduced masculinity of the boy. Preoccupation with more aggressive play and games, greater exertion of independence, more direct attempts at domination of other individuals and the environment in general, and stronger competitive tendencies have been viewed as the normal development of the male child. In respect to mental proficiencies, masculinity has been associated with analytic and logical superiority. Girls have been typed as more skillful in verbal communication and intuitive thought, and as more inclined to be nurturant, submissive, and dependent.

Studies comparing father-absent and father-present boys have found that the former turned out to be less aggressive and assertive than the latter, tended to have an unrealistic and feminine fantasy picture of what a father was or should be, behaved in a much more dependent manner, and reacted submissively and immaturely to peer influence.[13] The age at which a boy experiences father-unavailability also makes a difference with respect to his masculine development. It was found that boys who became father-absent before the age of four had a significantly less masculine sex-role orientation than those who became father-absent in their fifth and subsequent years.[14]

It appears that paternal nurture is mandatory for the unfolding of a masculine orientation and that the father's (or another older male's) availability is all-important. Only if a father is extremely inconsistent and rejective would paternal availability be a pathogenic factor. For a son, the vital function of a father appears to be that the boy can avail himself of an early and consistent masculine model. Studies show that chronic anxiety and poor adjustment are uncommon among boys who have solid identification with their father.[15]

In contrast, it was found that individuals who had experienced father-absence during childhood have a strong inclination toward depression.[16] Again, loss of a father due to divorce or separation (more so than due to death) during childhood has been found to be much higher in individuals who suffer from neurosis, psychosis, or personality disorders than for a number of different comparison groups.[17]

Findings also suggest that special attention should focus on the combination of absent or insufficient paternal involvement *and* maternal domination in a family. It may be assumed that most domineering Moms, in line with their particular needs and attitudes, marry extremely submissive men whose influence they can exclude from the child-rearing process. Hence there is probably a significant correlation between maternal overprotection and weak husbands. Sons in such situations have been found to be particularly susceptible to psychopathologies and tend to develop severe behavior disturbances.[18]

For example, it was found that transsexuality springs from situations where boys have extremely close physical relationships with their mothers, where mutual mother-child body contact during infancy and early childhood was especially intense, and where the mother reinforced many forms of feminine behavior. In none of these cases was the father "masculine" or involved with the rearing of the son.[19] Two surveys, appropriate as conclusions to these considerations, found that high paternal involvement and decisionmaking are uncommon in families in which there is a severely disturbed son.[20]

The impact of father-absence on the personality formation of the boy differs between the middle class and the lower class. It seems that the middle-class environment imparts to father-absence a particularly vicious quality. For example, it has been shown that middle-class father-absent boys suffer markedly from reduced masculinity while lower-class father-absent boys do not.[21] The lower-class boys', access to surrogate models gives them virtual immunity against turning feminine when a father's direct influence is removed. This may also explain the lack of evidence for maternal overprotection or overdependency among lower-class father-absent boys.[22] Moreover, while reduced masculinity in the middle-class boy lingers (and is still measurable during adolescence), reduced masculinity in lower-class children has adjusted to a normal level by the time they become adolescents.

When father-absent lower-class junior high school boys were compared with a matched group of father-present boys, clear-cut differences were found in either a masculinity-femininity interest inventory or in the teachers' rating of aggression and dependence.[23] Since similar comparisons with middle-class boys indicate a drastic reduction of masculinity in the father-absent groups, this finding seems to suggest that lower-class boys are not as dependent on their fathers for male models but have greater opportunity for model surrogates. Moreover, a lower-class mother simply has less opportunity to overprotect and feminize a father-absent boy than a middle-class mother because the former is usually involved in a full-time job. In fact, the lower-class mother who is without a husband (is divorced, separated, or deserted) is less inclined to react toward her child on the basis of feelings of guilt and shame, which have a way of encouraging a mother to overprotect her child.

In contrast, the middle-class mother is predisposed to feel guilty if her child, especially a son, is deprived of a father, for the ideal family consists of parents—both father and mother. Hence she feels partly to blame for the father's absence, particularly if this is due to divorce. As a consequence, she tends to overprotect and overindulge her child. Helpful and sentimental as these attempts may appear on the outside, such a mother is really using her child to alleviate her guilt feelings. Again, the child is not treated on the basis of his merits, or accepted as a growing individual who has a right to be unique, but as a medium through which the mother can achieve satisfaction for *her* needs. This emotional propensity of the mother sets the stage for the Momistic relationship.

Father-absence in itself, however, does not inevitably result in Momism. This is illustrated by many matricentric families in the lower class and among blacks where the father is absent and the mother heads the household. The mother tends to wield authority with a heavy hand, provides the income, makes decisions, and delegates duties—yet will not and *cannot* engage in the type of psychological manipulation that is central to a Mom's way of handling her child.

The middle-class boy, then, stands face to face with awesome perils to his emotional health. What advice, general though it may be, can we offer? As a rule, excessive maternal warmth and affection, motivated by a compensatory and making-up-to-the-child attitude, tend to hurt more than help the paternally deprived boy. It is important to realize that it is the *mother's ego strength* (where she has enough insight and sufficient control over her emotions to refrain from overpowering the boy's personality), *not* her constant demonstration of overconcern, which, in the last analysis, is the essential requisite for allowing the child a normal personality adjustment. The substitution of a close-binding, overprotective mother-son relationship for paternal deprivation will most likely result in stifling the son's personality and curtailing his ability for personal growth.

The Only Child

Momistic exertion can succeed only if the effort is focused and concentrated. It is psychologically and physically too difficult to spend the energy that is needed to tightly control and subtly manipulate more than one child, or at the most two children, to the intense degree Momism calls for. It follows, then, that Momistic practices are usually found only in small families. Any attempt at Momism in a situation of three or more children, unless they are very widely spaced, is likely to be fruitless, for the presence of siblings tends to insulate the effects of Momistic practices. Sibling interaction would create a variety of loopholes which the children would find convenient for escaping from Mom's totalitarian influence.

Population statistics indicate that lower-class families have a large number of children; so even if lower-class mothers made an attempt at Momism, it would not work. These mothers cannot effectively focus their control; their attempt at domination encounters too many hurdles and there are too many escape possibilities for the children. (The children can also use these loopholes to escape from father's domination, if need be.) It is not likely, under these conditions, to find Momistic practices in large lower-class families.

Moreover, lower-class mothers are too occupied with

the contingencies of day-to-day existence, especially when the father is absent, to have the time and energy to tightly control and psychologically manipulate the child. Unlike her middle-class counterpart, the lower-class mother cannot affort to "mother" twenty-four hours a day. Most likely, she goes to work, which in itself provides the child sufficient time away from an attempt at maternal domination or overconcern. For example, it has been found that more children with working mothers have disagreements with their parents than children with nonworking mothers. In spite of its negative connotation, this can be interpreted as meaning such children have a chance to acquire a healthy degree of independence and to develop their own ideas. They will be able to cut the emotional apron strings when the time comes.[24]

The Intellectualized Approach

Middle-class mothers tend to be college educated, and thus have been encouraged to approach problems and tasks from objective and scientific perspectives. This intellectualized outlook on life has most likely made a deep impression on them, for it is consistent with the style of reasoning with which they were familiar in their middle-class upbringing. Moreover, the intellectual way of looking at life had been shared with many other college students, their peers, who in interaction tend to reinforce each other's standards of scientific orientation.

Most middle-class mothers have this type of academic background, and come equipped with textbook outlooks on child raising. While this may sound entirely common and normal, it must be borne in mind that, historically speaking, this is a novel approach to child raising. During the preindustrial era, rural life and the large family set the tenor of child raising and created a nonacademic, work-focused, and survival-oriented parent-child relationship. The process of bringing up the child was coincidental to the family-life process as an entity;

no specific awareness of goal definition or means selection concerning child raising was cultivated. Even today we find this approach as the prevailing style of raising the child among lower-class, non-college-educated mothers.

A great deal of the information young college-educated women bring to the child-rearing enterprise is derived from textbooks that stress the importance of the personality development of the child. This theoretical treatment invariably belabors the importance of the child's proficiency in getting along with others. There is a tendency to judge the maturity of a person, even his total value as a person, on the basis of his ability to get along with others—to be congenial. (It is needless, perhaps, to point out that this reflects one of the major values of middle-class America, and that academia promotes it. While in many cases such academic support is desirable and serves humankind well, aspects of social pathologies and inhumanity may be unwittingly transmitted by the academic institution with equal effectiveness.) Their textbook training tells young women that "successful" child raising means to instill *congeniality* in the child's personality. This middle-class consensus threatens to add assembly line production to the child-rearing process. Perhaps an original parent is one who, luckily, did not listen to theories about what type of family produces "good" kids.

Ultimately, proficiency for parenthood is an emotional aptitude, and it cannot be acquired through exposure to prestigious theory. It *can* be acquired through the experience of growing up in an emotionally healthy family, where loving and accepting parents lay the foundation for the ability to, in turn, be loving and accepting of one's own children. *Good parents create good parents.* This presents a challenge to the attempt to promote formal parental education for young people. Can we really create good parents by such means? Perhaps we can help or enhance existing aptitudes, but normally we cannot *create* them once the individual has grown up and acquired his or her basic emotional inclinations. Probably the best we can hope to achieve through such formal nonfamilial education and training is to help participants discover whether or not they have the aptitude and inclination to become good parents.

This self-inventory process, nevertheless, definitely justifies the establishment of required parent-preparation courses for young individuals. Once they discover their proficiency, or deficiency, they have a more rational basis on which to come to a decision. If parenthood proficiency is not indicated, a person would be better off to stay away from it—and should be advised and counseled accordingly.

The foibles of the intellectual approach to child rearing were poignantly described by sociologist Arnold W. Green in his classic "The Middle-Class Male Child and Neurosis."[25] This report was based mainly on the insights and conclusions the author made as a child and young adult, growing up in Massachusetts in an industrial village composed primarily of immigrant Poles and their American-born children. The family life he observed among these working-class people was in sharp contrast with the style of "normal" American middle-class family life. Contrasting these two life-styles, and comparing the ominous differences in the results of child rearing, helped Green formulate a momentous and fruitful theory of the origin of neurotic distress in many middle-class boys. Green's comparison was an outstanding advancement toward recognizing the Momistic style, pinpointing the crippling peril and unveiling the hidden savagery of Mom's repressive transactions. His observations are so pertinent to our discussion that we shall go into them in detail.

The working-class families had a number of interesting features in common:

1. The European-born parents adhered to a simple peasant system of norms and values, which were alien to their American-born offspring.

2. In most cases the parents worked in factories and, consequently, were not at home during most of the day.

3. The children, who had many unsupervised hours, could roam the neighborhood, woods, and fields and associate with a variety of peers and adults outside their immediate family.

4. The parents were authoritarian and heavyhanded with the children, not sparing physical punishment on many occasions, and there were frequent confrontations between parents and children.

Green observed that these children did not suffer from undue anxieties, repressed frustrations, anti-individualistic docility, or other pathological symptoms that might indicate Momistic impairment. The explanation for this surprisingly healthy situation can be summed up by the following points.

1. Contact with many adults and peers in the neighborhood was not "obscured." The children had access to role models besides and beyond their parents; thus their identification process—and ultimately their identity—was not dependent on only their father or mother.

2. The children did not experience constant supervision by the parents, or by anyone in particular. They could pursue a wide range of activities without nagging admonitions about cleanliness, protection of furniture and appliances, and the social graces. As a result—and authoritarianism notwithstanding—the home atmosphere was psychologically nonrepressive.

3. The children were free to explore the neighborhood at will. Not only did they derive a gratifying sense of adventure from this but it also gave them a feeling of free will and power.

4. The children were not systematically conditioned

to repress hostility toward their parents, or any other person, and therefore were not trained in engaging in sublimations or substitutions for such repressed emotions. This may have saved them from, among other things, the necessity of rechanneling such negative emotions against themselves and acquiring excessive feelings of guilt, anxiety, and self-rejection.

5. The children were not forced, in any form, to show love and dedication toward their parents, nor was there any urging, demanding, or bartering for affection. The compulsive obligation to "love" one's parents was removed.

6. The children hit upon a variety of techniques for evading confrontation with parents, which enabled them to choose the more pleasant moments of parent-child association and to elude their parents when parental criticism or punishment was anticipated.

Green added comparison and contrast to the picture by turning to the American middle-class family *in general* and recognizing a number of its characteristics. (Some of the following points, merely hinted at by Green, are elaborated here to provide a fuller picture of the Momistic conditions in the stereotypical middle-class family.)

1. Middle-class fathers and mothers are usually well educated.

2. The fathers engage in a typical middle-class occupation where they experience pressure to succeed and where business and related social activities demand frequent absence from the home. In a sense, they are the property of the corporation and have to comply with time-consuming professional obligations if they desire promotion, prestige, and success. Their obligations might include a vast array of activities, such as attending parties, playing golf on weekends, joining clubs, attending conferences, traveling, etc. All of these activities reduce the time that fathers can spend with a wife and children.

3. The mothers suffer feelings of conflict because they visualize (frequently only vaguely) a possible career role which they regard as more suitable than the role of housewife. In the meantime, of course, they have occupied the position of wife-mother, and dissatisfaction about being limited to that role continues to bother them. They exhibit symptoms of ambiguity and discontent, which, beyond a certain degree, can be classified as neurotic. (Recall our definition of neurosis in Chapter 1.)

Many of the middle-class mothers express doubt, though usually indirectly, that choosing the wife-mother role is a wise substitute for the success they might have achieved in a career for which they think they have talent, skill, and proficiency. Interestingly, however, few mothers admit these negative feelings fully and openly —possibly because this would aggravate their frustration.

4. A similar style of sublimation can be observed among these mothers. Since they are unable to undo the *fait accompli* of parenthood, they resolve to turn motherhood into a career and become "career mothers."

5. They also believe that the work of a successful mother is reflected in the good behavior of the child. Unwittingly, the child becomes the "success test." In the final analysis, this means that the frustrated mother tries to live through her child.

6. The mothers agree that the best measurement of the progress of the child—and thus of themselves—is comparing him with other children. A vital implication of the comparison is that the mother keeps urging the child to compete with his peers.

7. The vast majority of the mothers are the constant and almost sole companions of the preschool child. Maternal supervision reaches into every detail of the child's daily activities, needs, and—if possible—thoughts.

8. It is apparent that the mothers try to raise the

child according to the latest thinking and writing of experts in child care. Most of them are familiar with the prominent child-care literature and make a serious effort to implement the theoretical advice.

9. Most of the mothers believe that it is wrong to inflict physical punishment on the child. If a child needs correction, it is to be done through "reasoning" and "explaining." The most noteworthy method, which is hidden behind these euphemisms, can be defined as manipulation of the child's need to be accepted and loved by his mother. This is the "conditional love" technique.

10. It is important to remember that the child's "need" must first be indoctrinated; otherwise manipulation obviously would not work. The mothers appear to have instilled this need perfectly; that is, they have convinced the child that he needs his mother's love—that he could not survive or be happy without it.

Mothers, then, find in the conviction (or need perception) a convenient lever which they vigorously operate to exact compliance and obedience—in short, "good behavior." Mother's disapproval of and disappointment with a particular form of behavior becomes synonymous with the threat to withhold her "love." And, conversely, "good behavior" is rewarded by the assurance that now mother "loves" him. Green emphasized that it is not an innate need for parental love, but "the constant threat of its withdrawal *after the child has been conditioned to the need* that lies at the root of the most characteristic modern neurosis."[26] This threat becomes powerful enough to make the child do whatever his mother wants him to do. Indeed, research findings indicate that maternal achievement pressures are more effective than paternal pressures because of a mother's application of the "love oriented" sanctions.[27]

It is precisely the use of these powerful "love oriented" sanctions (negative as well as positive ones) which, according to Green and other social scientists, forms the basis for many modern neuroses; that is, situations where unresolved conflict and uncertainty add up to so much psychological pressure that severe symptoms of anxiety and unhappiness arise. (We must emphasize that the way social scientists and especially psychiatrists discovered the causal process was *not* by observing a Momistic situation and then assessing its neurotic consequences in the child, but by first coming across all sorts of neuroses, usually in adolescents and adults, and *then*, coincidentally, tracing their origin back to the operation of a Mom.)

In short, the child is constantly reminded to be grateful for his mother's "loving care" and, in return, must "stay out of trouble" and do what pleases her; if not, he risks losing her all-important love. The child thus lives in perpetual anxiety about losing acceptance and affection, and knows that these qualities depend upon how he behaves in a given situation—that they are *not* something he can rely upon because of his worth as a total person. The activation of his sense of self-worth is hence anchored in the endless range of situational and external behavior and their ephemeral appraisal value by others, *and not in the core of his selfhood.* This nudges him toward endlessly seeking reassurance for self-worth from those around him by trying to do what is thought of as acceptable.

Once a child has been conditioned in this manner, the slightest controversy, argument, or disapproval may lead him to doubt his personal worth, and may generate acute reactions of fear, guilt, shame, and inadequacy. Such emotions can be built up to an agonizing complex of insecurity.

In order to reduce it, the child (or later the adult) will obey, conform, and remain a child forever—and, above all, desperately try to avoid being alone. Being alone would mean that the sources of potential approval and "love" are not immediately available and therefore cannot be readily activated. For many Momistically impaired persons—young or old—the total absence of potential sources of approval and love apparently is less bearable than having sources that harbor possible approval or disapproval. In other words, he'd rather be criticized than alone! This may be so because an outside agent at least offers the hope that it can be pleased if the right behavior is selected. Absence of the agent deprives him of any such chance, and he is left with a constant, nagging uncertainty about his acceptability and self-worth.

In overall terms, the resulting personality makeup is characterized by anxious self-tailoring to social expectations, which goes hand in hand with the search for security. This sort of individual, who is devoid of unique personality expression, manifests slavish dependence on his mother or, later, a mother surrogate.

The main conclusion we can derive from Green's observations is that lack of parental affection ("love"), authoritarianism, ready use of physical punishment, and unsupervised roaming will leave a child's personality relatively unharmed—whereas the intellectualized approach, with "love oriented" manipulation, will leave a child floundering with severe problems of insecurity and overdependency. In other words, "good" and "loving" mothers become dispensers of their children's neurotic anxieties—a ghastly irony!

What Will the Neighbors Think?

The old cliché, "keeping up with the Joneses," has always been the motto of the middle class. It refers to excessive sensitivity about how one appears to, and is appraised by, neighbors and the community at large. There is always the readiness to make amends if the family's social radar picks up a discrepancy between its condition or appearance, on one side, and the demands, tastes, and standards of the social milieu on the other.

Suggestions, though usually indirect and often only perceived as such, impinge on the family in myriad ways. For example, a neighbor lady's apparently casual inquiry about Jimmy's "strange" new friends from "another part" of the town may be sufficient to cause a mother to reconsider the wisdom of her boy's associating with the new acquaintances. On the other hand, hearing a favorable assessment of a new style or fad may trigger speedy imitation.

In this setting the child often finds himself used as a gauge by his parents to measure adherence to community standards. This becomes an acute issue for the mother who has decided, in the midst of all sorts of conflicts, to make motherhood the most important item in her success agenda. Norms as to what constitutes success seldom originate in privacy or in a social vacuum; rather, they are patterned on the sociocultural forces of the community. Community standards, then, become determinants which influence the "career mother's" production plans. In order to harvest success, there must be individuals who confirm it. And mother's job, first of all, is to sense the success criteria which significant persons in the community hold. Predictably, she will soon envision what the proper and desirable behavior of her child should be. This criterion becomes her goal, and she is determined to achieve it.

The significance of community influence becomes sharper when it is contrasted with the working-class setting, where sensitivity toward community standards is much more relaxed and the child enjoys greater freedom from parental achievement orientation and constant comparison. It would be unthinkable for most lower-class parents to visualize their small tots parading along a model's ramp, guided by mother's or father's hand, to be appraised by an audience and a panel of judges as to beauty, health, charm, and style of clothes. Yet this is precisely what middle-class parents do in many communities. For example, the Phoenix Soroptimist Club's annual beauty and health show included about 500 youngsters, age one to five, in 1970. It received wide publicity and picture coverage in the local press, which described, among others, fourteen-month-old W. D., dressed in a tiny bikini of blue daisies and wearing several daisies in her hair, entering her first beauty contest.[28] The report offers the understatement that it wasn't the little girl but her mother, Mrs. W. D., who told reporters: "I thought it would be fun and I wanted to see the other pretty babies." Mrs. M. T. had an even better reason: "I entered my child because we think we have a fantastic baby." Her son M., eighteen and a half months old, "was sitting in a stroller, a bottle to his mouth." This mother proudly added that over the past three weeks (the duration of the contest) her son had accumulated "more points [earned by tickets for the show sold by their mothers] than any other boy and appears to be in the lead for king."

The victors of the various age categories were announced at a Coronation Pageant in a large high school auditorium. Besides a king and queen, selections included a prince and princess, a count and countess, and a duke and duchess from each age group. It was noted—as the young children were paraded before a panel of judges—that some smiled, some squirmed, and some screamed. "Despite a mother's coaxing, all one little boy could do was hide his face in mother's skirt from the judges' view." Not all of the children reacted timidly; many were eager to smile and wave goodbye to the judges. One little boy offered to shake hands with a judge as he exited from the stage. Many little girls were prettily dressed up and hovered over by mom or dad. The mother of a twenty-one-month-old girl explained her reason for participation as "wanting to show her off." A four-year-old boy patiently awaited his promenade turn with his father while his mother was busy registering her two-and-a-half-year-old daughter. "This was all my wife's idea," the father explained. The little boy didn't seem that impressed: "He kept telling his dad all he wanted to do was 'sit down.' "

For most lower-class parents, this type of contest is meaningless and ridiculous. Their sensitivity to community standards is far less competitive and compulsive, thus eliminating the motivation to "use" children, least of all near-infants.

It is among middle-class families that we find the incentive for competition and achievement and, thus, the desire to control the child, to shape his behavior and, ultimately, his destiny. The family's prestige and social standing depend on how well the child compares to other children. A mother who suffers from oversensitivity will try to have her child look perfect in the eyes of the community and will work to accomplish this by any means. Actually, not quite "any means," because even the means must be acceptable, if not perfect. And here again we have the *psychological* style of child manipulation. It *works well*, given the additional conditions discussed elsewhere in this book, and it *looks good* because it does not use physical force or any other "barbaric" method to make the little boy the "best behaved" boy on the block.

In the final analysis, the mother lives through her child, aggrandizing herself and flaunting to the community that having a "top child" means that she is a "top mother." In the process, she appears to the community as a martyr who is sacrificing herself for a noble cause. But persons who appear unconcerned for themselves and, instead, make all manner of "sacrifice" in order to "help" another (they are looked upon as "unselfish") usually demand a terrible price in return, and usually *get* it: namely, absolute conformity with their wishes. As Sidney Howard says: "We are all familiar with the 'unselfish' mother who sacrifices all her own choices at happiness in order to help her son get through school. Would it not be ungracious if the son then, against his mother's 'reasonable wishes,' married a girl of *his* choice but not his mother's?"[29]

The Divorcee-Mother

Divorce *per se* is not unique to the middle class. In fact, social scientists could make the point that it is less so—that, statistically speaking, the family structure is more intact among the middle class than among the lower class. While this may be so, we must not lose sight of *accompanying* features that differ between the two environments. While the lower-class child, in a situation of parental divorce, continues to have access to other adults in the neighborhood, keeps "running around" with peers, and most likely goes on associating with a number of siblings, the middle-class child becomes much more isolated and much more acutely aware of the loss of a parent. The loss usually concerns the father, who in the past may have provided minimum balance to the mother's influence or domination attempt. It turns out that the fact of having divorced parents creates a much more limiting and confining arrangement for the middle-class child than for his lower-class counterpart.

Furthermore, the emotional interdependence and psychologized family style of the middle class prepare the stage for a shattering trauma when divorce hits. More often than not, there are profound feelings of confusion and guilt among *all* participants, including the child, whose feelings in reaction to the divorce are often considered secondary in intensity. This may be a mistaken opinion, though understandable, since the divorcing couple undergoes tremendous emotional stress and, in trying to sort out confusion and anguished feelings, may virtually ignore the reaction of third parties. They therefore often overlook the fact that the child may feel just as guilty or rejected as they themselves. The child's conclusion from observing the array of typical pre-divorce symptoms, such as whispers, yelling, dull silence, crying, petulance, and depressed moods on the part of the mother and father, adds up to "I'm scared. Maybe I've been a bad boy."

Of course, these are vague emotional processes which the child may not be able to verbalize at the time. To the young child, the parents are not ordinary human beings. They could do no wrong; they always had the answers to problems; they always were able to ward off fear, defeat, and uncertainty. And, most importantly, they represented the ultimate source of love and care. In short, for the young child they were Godlike.

The essence of this reasoning leads to the inability of the child to place responsibility for the parental disharmony on the parents themselves. Since the child—we are talking about a child not much older than five or six —cannot perceive his mother and father as being wrong, but rather as paragons of rightness, authority, and strength, he feels that it is *he* who must have done something dreadfully wrong—or, even, *be* wrong. The feeling of "being"—not just "doing"—wrong undermines his self-confidence and arouses essential doubts about his personal worth.[30]

Since, in the vast majority of divorce cases, the mother retains custody of the child, the child may develop an extremely strong need to be assured of at least retaining his mother. The fear of losing the remaining parent has been observed as nearly universal, and a common symptom is a clinging attachment to the mother. If the mother has a Momistic propensity, she can avail herself of this additional psychological leverage, making her influence all the more persuasive and powerful. All she has to do is intimate that "if you are hurting mother, she, just maybe, may also leave you," and typically she is assured the 100 percent cooperation of the frightened child. While this is not intentionally meant to be cruel but merely reasonable and expedient, the threat is apt to inflict severe anxiety on the child. The child, in this situation, is forced into a position of *super*dependency because the mother is absolutely all he has. His vulnerability is greater because there now is *no one else* upon whom he can rely. All of his needs must be filled by mother.

Given the impressive divorce rate in recent years, the importance of the effects of family breakups on children, especially in Momistic situations, can hardly be exaggerated. Yet there are no specific research data which provide insight into what goes on in children (especially preschoolers) in such Momistic-divorce situations. We can only surmise that they provide an even freer hand for a Mom to tie the child more tightly to herself, and that they better enable her to possess the child, live through him, and render him pliable.

The Rite of Passage—Or Missing the Boat

A "rite of passage" is a public ceremony that announces and celebrates a person's entry into a new status. Such rituals serve two major functions: (1) they inform the community about the new status and thus direct the proper actions and reactions of members of society toward the novice incumbent, and (2) they help the initiates develop the perceptions, emotions, and attitudes that go with their new status. A rite of passage thus facilitates identity formation. Such safeguards for status identity exist in many parts of the world but appear to be sparse in most urban-industrial societies, such as the United States.

In many cultures, especially small and rural "folk" societies, a helpful rite of passage is performed at the time a girl or boy ceases to be a child and is coming to be considered an adult. It substantiates the masculine and feminine roles in the self-perception of the young person, facilitates his or her assumption of adult stature, and in general helps combat uncertainty as to his or her identity. Sometimes these ceremonies have a sacred connotation, suggesting divine sanction of the new role and impressing on the youngster that the new rights and obligations are not merely man-made. In all cases these rites are public rituals, providing the young individual with the opportunity to make his or her bow to adult society.

A number of status transitions are universal, whether or not they are publicly indicated. For example, birth, puberty, assumption of adult responsibilities, marriage, parenthood, and death are universal transitions. Because of their universality, similarities can be observed all over the world in the ceremonies that mark these events. In a sense, this regularity of transition in human life resembles nature, from which neither the individual nor the society as a whole is isolated. A periodicity seems to prevail in nature that has its analogue in human life, patterning our orientation toward space and time dimensions. In the context of this book, the transition from childhood to adulthood is of particular significance.

It is a popular belief that this transition is indicated by the "puberty rite"; however, this is an oversimplification. It is more correct to distinguish between the "puberty rite," indicating physiological maturity and reproductive ability, and the "initiation rite," indicating entry into the adult world. In some cultures these two rites coincide; but in some cultures they do not, and separate rites are provided. These rituals have been described in anthropological literature.

For example, among the Masai of Kenya circumcision as a ritual of social puberty is performed as soon as boys are considered mature enough to undergo the elaborate rite of passage, usually between the ages of twelve and sixteen. This becomes a collective event every four to six years, with all eligible boys participating. This group of boys will then be known as a "generation," collectively bearing a certain name chosen by the chief. At the same time, the fathers of the boys also undergo a special rite of passage called "passing the fence," *elevating* them into the new status of "old man" and entitling them to be called "father of [name of the offspring]."

Other field studies have reported the initiation rituals among the Australian aborigines. At the turning point between childhood and adulthood, two aspects of the new role are publicly clarified and celebrated. They include the social consensus that now the young member of the tribe is marriageable and free from parental authority. He is henceforth allowed to move out of the parental dwelling and set up independent living quarters.

An interesting example of the independence of the initiation rite from the puberty rite is the bar mitzvah of the Jews. At the early and (usually) pre-puberty age of thirteen, the Jewish boy is ceremoniously introduced to adult responsibility and privilege—acquiring, at least ritualistically, adult status. However, it is obvious that the bar mitzvah within the American Jewish subculture has been reduced to a religious festival with little or no bearing on the public and secular life of the young boy. While in previous ages this ritual signified that the boy (young man) was allowed to marry and assume adult membership in the community, in modern times the boy is not afforded such privileges. Urban-industrial conditions, let alone modern law, simply do not allow a boy of thirteen to gain economic independence or assume political privileges. The decline of the bar mitzvah among American Jews may be, among other reasons, a consequence of the discrepancy between the implied transition to adulthood and modern society's prohibition against assuming adult standards at that age.

An extremely interesting parallel has been observed in cultures where, for various cultural or economic reasons, the mother-son relationship is unusually close. We refer to cultures where the offspring is breast-fed, sleeps with the mother, depends on her almost exclusively, and, in general, is in close physical contact with the mother not only during infancy but during an extended period of his childhood. Crosscultural surveys have disclosed that such cultures make their young males (usually during their teens) undergo an extremely harsh rite of passage.[31]

While this is done as an unquestioned custom, because it is part of the tradition of the people, the analytic interpretation of anthropologists suggests a definite reason for the particular harshness which is applied at the time of the ritualistic "weaning." This harshness may be a function of the unconsciously felt necessity for correcting emotions. It has the effect of correcting the emotions of the young men and aligning them with the cultural standards of masculinity. The striking aspect of this finding is a very significant correlation between the degree of mother dependency during childhood and the harshness of the rite of passage among the surveyed nonurban societies.

The sociological law that seems to unite these observations suggests that in order to neutralize or balance one social force, an equally strong social force has to be applied. More specifically, the boys have to learn to repress their earlier feminine identification. The ritual, initiating them into the world of the adult male, serves to shatter the remnants of feminine identity and firmly introduce the masculine identity. Many so-called primitive peoples have apparently hit upon this principle unconsciously and have intuitively institutionalized the required counterforce—in this case a definite and decisive rite of passage. It may involve painful hazing by the males of the community, tests of endurance and manliness, temporary seclusion from women, genital operations, change of residence (involving separation of the boy from his mother and sisters), and establishment of male authority.

Illustrations of initiation rites among "folk," tribal, or subcultural groups could be vastly extended. The ethnographic material on this subject is rich and fascinating,[32] and the examples cited above should demonstrate that, in many parts of the world, young members of society obtain help in defining their social standing, their sex roles, and, in the process, their basic identities.

No such unequivocal rite of passage exists for the middle-class child, or, for that matter, for a child in any socioeconomic class in the United States. Nevertheless, the debutante ball of the upper class has some elements of a rite of passage: publicity, emotionality, and the understanding that one is being introduced into the world of the adult. The lower-class teenager may also avail himself of a makeshift ritual when he enters adult status, even though this may consist of nothing more than quitting school at sixteen, getting a job, and acquiring a car. These changes, with their assumption of responsibilities, are a visible public phenomenon, acknowledged by peers and the neighborhood. A new status has been publicly established; the young individual (especially a boy) knows it; and the community respects it. The nonspecific and confusing adolescent years are thereby shortened.

This cannot be said about the middle-class youngster who has a long and tedious adolescence, during which, by definition, he is considered neither child nor adult. He must feel his way through a no-man's-land where status, status identity, and self-definition are tenuous. Thus it is more or less a normal reaction that he compensates for his vague standing in the adult world by turning toward a teenage subculture (or youthful counterculture) where he is able to derive—temporary though it be—a degree of identity among similarly troubled and "exiled" individuals.

Though it is true that for many middle-class adolescents the experience of bridging the gap between childhood and adulthood by joining the "in" crowd can be a helpful step in their liberation from family domination, this avenue is largely blocked for the Momistically dominated youngster. He simply is not allowed to venture out and away from mother's dominion. In addition, he probably won't even try to break the maternal bond. He is so thoroughly conditioned to adhere to his mother that he will forgo all attempts at establishing ego boundaries of his own. In the family situation where the mother had held the reins tightly, the child—right into his teen years, and often beyond—will be guided by his mother as the obedient child he was and is going to remain.

The assumption we make is that if American culture would provide a rite of passage at a given time during the teenage years, the young individual would be helped to wrench himself from mother-child bondage, liberate himself from stifling conditioning, develop his creativity and explore his personality potentials.

The significance of not having a rite of passage for the young members of our society ("puberty rite" or "adult initiation rite"—whatever terminology anthropologists prefer to attach to the process) must be seen *in combination* with the middle-class conditions discussed earlier. Mere absence of such a rite would be relatively insignificant; but its absence *in convergence with other conditions* robs a child of his last chance of escaping from a mother-imposed, continual childhood. This becomes especially acute for a boy who grows up without a father who helps him participate in the socialization process. Subsequent discussions will show how serious this condition can be for the boy who lacks a visible and realistic masculine model—for whom the absence of a rite of passage may mean a *coup de grace* to a faltering attempt at personality unfolding.

These, then, appear to be the major conditions the middle class affords, creating fertile ground for Momism. They are truly formidable.

The various middle-class circumstances must be understood as overlapping, reinforcing each other, and compounding into a complex issue. Their power can best be comprehended if we keep in mind that they combine to make a personality-molding *constellation* whose impact is a total experience for the young individual. Momism is systemic in nature; that is, it consists of interlocking conditions from which many children find it impossible to escape: a veritable labyrinth.

Chapter 4

*Each parent has a dream of what his child
will be, and it takes time to realize that a
child is not a dream but a person in his own
right.*—The Group for the Advancement
of Psychiatry

The Vulnerability
of the Boy

What makes the boy so vulnerable to Mom's influence?

It seems that his peculiar sensitivity is primarily due to the qualities of the masculine role and the method by which he learns it. To fully understand the dynamics of the mother-son relationship, we must look at the broader context of American child-raising practices, and its most obvious aspect, which immediately leaps into view, is the continuing sex differentiation in personality formation. Americans still value masculinity and femininity as the major and proper differences between human beings.

We shall discuss a number of incentives that persuade American mothers to perpetuate this contrast and continue the masculinity vs. femininity game. These persuasions emanate from the cultural heritage, with its linguistic bias, male-supremacist theology, dependence of

85

self-definition on sex identity, emphasis on the ability to relate with each other through "roles," need for a role blueprint with which to rear children, and the necessity to save nervous energy through routinized and predictable role behavior.

We call attention to the fact that the past decade has seen a reduced rigidity of the traditional role definitions and a modified contrast in role behavior. Enough changes have occurred to bring the divergent roles somewhat closer together: men act a little more like women and women a little more like men—in short, both act more like people. However, the loosening-up process was limited, so that we are now on a plateau of liberation from sexist traditions. In other words, the emancipation process has slackened because of ensuing confusion about what to do with the new freedom and how to cope with a society's inability to clearly define acceptable behavior in human relationships. The intimidating monster of normlessness (social scientists call it "anomie") typically follows on the heels of disturbance of traditional patterns.

This chapter includes a discussion of clinical problems and some of the pathologies that can arise in the masculine vs. feminine game.

The core of our discussion is the vulnerability of the boy. In the section "When Learning Masculinity, Don't Imitate the Teacher," we lay out a basic framework for understanding the intricate conditions under which the boy must learn his identity.

Finally, we discuss what might be called the male counterpart to Momism: Dadism. This speculative and innovative concept compares the pathological mother-son relationship with the pathological father-daughter relationship. This section is included to guard against the misconception that only the mother-child relationship is a problem in American society and to point out, as well, interesting similarities between the two types of relationships.

The Game's Still On: Masculinity vs. Femininity

Over the past decade the women's liberation movement has made appreciable inroads through the bastions of traditional male chauvinism. However, the vast majority of middle-class women have realized that full liberation is not around the corner. This realization—dim and emotionalized as it may be—motivated them to seek a substitute activity in the meantime: the "motherhood career." But it has backfired and turned into a misadventure.

In the preceding chapters we said that this maternal obsession has developed into a misadventure because of the mother's basic conflicts and frustrations and that the ensuing psychological manipulation leaves the child with an emotional handicap. Yet it is an even greater disaster in the sense that it has counteracted the most fundamental premise of the egalitarian aspiration of the emancipation drive. *Most mothers have retained, and further cultivated, the masculinity myth in their sons.* In a sense, they rigidly maintain a schizophrenic world: on one side they clamor for equality and unistandards and, on the other, they teach little boys how to become masculine he-men.

Can one condemn mothers for continuing this habit? Specifically, can one accuse the reneging mothers of hypocrisy—who presumably endorse the egalitarian aspirations of the liberation movement?

The persuasiveness to which they are exposed is formidable. They are up against thousands of years of sex differentiation in the division of labor, cultural dogma, character development, and child-raising practices. Probably not one aspect of Western civilization, reaching back to preliterate times, is not tinged with the male-supremacist attitude. Our language, for example, is a particularly accurate mirror of the sexist tradition, and we can hardly talk about a person without stumbling over pronouns that suggest a universe created and populated by males alone.

An interesting example, which is related to the subject matter of this book, is the style in which the various works of Dr. Benjamin Spock have been written. Throughout his writings he used the masculine pronouns "he," "him," etc., whenever he referred to "child." (There is no intention here of portraying Dr. Spock as an exceptional violator of egalitarian standards; he used the *customary* pronouns with which all writers of his time described a child *in general*.) Nor was it until the 1970s that Dr. Spock revised his books and replaced the formerly ubiquitous "he" with "he *or* she." Religious dogmas also reflect the male-dominated history of Western people: our male-oriented theology refers to God as "He," "Father," "Lord," "King of Heaven," and refers to "His Son" as the "Prince of Peace," etc.[1]

Can anyone change this sexist heritage or deactivate it within two or three generations? It is most likely that it will take many more generations, for the concern and striving for unisex standards have not yet permeated American society. They are still primarily a preoccupation of middle-class feminists who are up against defensive male chauvinists, as well as indifferent, nonsupportive, and even antagonistic women all across the socioeconomic spectrum.

But this may be the least obstacle on the road to liberation. It seems that during the last few decades of the twentieth century the women's liberation movement not only pursued the relatively tame aims of previous generations of feminists—who focused on equality in political life, before the law, and in the labor force—but an all-encompassing battle plan. Now the *basic sex-role differences*, including their rationale and justification, are under attack. This is an uphill battle if there ever was one. The counterforces are deeply entrenched (the major one being *subtle psychological nature*) and are found everywhere—among the ranks of either side.

Since time immemorial, one's sexual identification has constituted an important component of one's self-view, answering in major part the question, Who am I? Deletion of the sex-identification component from the overall identity of an individual would mean a drastic change from customary habits and rules—habits and rules that are deeply anchored in religio-cultural credos. Such a change would also call for a profound reorientation that would have to settle, at least provisionally, basic philosophical questions, including the most fundamental question of what a human being *is* or *should be*.

The process of formulating unisex standards and forming unisex personalities would entail extremely complex psychological dynamics. It would mean rechanneling an important part of our identity genesis: from gender to something else. What this "something else" might be is hard to say at this time; but reference is made to a *human personage*: before we are male or female, we are *human*.

But this may prove to be too vague and therefore frightening—at least during the initial transition from gender identity to a uniquely personal identity. Would one's social position, career, or professional status make up for the faded gender identity? Would it spring from some very private and idiosyncratic source of one's personality? Whatever the answer, it is not yet clear; it is still hiding in the future, in spite of the endeavors of fervent women's liberationists.

America is stuck with sex identities. It has retained

its rigidity to a much greater extent than modern egalitarian legislation would make us believe. After all, feelings and attitudes cannot be legislated. Departure from the traditional patterns is a slow process of modification, and initial modifications have a way of creating confusion, fear, and uncertainty.

As a reaction against uncertainty and confusion, American mothers, although often giving lip service to the principles of liberation from traditional sex-role distinction, continue to treat their sons and daughters according to the roles of our cultural heritage. Even though American society is less differentiated in terms of sex typing than many economically underdeveloped nations, its socialization practices and human interrelations still reflect relatively clear-cut sex differences. Social scientists agree that boys are still expected to be physically more aggressive, competitive, independent, and dominant, while girls are expected to be more nurturant, submissive, passive, dependent, neat, and verbally expressive. (Peer-group play and imitation of adult activities provide the opportunity to learn sex-differentiated behavior.) Boys are generally observed to prefer activities of a mechanical and analytical nature, such as building model racing cars and games in which speed, strength, and aggression are rewarded, as in contact sports. Girls seem to choose among the more sedentary and domestic activities, such as playing house and working in the kitchen.[2] (The issue of whether these are "innate" or "learned" preferences will be treated elsewhere.)

Another influence on a mother deals with social dynamics of an intriguingly subtle nature. Societies have always attempted to foster ease and lucidity of human interaction by offering prescriptions and formulas which outline the expectations for interaction. Thus we talk about *social roles,* which are society's blueprints for behavior for the incumbents of positions and for recurring situations. They spell out the rights and obligations of the interacting parties. Indeed, we are parties to such interactional situations every day. Even the seemingly informal and purely emotional relationship of a parent and child can be couched and described in the language of role interaction, which is not mere sociological pedantry but a useful tool for understanding the normal, expected, and recurrent qualities of the parent-child relationship.

The concept of role spells out the norms, the "musts" and "must nots," which we expect an individual to exhibit in his behavior, motivations, and personality. A role, then, is a blueprint for feeling and behaving in certain ways. It is society's way of making us distinctly social creatures who interact in an orderly and predictable manner.

Largely unconsciously, we adhere to numerous roles. If a society is characterized by large-scale abandonment of role adherence, it would suffer tremendous confusion, and possibly disintegration. Whether we are aware of it or not, most social interaction proceeds according to role understanding, thereby making the various transactions and communications relatively smooth and efficient. Normally, when there are two interacting parties, one's obligations are the other's rights, and vice versa. If the norms are clear and adherence is tight, confusion is at a minimum. This type of interaction takes considerable strain off our neural systems: we interact with a minimal expenditure of energy on trying to figure out the myriad "hows," "whys," and "whats" of each human encounter. The norms of many of these encounters are stringently programmed and outlined by cultural convention. Although this may be wearing on the creativity a person could marshal in a given instance of human interaction, it prevents friction and uncertainty.

The norms of many role interactions are highly specific, safeguarded by law, and formally sanctioned. For example, interaction between a doctor and his patient is expected to be based solely on professional functions and is surrounded by a legal aura. On the other hand, some role expectations are based on more informal and "customary" agreements and are informally sanctioned, such as the rules of friendship or neighborliness. Yet their purpose is just as important as the more formally agreed-upon roles: to maintain clarity and predictability in interaction. The desirability of these qualities is based on the need to conserve nervous energy, time, and social order. These powerful motivating forces exert a constant pull, like a social-psychological field of gravity, toward a clear, consensual, and predictable style of interaction. All human groups, in response to these needs of conservation, tend to work out agreements about roles and their interaction.

Men and women in society, when confronting each other, must cope with these needs. In an oversimplified way, one might say this is one reason why sex-role definitions were developed in the first place. (However, other very important factors include the biological and reproductive differences and the necessity of the division of labor in pre-industrial living.) In any case, the social, psychological, and even neurological needs for clear norms of interaction *exist*; they demand patterns, regularities, and a certain style, according to which logical generalizations can be made without the necessity of totally reassessing each situation. This, then, presents another pressure for the mother to go along with the age-old masculinity-femininity pattern. A mother derives a degree of certainty from these standards, a sense of direction, and a feeling of being on familiar ground on which she can treat her son as a socially defined and approved object. In other words, she has a blueprint by which she can proceed with minimum confusion and wasted time.

One could turn the psychological process around and approach it from the need for control *in general*. In order to exert control, adherence to a blueprint—of whatever type—is imperative. Many mothers find the conventional masculine blueprint quite convenient for controlling the child. In fact, they may endorse the blueprint's *procedural guidelines* because they give them a good measure of control, while throughout all their labor of bringing up the boy the *goal* of masculinity may play a relatively minor role.

These, then, are some of the major incentives that explain why mothers teach children very early in life their roles as males and females. These roles are assigned right after birth and are continuously reinforced as the children grow older. We now know that the first two or three years of life are of crucial importance in the formation of an individual's sex-role orientation. Clinical observations of patients with physical-sexual incongruencies have revealed that self-conceptions relating to sex role are extremely difficult to change after the third year of life.[3] Children grow into a gradual understanding of male and female roles and reflect their knowledge through sex-appropriate action. Behavioral scientists have determined that eight- to eleven-year-old children generally have completed the process whereby definitive differences in sex roles are established in their own minds.[4]

Modification of the Game

We must insert a word of modification here: there is indication that sex-differentiated indoctrination has lessened over the past decades. In the 1930s, Professors Lewis M. Terman and Catherine C. Miles worked out a scale for measuring femininity and masculinity (which became one of the standard measurements of its kind) that included a large variety of items which were, at the time, reliably sex differentiating.[5] A retesting of the internal consistency and validity of the items in the 1960s disclosed that a majority of them no longer discriminated between female and male behavior, manners, attitudes, emotions, and aspirations.[6] The discovered changes were in the direction of more diffuse standards between the sexes.

While these changes have had some liberating effects, especially on women, they have also made conduct between the sexes more complex. More and more, the determination of proper action and reaction toward a member of the opposite sex has come to be based on knowing the individual personality involved, with its unique makeup, needs, and aspirations, rather than on the old-fashioned stereotypical approach which offered lucid and neatly packaged recipes as a way of guiding relationships between the sexes.

Conscious efforts are made today in trying to reduce the sexist tradition. One of the most significant thrusts in that direction is aimed at preventing children from being indoctrinated with contrasting sex roles. For example, the New York Women's Action Alliance has prepared a new child-care project which tries to eliminate sexist elements in the curricula of day-care centers. A groundwork was laid by researching sex-role stereotyping, then meeting with parents and teachers at various centers, and then revising stereotyped materials, toys, equipment, etc. The latter step necessitated redesigning and hand-producing early childhood materials, including such things as puzzles, block accessories, photographs, and lotto games. The result was a set of highly innovative toys that were aimed at breaking down stereotypes in a wide variety of jobs, statuses, and activities.

Family life was portrayed by showing situations in which both men and women engage in nurturing roles. The traditional play situation in which "boys are doing and girls are watching" was restructured to depict girls and boys together in active play.[7]

Other efforts include the rewriting of children's books. Stan and Jan Berenstain, for example, created *He Bear, She Bear*, a book for preschoolers with simple, lively pictures showing sexual equality and saying, among other rhymes: "We bulldoze roads, we drive cranes, we drive trucks, we drive trains. We can do all these things, you see, whether we are he or she."[8]

But such efforts are few and far between. This, at best, is the embryonic stage of changes to come. All over the nation, the usual day-care center is still blatantly sexist oriented. Hence such observations as those listed above should be understood as adding up to no more than a relatively minor modification of the traditional social patterns between the sexes at this time.

There are at least two primary reasons why the traditional sex-role distinction is still intact in American society. One reason deals with the *degree* of change that women's liberation has made on traditional standards. There has been much more lip service and verbal attack than formulation of new patterns when it comes to reorienting the children to unisex standards. The second reason takes into account a general social truism: a touch of anomie (social normlessness and confusion), after an initial period of nonsystematic and halfhearted attempts at abolishing or reducing time-honored standards, usually results in the *hesitancy*, at least temporarily, to proceed further with the liberation movement.

(This coming-to-a-temporary-halt phenomenon is often identified as the so-called *backlash*. This concept reminds one of the rallying cry and resistance of the opposition, which usually marshals its forces precisely at the time the movement shows a slowdown in momentum. In fact, the forces of the backlash may be invited or encouraged by the slowdown to strike back because of apparent uncertainty among the ranks of the opponents.)

In our case, rather than risk further chaos in human relationships, the truncated revolution (which was largely verbal anyway) seems to have settled for a reprise, for a degree of adherence to sex-role behavior. In other words, the fact that sex-role behavior is still widespread, and most likely will stay with us for generations to come, is due, first, to insufficient progress on the part of the feminists and, second, to the reaction to the confusion arising from the initial battle.

Social scientists have found that sex-role differences have remained remarkably stable. Especially from the child's viewpoint, there have been hardly any changes: the child continues to visualize the world as split down the middle and dividing things, events, and behavior between the masculine and the feminine.[9] As a young mother, a dismayed women's liberationist, exclaimed: "It's no damn wonder—just sit in on a kindergarten class some afternoon!"

The kindergarten is only one example of society's many powerful bulwarks against unisex development. Children who attend the average kindergarten are treated in accordance with traditional boy-girl differences. Boys learn that "boys don't cry" and girls learn that "girls don't boss boys." Toys are assigned according to the traditional boy-girl distinction; speech patterns, aggressiveness, innovativeness, and a myriad of perceptions are likewise reinforced. In short, two different life-styles are introduced and encouraged.

Essentially, then, we can say that the game is still on. Americans still value, inculcate, and practice the difference between masculinity and femininity.

Disasters of the Game

The halfway-emancipated middle-class mother is no exception: she "goes along" and helps with the indoctrination of the conventional sex-differentiated roles; but she does so with considerable conflict. The conflict may symptomize itself in various ways. She may basically identify with the old feminine role but exhibit (perhaps in a compensatory mood) masculine interests and activities. Or she may identify much more with an egalitarian, perhaps even masculine, role but exhibit feminine interests and activities—possibly as a guilt-created coverup. The child will function like a seismograph of his mother's personality conflicts, and will inscribe his personality with the Richter-scale readings of her confusion.

It has been noted that boys are quite differently affected by a mother who is involved in relatively masculine activities and interests, on one hand, and a mother who identifies herself with the basic feminine role on the other hand. While the degree of femininity of the mother's *interests* does not appear to be critical, the *general role* she assumes in her family makes a difference. For example, a mother can express feminine interests (such as mothering and housekeeping) and yet feel insecure about being a woman and mother. Conversely, she may engage in masculine-type activities (piloting a plane or fishing) and yet convey a feminine-nurturing attitude. While the type of a mother's *interest* does not influence the boy's development of masculinity, her *role identification* does. If a mother does not identify herself with the feminine role, the boy's masculinity usually suffers and he exhibits more feminine traits.[10]

It appears that the least complicated way for a boy to acquire masculinity is directly through his father (or another adult male). It does not matter so much how his mother behaves; what *does* matter is how her behavior and orientation are balanced by the father's presentation of himself. So mother may act feminine or masculine, be overprotective or permissive, conflict ridden or relaxed. The impact of these personality traits can only be fathomed if we know the balancing qualities of the father.

A reliable generalization emerges from the various studies and observations: it is extremely difficult for a mother to successfully substitute in a father's role. She may be able, through conditioning, to inculcate a sort of masculine behavior, but, most likely, it won't be genuine and complete because it is not acquired through the first-hand and more fail-proof method of imitation. All relevant studies indicate that the pathological effects a child acquires through association with a pathological mother are able to gain a foothold in the child's psyche only if the father stands back and, in a sense, "lets it happen." The preceding as well as the following considerations must be understood in the light of this generalization.

Observations show that mothers with severe sex-role conflicts have a profoundly discouraging effect on the boy's masculine development.[11] Vital help in learning one's sex role derives from learning how to interact with the opposite sex, but the boy who has a nonfeminine mother is deprived of such help. His relationship with his mother does not activate the many subtle elements of psychological complementarity. Hence he cannot use his relationship with his mother as the foundation for adequately initiating and maintaining relationships with other females. In short, he has not learned the complementarity of male-female interaction. Since such a mother's conflict frequently expresses itself in attempts at dominating males, including her son, she may curtail development of the boy's masculine assertiveness. In contrast, research shows that a boy's masculine development is greatly fostered if his mother is secure in her femininity.[12]

It is also important to note that the demands on the masculine role are harsher and more restrictive than those on the feminine role. Myron Brenton, in his book *The American Male*, talks about the "masculine straight-jacket."[13] A girl can spread her behavior style across the traditional boundary between the sex roles and not be punished for it; the "tomboy" is acceptable and is not thought abnormal. In contrast, if a boy acts across the sex-role boundary, he is defined as a sissy, found unacceptable by both males and females, and possibly even thought abnormal. This means that sex-role behavior is not symmetrical but considerably one-sided.

Because the realm of acceptable behavior is larger and more diverse for the girl than for the boy, girls may indulge in activities, professions, and styles that used to be strictly in the male domain. Perhaps the most obvious example is that girls may wear pants *or* skirts but boys may wear only pants. Another manifestation of this interesting one-sided permissibility was revealed by a unique survey on *who* cusses and *how*. A professor of linguistics at the University of California at Berkeley observed that as emancipation moves forward, the linguistic changeover is a one-way street: women adopt more and more of men's cuss words but few men adopt words with traditionally feminine connotations, such as "chic," "fine," "divine."[14]

Further, the psychological demands are more stringent for the male. We say to a boy "Boys don't cry." We don't tell a girl not to cry; neither do we encourage her and say "Girls cry." She may behave one way or the other—no matter. We say to a boy "Have courage and act like a man." We don't say the corollary to a girl. To boys and young men we promise that discipline will "make a man out of you." We don't admonish girls that way. To males we say " *Try* to be a man"; to females we simply say "Be a woman."

Such cultural attitudes may explain the commonly observed fact that young boys are more likely to have difficulties in their sex-role development and adjustment than girls.[15] Actually, this is no wonder if we consider the frustrations boys must suffer from being encouraged to be aggressive, innovative, independent, and explorative on one hand, although they are quickly reprimanded if they transgress the narrow line of masculine behavior on the other hand. In fact, this is a learning process in which one stimulus tends to counteract another—and it has been shown that even a dog can be driven into a schizophrenic reaction by this method.

It is therefore understandable that boys' difficulties in adjusting to their roles are, at least in part, a consequence of their suffering greater frustrations while learning their masculine role than girls experience while learning their feminine role. The young male's frustration may spread into every sector of his life. For example, it has been found that boys have more difficulties in school than girls and are more often classified as emotionally immature or delinquent.

The boys' difficulties in adjusting to the role requirements are symptomized by a low tolerance level for deviation (which is a reliable sign, in any situation, that a person feels insecure). It has been observed, for instance, that female as well as male students disapprove of opposite-role behavior—but males disapprove far more emphatically.[16]

Specialists have also noticed that considerable anxiety results from the fact that boys are more severely punished than girls for deviating from sex-role expectations. Many boys worry excessively about stepping outside the sex-role-appropriate behavior. Often, they overcompensate in trying to prove their masculinity, and virtually panic when caught doing anything traditionally defined as feminine.[17]

This reaction becomes even more plausible when we realize that, generally, "feminine" behavior and interests have historically not merited esteem—neither for girls nor for boys. Hence a reason why girls are tempted to pursue masculine activities lies partly in the greater prestige and esteem ascribed to such forms of behavior. It is more prestigious and acceptable for a girl to engage in "superior" activities than for a boy to engage in "inferior" activities. (Of course, this process is not on the awareness level but is an unconscious reaction to a cultural archetype.)

An interesting theory follows from this assumption. Since it is the girl-like activity or style that elicits punishment for the boy, to preserve his sex-appropriate behavior it is only natural that he comes to dislike such activities and reacts with dismay and anxiety if he is caught, or catches himself, engaging in such inappropriate behavior. It is a "natural" reation in the sense that humans and animals alike develop fear and dislike of an activity that regularly results in frustration and pain. An extension of this reaction leads to an even more radical dislike: the boy may associate the unpleasantness with the persons in whose life-style he sees it reflected. He develops dislike not only for the behavior form itself but for the agents who display it. This means that the boy learns to dislike not only feminine behavior but girls in general. This is a case of generalizing hostility from the disliked role to the persons who represent that role.

This hypothesis cannot plausibly be reversed and applied to females' disliking males for similar reasons, since there is not that extreme pressure on girls to avoid opposite-sex-role activities. (This, of course, should not obscure the fact that females may harbor hostilities because of other reasons.) Girls are not punished as early or as severely for trespassing upon the traditional masculine style. In fact, their permissibility is broad enough that one can hardly describe such behavior expansion as trespassing.

The major hypothesis that emerges from these considerations is that boys tend to harbor stronger feelings of hostility toward girls than girls toward boys. At this point the hypothesis must be considered moot because there is as yet no reliable way of testing it, but certainly it makes for animated thought and speculation. If the motivating emotions back of the hypothesis really exist, then, with gradual abolition of the contrasting sex roles, hostility should abate. If this is one of the results that women's liberation will bring about, we can only welcome it.

The boy's concern and anxiety about engaging in appropriate behavior forms are accentuated when he lacks a reliable and consistent male model—as we have stressed. Such anxiety and strain seek alleviation through compensation; but compensatory attempts may not meet with the approval of society. Indeed, they may be categorized as excessive, pathological, or delinquent. It is therefore paramount for the boy's psychic equilibrium that he has a model from whom he can derive assurance that he is acting correctly. Again, we recognize that the pivotal point for the boy's feelings of certainty and adequacy is the role his father plays in his life. If this role is salient, strong, and tangible, personality problems for the boy (including Momistic encroachment) can be warded off.

If the father's masculinity is not an available guideline, the boy may become overdependent on his mother for teaching him the proper sex-role behavior. The easily aroused anxiety associated with his eagerness to find the right sex role constitutes another psychological lever with which a Momistically inclined mother can influence and manipulate.

When Learning Masculinity, Don't Imitate the Teacher
Why is it the mother-son relationship, and not the mother-daughter relationship, that appears to be the most frequent setting of Momism?

It may well be that the inherently different dynamics of the mother-son relationship hold the answer. If a girl is exposed to a Mom, she will rarely suffer the harm that befalls her brother because she can escape from being a stifled personality by imitating the mother's ways. The girl can adopt her manners with relative ease and social approval, and can imitate her domineering or overprotective role. In this way the girl's personality development finds a *direction*—perhaps not a very desirable direction but a direction nevertheless. She can grow up and become a Mom herself—which, in fact, is the way many Moms are created. (There are, of course, many Moms who were created through different processes, as when frustrated women tried to develop their creative drives by attempting to turn a captive child into a superior "product.")

A classic example of this principle of greater male vulnerability was found by the Arizona Child Evaluation Center in a scenario that involved a household consisting of a sixty-five-year-old mother, her twenty-nine-year-old daughter and five-year-old grandson, and her two sons, ages twenty-seven and twenty-one. The husbands of the two women were not part of the living arrangement as they had been divorced many years ago.

Attention was first directed to this group by the five-year-old boy, whose mother brought him to the center for evaluation. He seemed to display the bizarre behavior typical of autistic children, but extensive psychiatric testing found that his I.Q. was above average and that his mannerisms were due to an unbelievable isolation. He had never been allowed outside the house—

even to play in the yard or associate with peers. As a result, his emotional and social development was severely retarded. Equally retarded was his motor control, and at age five he could not pick up a pencil correctly (his mother did such things for him). Nor had he been taught to control his bladder or bowels, so that he wore diapers at all times (and had constant urethral and bladder infections as a result). Most suprisingly, however, the boy was extremely advanced in mental skills: he could read, write, and do arithmetic on a ten-year-old level and was well into learning three languages. His mother and grandmother, both school teachers (!), had taught him these proficiencies. In sum, the boy's personality makeup consisted of an artificial and contrived intellect and atrophied emotions.

It was through this child that the social workers obtained access to a bizarrely pathological home situation, and discovered that the two young men were equally emotionally (not necessarily intellectually) retarded. They had been living isolated lives, depending entirely on their mother and sister, and their most "important" activity had consisted of sitting at home and watching soap operas on television.

The mother had achieved a striking degree of infantilization in her sons. The social workers discovered that the twenty-one-year-old was fed baby food, slept in the same bed with his little nephew, and was homosexual. In fact, it was only then, at age twenty-one, that the young man changed from baby pabulum to other varieties of food.

This case study makes a number of obvious points. It is very apparent, for example, that a person who is intellectually capable is not necessarily emotionally mature or healthy. For our purpose, however, the main point is that an overprotective and domineering Mom can wreak emotional havoc on her sons and grandson, casting them into incredible dependence and immaturity, and yet have a daughter who is domineering—in fact a Mom. From all indications, the daughter was an emotional carbon copy of her mother and had learned to become a Mom by imitation.

Boys may not imitate their mother. Not being allowed to identify with his mother renders the boy helpless against her guiding powers. He depends on being *told* how to act; he cannot *see* most of the time what he is supposed to be or do; he has no choice but to take his mother's word for it. This, in a sense, calls for blind trust. And once blind trust is established, the boy will surrender and let himself be guided; otherwise he would not know how to live and which way to turn. He is caught!

Such blind trust, it must be remembered, is necessary for the boy only if the most decisive condition of Momism is fulfilled: *if his father is absent, remote, or ineffective.*

In the technical language of psychoanalysis, the fundamental difference between boys and girls in learning their sex roles consists of the following elements. The earliest agent who conveys pleasurable experiences to the human young in a normal family situation is the mother. She is the one who provides comfort, warmth, and food—and in the process the child zeroes in on her with consummate attachment. It seems to be a universal tendency for girls *and* boys to make the mother the object of intense attachment and the object with which they would like to identify. In other words, they want to become like the agent who nurtured them so intimately. But this is where the path for little boys and girls diverges.

While girls may equate the object of their attachment with the object of identification, boys may not do so. During early childhood—anywhere between three and six years of age—there is a crisis of identification for the male child, but not for the female child. For the young male, identification is expected to shift to a male model, but the girl may retain the mother as her model. This makes acquiring her sex role a lot easier. Learning about oneself and what one is expected to be now proceeds in a sex-differentiated manner. The girl has the opportunity to learn through personal, direct, imitative contact; the boy is forced to learn in a much more abstract and impersonal fashion. While the girl can proceed with greater intuition and vicarious understanding, the boy's process of learning seems to demand greater reliance on logic, inference, and mental computation. When it dawns upon the male child that he does not belong in the same sex category as his mother, he must direct his attention toward finding the proper goal of his sex-role identification.

So the boy must *figure out* a goal, and goal defining is an abstract process which requires considerably more independent thinking than a process of learning that is based on direct imitation. We may hypothesize that sex-differentiated personality traits stem from the different ways boys and girls learn to cope with their intimate social environment early in life. In other words, when boys and girls go through the learning processes whereby they acquire gender-appropriate behavior styles, they acquire separate *methods* of learning—methods which gradually become their distinct styles of learning *in general*.[18] And it is these different approaches to problems and tasks which become core characteristics of what we call masculine or feminine.

Further support for this interpretation of typical male vs. female behavior can be derived from numerous research observations that have consistently found that daughters' resemble their mothers' personalities to a significantly closer degree than sons' their fathers'.[19] The personality similarity between daughters and mothers is probably a direct result of the girl's being allowed to use her mother not merely as the object of attachment but also as the object of identification. In this way, Momism can be perpetuated through the daughter's ability to model herself after her mother's behavior.

Further comment on the inbornness vs. the learnedness of masculinity and femininity is derived from studies that show the seemingly innate quality of the male's analytic and logical propensity is drastically reduced if he has been without the model of a father or another adult male.[20] Even if the father is accessible to the boy but is a weak and nonmasculine male, the boy's analytic capacity is equally reduced. If the father is available and represents a powerful masculine role, the mother-dominated learning process can be replaced, or at least significantly modified, by the boy's direct and personal imitation of his father.

As a result of normal father-son interaction, the boy has the opportunity to achieve a normal level of analytic/ logical ability, which, otherwise, might have been repressed by a domineering Mom's replacing of imagination and experimentation by detailed instruction of how to think and what to do. This, in turn, suggests that it is the *learning process*, by way of having a masculine model, which endows the boy with these traditional masculine characteristics.

Interestingly, it is found that father-absent boys tend to have a normal, if not superior, verbal aptitude. This proficiency seems to derive from their middle-class mother's strong influence on their intellectual functioning. Boys who have lost their father during childhood also tend to be highly successful in their academic pursuits because of a conspicuous overdependence on their mother. Evidence mounts that high verbal ability in boys (generally found to be a typical female characteristic) is often associated with a close and restrictive mother-son relationship.[21]

The above portrayal (including the research examples) of the differential acquisition of sex roles and their contrasting manifestations in the personality make-ups of the boy and girl is in line with the assumptions of those behavioral scientists who endorse the theory that it is the environment that creates these differences, and not genetic and inborn catalysts. Feminists would readily endorse the environmental theory and point out that gender differences are solely the product of conditioning. They would expand the argument and emphasize that if the role is the end result of conditioning, different conditioning can result in different roles. From their viewpoint, these different roles should be more equitable and sane.

However, to be fair, we must warn that the environmental argument is only one side of the ledger and that a rebuttal of the theory could introduce numerous medical and psychological data into the arena. These data would attempt to show that hormonal and cerebral functions differ between the sexes and that these differences account for the sexes' different mental and behavioral styles. This genetic or archetypal theory maintains that it is not the environment that determines the typical male and female personality traits—that these traits are largely unlearned and genetically inherited impulses.[22] The controversy whether femininity and masculinity are inborn or learned is essentially unsolved at this time.

Regardless of which theory is applied to interpret the phenomenon, the empirical world presents the interesting fact that normally there comes a time when a boy makes an enormous effort to liberate himself from his mother's influence and whatever remnants of feminine identification may slumber in him. He does this, quite unconsciously, by being brash and overly masculine. This is the time when his mother's physical affection or caress would embarrass him profoundly, and he is apt to reject such intimate approaches with a spectacle of masculine aloofness. This is an entirely normal and healthy, in fact *necessary*, reaction of the boy. It is a manifestation of his effort to rid himself of the tendency to relate to his mother as an object of identification and inadvertently slip into feminine behavior. Masculine overreaction normally gives him the necessary emotional momentum to accomplish such liberation.

It is not entirely clear what generates the impulse behind the boy's exertion and "declaration of independence." There is probably little valid support for explaining it by specific "innate programming"—although some famous writers maintained just that. For example, G. Stanley Hall in his classic volumes on adolescence asserted that the individual goes through a number of developmental stages and that in each stage certain behavior forms emerge "instinctively."[23] Along this train of thought, it is possible to hypothesize that the rebellion of the little boy announces his arrival on an "emancipatory plateau."

More acceptable to modern social scientists, however, is the notion that such rebelliousness grows out of the boy's awareness of the differences between the cultural dicta and the actual mother-son situation. The latter, even in a normal relationship, is replete with major and minor abrogations of what the cultural stereotype prescribes as masculinity. The boy, rather intuitively, reacts against the discrepancy and tries to achieve image consistency. In other words, he tries to make an adjustment between the two patterns (one cultural and the other individual) and integrate them into some sort of a consistent self-image. His rebelliousness, overreaction, and rejection of female intrusion across his ego boundary serve to establish such integrity. (Gestalt psychology offers a suitable framework for further examining this process; its premises assume that human beings have a general need for consistency, integration, and closure of a structure.)

But in a situation of Momism, the mother will not allow such masculine emancipation. In fact, she has conditioned the boy to the point where even his desire to make a stand of brashness and overmasculinity is precluded. His conditioning has been so thorough that he does not dare to stand up against his mother, or any other female, and is unable to separate his male ego from the overwhelming intrusion of female possessiveness. He has never been allowed true self-expression; and later, even if he should want to try, he would have insufficient will power to adopt the cultural image of masculinity and make it a personal and unique part of his personality. The cultural image of masculinity (as well as all other cultural standards) has been preempted by Mom: interpreted for him and systematically inculcated. The version of masculinity that Mom has instilled in the son is, then, a censored superimposition; it is empty and broken in spirit, a mere abstract pretension, the proverbial Potemkin village where grand facades hide poverty of reason and emotion.

Momistic conditioning, it must be realized, amounts to *complete* domination. If the domination and accompanying isolation of the boy are incomplete, he will have a chance to liberate and align himself with the cultural image of masculinity during the period of mutiny described above. In that case, a crass overacting of the masculine role has the potential to guide him onto the path of masculinity and keep him going in that direction. It is therefore the initial action (or reaction) of supermasculinity that provides the momentum that is of crucial significance for assuming and adhering to the proper sex role. This is why we said this is a "healthy" and "necessary" expression at a certain time in the boy's childhood.

It is interesting to note that this show of overmasculinity differs in strength, relative to the degree that his mother tries to control and dominate him.[24] For example, to overcome strong domination, strong resistance is needed. Conversely, minor domination calls for only minor resistance. (This represents what social scientists call a direct correlation of two dimensions.) However, at and above a certain point of motherly domination, *no* resistance is offered because a point of no return has been reached where the boy's subjugation has been achieved to the extent that an attempt at shaking off the yoke is either perceived as useless or is not even thought of. Probably, the sense of futility of resistance on the part of the boy is not a conscious assessment of the situation but a general feeling of powerlessness that has become part of the way of life of the Momistically suppressed youngster. When this point of nonresistance has been reached, it means that mother domination has evolved into Momism. (Social scientists, if they consider the complete spectrum of domination, call this a curvilinear correlation.)

In summary, the potency of Momistic power depends to a large extent on the remoteness of the father from the everyday process of bringing up the boy. The venom of the Momistic embrace becomes particularly effective if it is not counteracted by the father's or another adult male's influence—and such countermeasures appear to be frequently absent from the lives of American middle-class boys. All too often these boys' fundamental learning process is left exclusively to females—the mother, the Sunday school teacher, nursery and kindergarten personnel, and the elementary school teacher. Thus boys are exposed to the continuous authority and teaching of agents whom they may not imitate, but whose guidance and information about what they should be they are expected to accept and practice. Because of the domination of the mother, the authority of other women, the remoteness of the father, the absence of close male models, and the culturally enforced sex-role differences, boys confront a powerful array of forces which can easily enmesh them in Momism and its life-long deleterious consequences.

Throughout this discussion the assumption was that Momism is a mother-son process. If some allowance was made for Momism affecting the female child, the effects were diagnosed as usually different from those of the boy because of the cultural permissibility for the girl to imitate and identify with her mother and, hence, become a Mom herself. But this is largely speculation and is in line with what we know *generally* about the identification process with the same-sex parent. It necessarily remains speculation since there is a startling paucity of research concerning the mother-daughter relationship. Social scientists have focused primarily on the mother-son relationship, and hence we are able, to some extent, to portray the phenomenon of Momism.

The father-child (boy or girl) relationship is almost entirely devoid of study. For example, a survey of American family research literature showed that between 1929 and 1956 there were only eleven publications pertaining to the father-child relationship but 160 focusing on the mother-child relationship.[25] This may be due to a nearly universal tendency to associate mothering with the feminine role, but not fathering (in the sense of socializing the child) with the masculine role. In other words, by general definition the father's masculine role neglects the child-rearing function. This is reflected in our everyday sociological parlance: we say "maternal deprivation" but merely "father absence"—as if the latter does not imply deprivation.

There are additional reasons why the father-child relationship has not had much scrutiny. In the *father-son* relationship, the same principle as in the mother-daughter relationship applies: the boy can imitate the father, and assume his masculine behavior, even if the father is overbearing and authoritarian. The boy can prevent his personality from being absorbed and squelched through imitation. Thus no particular pathological consequences may come to the attention of social scientists or the public in general. But this, we should note, may constitute a cultural blind spot, where a destructive practice and its invidious outcome are ignored or tolerated. This tolerance is a function of the male-dominated society. For example, the extreme male domination of the "German era" led to the holocaust that destroyed the lives of millions of people.

In the *father-daughter* relationship, the consequences of an authoritarian and supermasculine father may also go unchallenged. Again, a cultural blind spot is operating; that is, the outcome—the squelched and noncreative personality of the female child—is in line with culturally acceptable and even recommended norms of femininity. Since, to date, the feminine outcome has not been interpreted as a social problem, behavioral scientists have had little incentive to examine it. Issues that are not defined by society as problems are usually overlooked, and simply are not defined as such by social scientists.

If, in spite of the imitation-inviting opportunity, Momism should have effects on the daughter resembling those of her Momistically oppressed brother (the typical insecurity-overdependence syndrome), then, again, such characteristics would not show up as problems. They would be interpreted within the norms of feminine passivity. Generally, however, the father is more effective in planting such traits in the girl. His exertion of masculine power brings out her complementary feminine subservience.

In addition to the "normal" display of masculine power, a father may also have idiosyncratic needs to prove his masculinity through the domination and "possession" of the female child. In such cases we are dealing with a neurotic parent who is likely to inflict severe complexes on the child. In other words, we are facing the male counterpart of Mom. And this may be the time to introduce the concept of Dadism.

Dadism: What Happens to Little Girls?

Although the focus of this book is Momism, a brief description of its counterpart is justified; otherwise, we would imply that only the mother-son relationship is of vital importance to child-raising practices in American society. If our focus is on the mother-son relationship, it is primarily because of limitations of time and energy. Perhaps a future book will more fully explore the father-daughter relationship. Here, then, is an attempt to see the parallels or nonparallels (as the case may be) between the Momistic relationship and the father-daughter counterpart. Whatever generalizations follow ought to be understood as hypotheses yet to be tested.

What precisely do we mean by the "male counterpart" to Mom? We intend to focus on the type of father who socializes his daughter in such a way as to inflict personality problems similar to those of the boy in the Momistic situation, that is, a personality charged with doubts about her self-worth, full of anxiety, unable to make personal decisions, and lacking adult maturity. There are a number of similarities between Dadism and Momism, but there are a few dimensions that differ between the two situations. Therefore Dadism is not exactly the obverse of Momism.

Dadism must not be equated with authoritarianism. As we saw in Green's study of male neurosis, an authoritarian father or mother (as in many lower-class matriarchal and matricentric families) does not automatically imbue the child with neurotic anxieties. It is in conjunction with other conditions, such as the conditional love technique, that the mental health of the child is adversely affected. Also, similar to a son's being exclusively subjected to a Mom, the severity of a father's impact on the daughter's personality increases if the mother is a weak and submissive person. This gives the father freer rein to inculcate his daughter with the ways of submissive femininity. And to all appearances it is done in good taste and style: he is merely producing a feminine personality with society's stamp of "good housekeeping." The little girl will receive top grades from her father (later from her teacher, boy friend, and spouse) for growing up to be timid yet "sweet," indecisive yet "compatible," dependent yet "supportive," unsure of herself yet "loving"—in short, "very feminine." This is the way society has camouflaged the stifled personality of females. They cause no problems. They fit a system of male supremacy.

This type of conditioning introduces intriguing psychosomatic symptoms, some of which are almost bizarre. The feminine acquisitions do not stop with the patterning of mental attitudes but extend to external behavior and deportment—to a woman's total body language. In walk, gesture, posture, facial expression, and tone of voice she will reflect the feminine etiquette. The teenage girl will learn to identify with many traits that are "known" and favored as "feminine"—from a mellifluous voicelet to an ostentatious headache when her period is due.

In order not to miscast the father's techniques, we

should point out that he does not usually achieve his daughter's compliance with his wishes and her alignment with the feminine role through gruff and open authoritarianism, scaring her, so to say, into submission. On the contrary, he will bribe her by offering love and tenderness, by talking to her as culture has traditionally suggested that a man talk to little girls, by giving affection to her as is "customary," and by coaxing her into obedience rather than ordering or forcing her. In short, the process adds up to trading "love" for being a "sweet little girl." The resulting product can best be described by the concept of "Daddy's little girl."

The consequences of introducing the child into the feminine game usually last a lifetime. She—just as the boy under the reign of a Mom—is doomed to perpetual childhood and noncreativity. This unfortunate outcome has been confirmed by recent research. When a sample of several hundred college students was tested to determine the connection between their parent-child experience and their creativity as young adults, it was found that the group with the *lowest* creative potential were coeds who grew up under highly protective fathers. With respect to girls, protective fathers clearly had an edge over protective mothers. The interpretation was that paternal "love" and possessiveness stifle creativity and foster dependent minds.[26]

Just how awesome and lingering the effects of a daughter's dependence on a father can be was demonstrated by a unique study of three groups of adolescent girls and boys. The first group of girls had grown up with both their father and mother present in the home; the second had grown up with only their mother, due to the father's death; and the third also had grown up with only their mother, but because of divorce. It was observed that the seating arrangements the girls chose, vis-à-vis the *male* interviewer, differed greatly between the groups, as did their attitudes and manners. The majority of the girls whose father had been divorced took the chair closest to the interviewer, acted clumsily erotic, and showed signs of sexual tension and general seductiveness. (This conclusion was arrived at by interpreting posture, style of leg crossing, other bodily movements, and comments made by the subjects.) The majority of the girls whose father had died took the chair farthest from the interviewer and showed shyness and sexual anxiety. The girls who had an intact family took intermediate seating and behaved relaxedly.

It is interesting to note that the two groups of father-absent girls acted aggressively or withdrawingly only if the loss of the father had occurred *before* they were six years old. Girls who had lost their father *after* that age did not behave differently from the girls who had not lost their father. The study also showed that the effects of father-absence manifested themselves considerably later in the lives of the girls, usually during adolescence, and remained with them; while in the case of the boys the effects revealed themselves early, during childhood, and diminished with age.[27]

For the daughter, the father is representative of all men. He leaves a deep impression on her personality, shaping her attitudes, feelings, and expectations, which she carries into her relationships with other men. In the case of Dadism, the girl transfers her dependence on her father to her husband, accepting chastisement for showing initiative and independence (if any is left) and believing that her lovability depends on pleasing the man— once a parent, now a spouse. We might also point out that girls from mother-dominated families have great difficulties relating to the opposite sex and are disliked by boys,[28] while girls from homes where the father plays a salient role display a high degree of femininity and get along better with boys.[29]

Interpretation of these findings suggests that the mother-dominated girl has adopted a domineering demeanor and reflects a touch of the Mom, while the father-dominated girl is hewn into the complementary feminine role that does not cause adjustment problems with the opposite sex—as long as the traditional role behavior is expected. The proper psychological matching of the two types of girls calls for a weak and submissive male in the first case and a strong and assertive male in the latter case.

A common feature that emerges from the comparison of Momism with Dadism is the psychological manipulation of conditional love. It is more important for girls to feel "loved" and accepted than it is for boys. Every nook and cranny of our Western heritage abounds with the "necessity" of a girl's being loved. This, later in life, becomes the great Love Myth for a majority of women, so that "to find one's love" is the all-consuming and overwhelming desire. The "love" process in American society, especially for women, often includes complete abolition of ego boundaries, a merging of selves, a loss of separateness, and a surrender of individuality. The far more healthy and creative view, that selves can and must be partners instead of "mergers" (where egos collapse into a romantic and unrealistic oneness), is largely unrecognized.

For the sake of the Love Myth, girls can be easily persuaded to neglect their identities as unique and creative persons, forgo their ambitions, forget their talents, and marshal all their competitiveness and aggressive drives for playing the femininity game. Girls learn the game early. With the exception of lesbians and the most determined women's liberationists, they go on playing it, and play it a lifetime. The ultimate score is a man and, traditionally, marriage. The tactics consist of charm and guile, clothes and cosmetics, and, hopefully, physical measurements—which will be thrown into the game when all else fails.[30] Those who play the game impatiently anticipate the most important payoff: "to be loved by the right man."

For a child, the "right man" may be a "loving Dad." And he may exploit this love syndrome to the fullest, basking in the thoroughly cultivated femininity of his daughter, who, in the process, reinforces his masculine ways. The Dad-oppressed daughter *learns her role by contrast*, almost automatically slipping into complementary behavior patterns. Seeing the feminine counterrole develop in the female offspring creates a contrapuntal reward for a father's masculinity. This becomes even more important to a father whose wife does not provide these rewards, whose femininity does not thrive on the demonstration of his masculinity—who, in short, does not make him feel "ten feet tall." Similar to Mom, the Dad uses the daughter, lives through her, and in a sense takes possession of her. This is the father who, later in life, develops profound jealousy and neurotic concern when the daughter begins to date. It is not uncommon for this type of father to try to prevent, or at least postpone, the serious attachment and/or marriage of the daughter. He will find fault with each suitor, restrict dating hours, demand reports, etc. He unconsciously feels that she is "his girl."

It would be misleading to believe that Dadism and its peculiar "feminine" product will go unchallenged forever. The attack upon the traditional feminine style by the women's liberation movement appears to be making inroads on the desire to adopt this subservient style. In the future, this style may (at best) be accepted as merely one of various alternatives. A girl who chooses the old style may be looked upon as "old fashioned," unsophisticated, and even ridiculous. When this occurs, Dad's indoctrination program will surely come under fire. With advanced emancipation, this unintentional power play will be thought of as interference with the process of a girl's unfolding her true potential and unique personality. In short, it will be branded as hindering a young woman from developing her *personal identity*.

While this superpaternalism, as a culturally sanctioned approach to the father-daughter relationship, has hardly been noticed in the past, it will be seen as dysfunctional in the future, when more and more adult expectations will be exacted of the American female. As soon as such characteristics as independent thinking and decisionmaking become as expected a way of life for the mature woman as for the mature man, Dadism will be recognized as just as neurotic and destructive as Momism.

Women must have felt the oppression in the past— the helplessness, the limited life-style. But no one, including themselves, understood the feeling. As Betty Friedan said, it was a problem without a name, but it has a label now: sexist oppression. It comes in various forms, but Momism and Dadism are two forms that directly affect children.

In summing up the process of Dadism, a number of points can be made.

1. The father reflects strong, traditional masculinity.

2. He assumes a major role in rearing the child.

3. He is not necessarily overtly authoritarian; rather, he uses the conditional love technique to retain the girl's love and loyalty.

4. The wife is weak and passive, and plays the traditional submissive role.

5. The girl is molded into the complementary role (vis-à-vis father's), a process that is facilitated by imitating the "feminine" mother.

6. The girl learns to repress her creative and independent impulses, and grows up to embrace the "feminine mystique."

7. She will look for and find, a traditional masculine

spouse and engage in the traditional complementary marital role, similar to the one she observed in her mother. She will be relatively passive and submissive in her marriage.

8. The traditional adjunct to the traditional wife role is motherhood, and most likely our young woman will opt for it. If she has a daughter, the cycle will repeat itself: another little girl will be raised under the tenets of the feminine mystique.

What are the parallels between Dadism and Momism?

1. In both situations the child may not identify with the major socializing agent. That is, in the case of Momism the boy may not reflect the feminine role; in the case of Dadism the girl may not reflect the masculine role. (It must be remembered, though, that the wider behavioral range permitted the girl is a modification of this generalization.)

2. In both situations the spouse is weak and passive. In Momism, it is the husband; in Dadism, it is the wife.

3. Both the Mom and the Dad manipulate the child's desire for love.

4. In both situations the children develop personality problems whose symptoms are similar. Primarily, both have a profound need for "love" and seek constant assurance of their self-worth.

5. Both the girl and the boy will grow up and seek Mom or Dad surrogates who will make decisions for them, protect them, and give them answers and purposes. In short, both suffer from overdependence and neurotic anxiety. Their preferred method of alleviating anxieties is by attachment to substitute agents, which can be of myriad forms—all serving to prolong the psychological servitude they have experienced as children.

But there are also a number of dissimilarities:

1. While the typical Mom is a halfway-emanicipated

female, no equivalent circumstance applies to Dad.

2. Dad is not a homemaker; he holds a full-time job elsewhere. Thus his presence at home is more limited than that of his wife, which gives her more opportunity to be with the children and influence them. (One might hypothesize that, for this reason, Momism works more thoroughly on the boy than Dadism on the girl.)

3. Dad's style of child raising is not as motivated by the success principle as Mom's. His emotional needs deal more with a desire to dominate—to have his masculinity verified and enhanced.

4. While the typical Mom is generally dissatisfied with her husband, possibly to the point of rejecting and despising him, no such feeling is necessarily part of Dadism.

A host of questions about Dadism remain. For example, how different are Dad's needs from Mom's? What are his techniques for retaining the loyalty of his daughter? What, precisely, are the consequences of Dadism in the grown daughter? How are Dads created?

The attempt to answer these questions in detail would expand this book excessively, and the course we are steering bears directly on Momism. Thus it will be for another book to devote itself to the exploration of Dadism—a novel concept that has not yet emerged in the social science literature.

We hope that, with this chapter, the theoretical part of the investigation of Momism (and to a limited extent Dadism) has been largely completed, and that it will give the reader a useful framework in which he can order his observations of Momism in actual life. Beginning with the next chapter, and especially in Chapter 6, we will deal more explicitly with *direct* observations and examples of Momism.

Chapter 5

The notion that the maternal wish and the
activity of mothering are instinctive or
biologically predestined is baloney. Try
asking most sociologists, psychologists,
psychoanalysts, biologists—many of whom
are mothers—about motherhood being
instinctive; it's like asking department-store
presidents if their Santa Clauses are real.—Betty Rollin

Types and Techniques of Moms

The various processes whereby Momism anchors itself in the child's personality are kaleidoscopic and would do honor to any museum of psychopathology. Although, as repeatedly mentioned, the principal technique applied by the Mom to render the child captive is the conditional love technique, this strategy may hide its true face under many-splendored camouflages. Many of them cleverly conceal the technique, which appears quite harmless, and even commendable, on the surface. This chapter takes a sharp look at the varied expressions of the technique.

But before we begin this investigation we must briefly touch on why so many mothers appear to adopt these perilous techniques. The circumstances that produce a Mom are, of course, a burning question, and in earlier chapters (especially "The Rise of Momism") we outlined the social and psychological features of our time that seem to be responsible for so many late-twentieth-century Moms. But the discussion dwelled on broad societal themes and trends and provided little in terms of examples and personal description, because to trace the background of a Momistic mother is much more difficult than to follow the history of her victimized offspring, since the former does not usually see herself as a problem and thus is not open to analysis.

Further, the general societal antecedents are relatively well recognized and suffice as reliable determinants of the Momistic inclination.

Moreover, there are limits to concentrated study and available material.

This book, therefore, prefers to be slanted toward a description of the victim and his problems. Suffice it to say that the causes that make a Mom can be embedded in any one of many—or, more likely, a combination of—background factors. A number of such possibilities are indicated below.

1. The formation of a Mom may be influenced by the opportunity of imitating one's mother, who is the Mom type. This may be the explanation in many cases.

2. The opportunity to imitate may have been combined with experiences that generated hostility against males. As mother, the young woman—probably unknowingly—may ruthlessly suppress the personality development of her son. She may have acquired enough animosity to be motivated to apply the suppressive technique she has learned. Sometimes her Momistic ways can be a veritable revenge for disadvantages or harm, real or imagined, she has suffered at the hands of one or several males. It is possible that her father played the salient role of villain in her young life.

3. The outstanding background feature which stimulated the Momistic development may again be the father, but a different type: the weak and submissive

father. As a girl, she may have witnessed her mother acting in a domineering and overbearing manner toward her father, with the result that she came to perceive men as weak and indecisive creatures. She may have consequently developed an attitude of superiority in her relations with men. Later she sought to marry a similarly weak and subservient man to fit the pattern with which she was familiar and in which she had learned to function relatively effectively. As wife and mother, she perpetuated these attitudes and directed them toward her husband and son. Her domination and overprotectiveness gave the child little chance to grow up and become an independent person.

4. The Momistic tendency can possibly be traced to extreme experiences of powerlessness in a girl's life. As a grown-up in the position of motherhood, the young woman may compensate by wielding excessive power—seeking an antidote for her former powerlessness by reigning mightily.

5. Momism may result from having experienced emotional neglect in childhood, so that the love and care that were not found in early life are lavished on one's child. But there is a "catch" in this type of "love": by identifying with the child, the love the mother extends becomes *self-love*. Up to a certain point this can be a relatively healthy and even creative compensation, but beyond that point it becomes narcissistic. In effect, the child is used as a mirror of love, who is not treated as a separate entity endowed with a potential uniqueness. This type of love, then, is not real love; it does not accept the child in his own right. Instead, the mother projects her needs onto the child and addresses herself not to his personality but to the needs of her own personality. Like Narcissus looking into the water and becoming infatuated with his own features, such a mother uses the child as a medium for her self-reflection.

6. A mother may take a turn toward Momism because of a disappointing and impassive husband who does not fulfill her craving for intimacy—sexual and otherwise. Her demand for intimate communication, personal attachment, and affection drives her toward the child, from whom she expects the surrender of his preference for age-appropriate intimacy with his peers. Such a mother demands his time, affection, and loyalty. Under the guise of personal dedication and "closeness," she uses the child as a substitute for a nonresponsive husband.

7. Another way for Momism to emerge deals with the complex psychodynamics of the "reaction formation," in which the mother, who is the classic pretender of love and kindness, harbors hostility underneath. In fact, her hostility may be so intense as to be hatefulness; but hatred is a frightening thing for everybody involved, including the mother. The emotions of hatred can be so powerful and frightening to the mother that she must suppress them, since awareness and admission of them would endanger her ego ideal; that is, the way she would like to be. Hence, she practices deceit with herself.

How can such negative feelings be hidden? Or how can they be hidden *and controlled* at the same time? The opposite feelings lend the necessary counterforce, which, in this case, is the convincing display of a fervent belief in "love." It is symptomatic of a reaction formation to constantly and insistently proclaim that the counterforce (which the enactor, of course, does not recognize as the counterbalance it is) is the only proper behavior. In other words, the reaction formation can frequently be detected by its compulsiveness, obsessiveness, and repetitiveness.

Again, the child is *used*. He becomes the focal point for his mother's neurotic compensation and the medium through which she tries to obtain relief from her guilt and anxiety, which are generated by her frighteningly negative emotions. Her reaction formation zeroes in on an innocent and utterly helpless individual.

8. Still other women become Moms because they are, quite plainly, in search of a cause—any cause—and it happens that their cause becomes the child. These are the mothers who flaunt motherhood as a noble devotion and use it as a safe island in an otherwise empty existence.

Again, the child is used as a means. It is he who must fill the void—the otherwise meaningless and purposeless existence of his mother. This is a big order, and in the process, the child is made to experience excessive feelings of inadequacy and guilt. In essence, the child is called upon to provide something that not even God can provide. Every human being must figure out and determine his or her own meaning and destiny in life.

And so it goes. A near-endless assortment of causes and combinations of causes could be listed, all capable of describing the origins of Moms.

One short-range generalization that can be derived from a discussion of why mothers enact Momism concerns their common need and tendency *to live through the child.* Whatever varied background circumstances lead to the final outcome of producing a Mom, the essential emotional orientation is the same; she uses the child as a medium for compensation and as a palliative remedy. Therefore, though the techniques abound in number, the colorful versions serve one and the same goal. Behind the various expressions lurks a mother who is characterized by a typical psychological makeup: emotional immaturity, lack of the ego strength to draw a boundary between her own ego and the ego of her child, and inability to grant her child emotional and intellectual independence. She does not understand how detrimental it is to attempt to shape the child into the realization of *her* dreams and to deny him the right of becoming the realization of *his own* dreams. (Some dramatic consequences of Mom's forcing an alien dream onto her son will be described in the next chapter.)

If we should generalize as to the cause of her Momistic affliction by saying it is her parasitic ego, we immediately open the door to further questions and begin to wonder what caused this cause. Why did she develop this parasitic ego? Most likely the answer will involve her parents and the way they brought her up. But we realize that now we are talking about the victim's grandparents. Thus we could delve deeper and deeper into the background circumstances, roaming a never-ending labyrinth of inquiry. Probably only in a detailed case history could the unique circumstances that produced a Mom be fully grasped.

Throughout this chapter we shall examine several brief case studies that, once in a while, allow a glimpse of the causative background of Mom. But, in general, this chapter deals less with trying to determine *how* a Mom evolves and more with recognizing the *type* and *technique* into which her background experiences have cast her. This means that we are more interested in understanding *how* she operates than in how she has *evolved.* This interest demands a shift of focus to her techniques; so when we talk about a "type of Mom." we are talking mainly about the preponderant technique she uses to enslave her child. In short, the typology is an enactment, not a development, of Momism.

This, finally, leads us to the core question of the chapter: How does the Mom accomplish compliance with her dreams and demands on the part of the medium? After all, he is not impersonal clay, to be kneaded into an arbitrary form, but a young human being, presumably endowed with will, aspiration, and reason. The question, then, is, What is the formidable method whereby he *can* be cast into the form of his mother's dreams?

That method is the conditional love technique. It is the strategy applied by nearly all Moms, regardless of origin. They use it because it works. Through it, they come closest to achieving satisfaction, alleviation, and compensation for their real or imagined hurt and deprivation. Moreover, this strategy not only works, it also looks good. Modern Americans frown on corporal punishment or similar coercive means for conditioning and educating the child. Aversion to such "barbaric and savage methods" has been sounded out by almost every popular author or child psychologist in the country.

One such prominent spokesman is Dr. Benjamin Spock, who said that the child is easily brought in line by his need for love and social approval. One of his chapters, "The Question of Punishment," has a section on the *method of punishment* that opens an ominous Pandora's box by encouraging parents to consider the giving or withholding of love as a means of influencing the child. Dr. Spock referred to the child when he said, "Knowing how good it makes him feel to be loved and how uncomfortable, by contrast, to be disapproved of, he also behaves himself to keep people liking him."[1] While Dr. Spock cannot be held responsible for intentionally encouraging the conditional love technique, his words can easily be construed (or misconstrued) to lead to a facile embrace of a psychological mechanism whereby mothers accomplish control and discipline among their children.

Our point is that prominent authors and child-care experts, such as Dr. Spock, have made unwitting contributions to the conditional love manipulation and have helped establish it as an accepted and widespread strategy among America's mothers. For the typical Mom, this was a windfall.

The various shades and nuances of the strategy depend on the Mom's personal resources, such as her temperament, intelligence and sophistication, and availability of means. On the bases of resources and differing compulsions, a simple typology is suggested below. It must, however, be remembered that some Moms resort to more

than one method and achieve the Momistic effect through
a combination of manipulative tricks. It is only to facilitate discussion and communication that types are introduced here, to show the styles by which Moms achieve
possession of their children's personalities. Obviously,
in actual life they overlap and differ in degree.

The Overprotective Mom

This type of mother seeks to control the child by
suppressing his ego development. (The ego has been defined as the ability to recognize and cope with reality.)
In this case it means that the mother does not give the
child an opportunity to grow up, explore the world, and
learn through his experiences. The mother curtails the
child's process of learning reality by forcing herself on
him as the mediator between the world and his inquisitiveness. While mediation is of course a natural and necessary part of mothering, the Mom seeks totalitarian
mediation. In a sense, she functions as the child's ego.
She does not entrust the child with any personal exploration and decisionmaking. This is all done under the labels of love, care, and protection. In the process, the
mother uses "love" as a tool to enforce the child's dependency on her.

In his famous report, Maternal Overprotection,[2]
psychiatrist David M. Levy discusses four dimensions of
overprotection that were noticeable in the maternal behavior of mothers who had raised sons who had extremely dependent and irresponsible attitudes and behavior patterns.

1. *Excessive contact.* The mother extends excessive
physical care and contact to the child, which may include
excessive fondling, common sleeping arrangement, helping the child with washing and getting dressed, and prolonged dependence on breast-feeding. These forms of
physical contact are extended far into the childhood

years. The mother provides uninterrupted companionship in terms of her constant physical presence and assistance, the decisive point being that this is still done when the child reaches an age when he should be weaned and freed from physical dependence on his mother.

2. *Infantilization*. In addition to insisting on protracted physical closeness, the mother tends to treat the child as an infant *in general*. She will continue childcare practices beyond the time when such practices are actually needed and culturally recommended. She will not expect independent thinking and acting. On the contrary, she will think it "natural" to wait on the boy and do things for him.

Examples of infantilization include a mother's not allowing her fourteen-year-old son to go to the swimming pool with his peers, except with herself and under her watchful eyes; not permitting him to play with his peers at any place other than home and under her supervision; demanding that he sleep an hour after lunch; picking out and buying his clothes for him; carefully censoring every book or magazine he reads; and frequently contacting his teachers to inquire about and ensure his welfare at school. When asked about such protectiveness, this type of mother is most likely to say, "You know he is all I have," or "I want him to have a better childhood than I had," or "I want him to know that I love him."

3. *Maternal anxiety about the welfare of the child*. Overlapping the previous point, this dimension becomes particularly obvious in the mother's refusal to let the child take any risks. At the slightest indication of the child's experiencing difficulty, trouble, or illness, the mother immediately mobilizes her maternal resources to ward them off.

As mentioned above, she is inclined to pester her son's teachers with inquiries and entreaties. Less than favorable grade reports and complaints by the child about a teacher or fellow pupils (or vice versa) will trigger the mother's overconcern. She will contact the person or persons involved and work out *for* the boy the problems he normally should work out by himself.

Likewise, physical symptoms are quickly interpreted as danger signs, and the boy is importuned to rest, stay in bed, swallow medicine (at least aspirin), accompany his mother to the doctor, etc. Such oversolicitude is quickly elicited, not only by real but often by imagined dangers or illnesses, and by the thought of future problems that might befall the offspring. It is a transferred and misplaced hypochondriasis whereby the mother imagines and/or feels all the symptoms of the child—symptoms that often exist so minimally as not to warrant excessive worry, or symptoms that do not exist at all.

4. *Prevention of social maturity.* Maternal overprotection prevents the boy from developing responsible and considerate social behavior. He is accustomed to having his problems solved for him and not being called upon to help and understand other human beings. The mother has segregated the child from difficulties, frustrations, and responsibilities, and hence stifled the natural aggressiveness and sense of exploration that all living organisms exhibit under normal conditions. Unwittingly, she has preserved the child's dependent and egocentric attitudes. He is not prepared to cope with the inevitable conflicts of everyday life that require aggressive, imaginative, and independent thinking. The chances are that later in life he will look for a substitute Mom who is willing to take care of him and solve his problems.

Some behavioral scientists have called the stifling of the natural aggressive tendency the key explanation for this type of Momistic effect. They feel that aggression is a natural, necessary, and healthy attribute of the human race—especially in the young. Aggression, they believe, emanates from the innate inclination to grow and explore life. As such, aggression is not to be equated with de-

structiveness. Only when this life tendency is thwarted
do anger, viciousness, and hate become attached to it.
Moreover, the opportunity to express aggressiveness is
necessary for normal personality development. The parent who it too protective gives the child nothing to "come
up against"—eliminates the hurdles in life that normally
provoke and test his aggressiveness and provides no impetus to the innate urge toward independence.[3]

Also, his mother has shielded him from serious problems and perplexing issues (including responsibility, sexuality, death, the complexity of loyalty, etc.). If called
upon to justify such defensive evasiveness, she might
argue that "he will learn the cruel facts of life soon
enough anyway." In this version of child raising, the
mother will bind the child to her so that he finds it impossible to turn away because he needs her continuing
service and guidance. The mother figure means total security and warmth: a problemless existence.

The continual ignoring of reality becomes a self-
perpetuating mechanism. As the child grows older, the
tasks he confronts—and which he should be able to cope
with—become, naturally, more and more complex and
demanding; but since he has not learned to cope on the
simple levels, coping on the complex levels is all the more
difficult, if not impossible, for him. In the end, the young
man cannot function as an autonomous individual; he is
severely dependent on an outside agent for security and
problem solving. He is condemned—psychologically if not
physically—to adhere forever to his mother or some kind
of mother surrogate.

Taken together, these four intertwined dimensions
or factors make for a formidable stifling of personality
development. But their exercise, as well as their effects,
has not always been interpreted negatively.

There was—and still lingers on, it appears—a romantic perception of this process. It views overprotection
as a natural symbiosis between mother and child whereby

a mystical oneness of the two individuals is accomplished that extends beyond the severance of the umbilical cord. A psychological union, or "emotional symbiosis," continues —so the romanticists say. Mother's love takes the place of the placenta, nurturing and protecting the offspring. This psychological analysis was inspired by poets and novelists and was promoted by numerous popularizers of certain psychologies who visualized an emotional symbiosis that keeps feeding the psyche of the child until he has matured and is psychologically born, as it were. Thus the writers and orators of mother love depict a state in which the mother and child retain a mystical oneness.

The innocuous facade of this romanticism gives way to a dismal revelation when the clinical results of such a "psychological symbiosis" are read. The pathological effects of the mutual parasitism have become visible in case histories of disturbed children. They suffer from a psychological version of parasitosis: the effect of having been infested and debilitated by a parasitic mother— the overprotective Mom. Once the effects have become severe enough to be brought to the attention of psychiatrists and counselors, the cure is infinitely difficult. There is no convenient parasiticidal medicine to restore the ravaged emotional maturity of the individual. "Restore" is really not the correct word because, in the classic case of Momism, maturity has never existed in the afflicted person; therefore nothing can be restored. Hence we are facing therapy that calls for some sort of miraculous transformation, from an individual who has never been a separate self, or an independent ego, to an individual with a self-contained personality.

Of course, there is no instant transformation. At best, the Momistically impaired person may slowly learn how to "walk" by himself—with the patient and prolonged assistance of a number of agents, including professional counselors.

Two fields of abuse are involved in this mutual

mother-son parasitism: the son's feeding on his mother's overprotection and basking in the resulting infantile security, and the mother's making use of the offspring to alleviate her frustrations and have her dreams "acted out." The "acting out" concept normally refers to behavior whereby a person expresses unconscious desires and fantasies, but this behavior becomes pathological when it reflects infantile and immature tendencies and violates the reality of the situation. It is interesting to note that Mom can be a veritable con artist in getting her child to do the "acting out" for her. Strangely, this transference has rarely been considered pathological for mothers and fathers in the past; it used to be defined as the problem of the victim, who made the actual demonstration. It was simply *his* behavior that was considered pathological—with little thought or question about the neurotic inducer of the pathology.

It has been only recently that psychiatric experts have become aware of the true nature of this transference and recognized the disastrous consequences on the child's personality, when his reality has been distorted by the imposition of the parent's dream. Case studies describe the boy who was pushed by his mother into marrying when he would have been better off staying single, or the boy who was coerced by his mother to lead a lonely bachelor life when he might have become relatively happy in marriage. And there is the case study where the unconscious wishes of the mother made her offspring lead a life of prostitution. Another case history tells how the son was manipulated to stay addicted to heroin so as to be rendered economically dependent on his mother and thus manipulatable by her. Still another case study describes how a child was subtly persuaded to enact the condition of a cripple who needed the complete care and nurture of his mother—a most extreme case of infantilization, where the somatic constitution was so conditioned as to allow the mother to continue treating him as if he

were still an infant. With increasing frequency, therapists are able to trace the steps whereby a mother uses
and abuses the child to satisfy her neurotic dreams and
unconsciously pushes him into life patterns that are destructive to his emotional development.

To sum up the theoretical aspects of the discussion,
we can conclude that this destructive symbiosis is an in-
herent part of Momism. It involves two neuroses, with
the two diseases feasting on each other. Inducing the boy
to evade the tests of reality, such as assuming responsibilities and commitments, it arrests his development at
the infantile level, short of personal identity and without
clear ego boundaries. His self is diffused, as by parasitic
demolition, and his self-security depends on merging into
his mother's or a mother surrogate's field of force. He
will be tempted to engage in "vicarious living," consisting of continual repression of his personality and incessant endeavor to substitute another personality or the
ideas and dicta of some group or movement.[4] (The dangers of the True Believer syndrome, as related to "vicarious living" and collective phenomena, will be discussed
in the next chapter.)

This emotional condition involves the suppression of
all those genuine impulses which reflect unique thinking
and synthesizing, and leads to irresponsible (often illog-
ical) and very often purely hedonistic behavior. Such
"vicarious living," even if it is nothing more profound
or concrete than a popular cliché of the time, is at the
very heart of the effect of Momism.

A colorful array of observations, reported in the
professional as well as general literature, presents striking illustrations of the transactions of the overprotective
and possessive mother. For example, interesting information about the schemes, desires, and behavior of a
number of Moms was obtained through the Arizona State
Department of Mental Retardation. Repeatedly, mothers

would bring their teenage offspring (especially girls) and request their sterilization. They felt that their retarded children lacked the necessary understanding of sexual and reproductive behavior, and feared that unwanted pregnancies might result. In many cases the investigating personnel were reluctant to order or perform such surgery, since the I.Q.s of the presumably retarded youngsters were either not clearly established or not low enough to warrant the label of retarded. On further investigation it became clear that the real trouble rested with the mothers, who were overprotective and overconcerned.

There was no reason to suspect that the hovered-over boys and girls would have an opportunity to engage in sexual activities or promiscuity, either at the time or in the near future. Most important, it was determined that the retardation was not severe enough to indicate such drastic surgery—and, indeed, that the retardation appeared to be induced by the mothers, who did not let the children unfold their emotional and intellectual abilities. Systematic ego suppression and the resulting narrow limitations of reality comprehension underlay the so-called retardation.

Interestingly, the fathers of these children exhibited different attitudes; generally, they dissented—though rather passively—from the views of their wives and did not believe their children were retarded. It was apparent that in many cases the mothers did not want to let go of the children and that their ostentatious show of concern and protection was a symptom of their possessiveness. In fact, the doctors, nurses, and psychologists at the state agency had more problems with the mothers who clung to their children than with the retardates. The mothers tended to constantly interfere with the process of diagnosis and treatment of their children. They insisted on treating their teenage retardates as if they were babies.

A notable example of the retardation influence of a mother was observed when she brought her four-year-old son, complaining that he was (1) "abnormally small" for his age and (2) "mentally unresponsive." However, it was immediately determined that the boy was within the normal range of physical development, and testing and observation established that he was alert and well oriented, although his language progression seemed somewhat slow. The explanation for the latter was soon found: his mother always tried to say things *for* him. He was not given enough opportunity to express his thoughts.

A case study that was prompted by parents' shattering discovery that their eighteen-year-old son was a homosexual is another poignant example of what can happen in a situation of overprotective and possessive motherhood, especially when it is not checked and balanced by the father.[5] This mother, unaware of what she was doing, had feminized her boy, Jed, almost from the beginning. She discouraged him from becoming interested and involved in masculine activities, tied him closely to herself, encouraged him to join her in doing feminine things, and prevented his becoming emotionally interested in girls. His father, who played a weak and passive role, was dominated by his wife and presented no strong masculine model for the boy to emulate. Jed developed no particular respect for his father; he neither felt he wanted to become like him nor do the things he did. As happens so often in the lives of homosexuals, the combination of these two variables, the overprotective and excessively possessive mother and the detached and weak father, was at least in part to blame for Jed's sexual deviation. They were considered the major etiological factors, according to the investigating psychiatrist. Jed's mother, an only child, had spent many lonely hours by herself because her mother was a busy interior decorator.

Moreover, she was an unplanned and unwanted child, who was born when her mother's career was at its height. When the lonely girl grew up, she vowed to herself that when she became a mother she would give her child all the love and attention she herself had yearned for. So, from infancy, Jed became the focus and most significant "issue" in the life of his mother, who insisted on his exclusive care, never allowing her husband to feed or diaper him. Her attitude was that "babies need a mother's touch."

As Jed grew older, his mother's touch did not lighten. Making excuses on the grounds of a mild digestive ailment that barred starchy foods from the boy's diet, she kept him with her constantly. She did not permit him to have playmates—*she* was his playmate. The exclusivity of her companionship continued after the disease ended. Even after her second child (a girl) was born, she continued a careful watch over Jed. For example, as a six-year-old, he could not have roller skates or a tricycle. Rather, the mother selected home activities to keep him busy and involved, including taking care of the new baby. While other six-year-old boys played outdoors, Jed happily spent all his time helping his mother powder the baby, prepare her bath, and fold and count the diapers. As Jed grew even older, he could not develop much interest or ability in sports and outdoor activity. He was known as a rejected "sissy" among his peers and was the target of their ridicule. This alienation and isolation from potential playmates drew him even closer to his mother. He adopted her interests, which included (among others) antiques, fabrics, and fabric design. Mother and son spent many weekend afternoons in shops, museums, and drapery establishments. An occasional demonstration by the father, such as "Don't make a sissy out of the kid," was met with rebuke and the refusal of his wife to speak to him for several days. He would let it be at that, being a weak and passive male. Thus Jed was a perennial witness to father's passivity and indifference, realizing that he did not bother to make himself count in the home.

Jed's mother downgraded girls. When, now sixteen years old, he made several dates with girls, his mother found fault with all of them. One of them had an "absolutely dreadful" taste in clothes, another was "unbelievably stupid," and a third, the daughter of a working-class family, was not in his social class. In essence, Jed's interest in the other sex was shamed and discouraged; and a life of sexual maladjustment commenced. Taken together—Jed's feminization, the rebuff he experienced by his peers, the contempt he was taught to hold for girls, the lack of an adequate male model—these conditions were enough to prevent his sex drive from taking a normal direction.

Jed was a high school junior when his horrified mother learned that he was involved in a homosexual relationship. The disclosure came all at once and was a great shock to her. Fortunately, the shock carried her through the initial steps of seeking help and a cure for Jed—and for herself, as it turned out. At the beginning it was extremely difficult for her to understand that she bore the main responsibility for Jed's being a sexual deviate. She found it almost impossible to believe that her "love" and "protection" of her child could have created such damage. Yet, gradually, she understood. A long period of counseling and therapy followed, involving mother, father, and son.

The final outcome appeared to be successful, with the participants in this family drama learning to disengage from destructive behavior and engage in more normal and creative relationships. Jed learned to establish normal relationships with the opposite sex; his father assumed a more salient place in the home and played a healthier role in relation to the younger children (another daughter was born) ; and the mother overcame—or at least controlled—her neurotic attachment to her son. When she was interviewed a number of years later, she said something very significant, indicative of the terrifying force a neurotic desire can exert over a person: "Finally, after I had understood the causes of the problem, I was ready to fight and cure myself. I felt like an addict, struggling to rid myself from something that, it seemed, every fiber of my whole being demanded. I went through painful emotional withdrawal symptoms. I had to fight with myself to cease smothering and possessing my son."

Only a fraction of the families who experience the consequences of an overprotective mother and a passive father recover so successfully. The others remain crippled for the rest of their lives. The shadow that had moved from this particular home can descend on another home. But then it may *not* move on, and emotional darkness may settle in to permanently stifle lives that otherwise might have had a chance to live more fully and happily.

The Overindulgent Mom

Unlike the overprotective mother, who suppresses the ego development of the child, the overindulgent mother focuses on his id forces; but rather than suppress the id (the hedonistic and selfish demands of the child), she caters to it. In seeing to the gratification of his egotistic demands, she establishes the offspring's tenacious dependence on her rather indiscriminate nurturing. Other differences between the overprotective and the overindulgent mothers consist of the former's bordering on the domineering Mom: not being permissive and not allowing individuality; while the latter type is clearly permissive: not domineering (at least not in a direct way) and, in general, providing a laissez-faire atmosphere. One of the important underlying needs of the overindulgent mother is her craving for the child's love and loyalty. This craving is often symptomized in forms that overlap the martyr type, where the mother tries to impress the child with her altruism, or even suffering, for him.

Although the overindulgent method differs from the overprotective, the overindulgent mother achieves a similar lack of individuality in her offspring by not demanding that he assume responsibilities and commitments. Actually, he has no need to learn such a discipline because his mother provides every service for him. There is no need to be neat and orderly—his mother cleans up after him. There is no need to work—his mother provides everything, including room and board, clothes, and spending money. There is no need to be punctual—his mother doesn't mind waiting. There is no need to straighten out his own affairs and problems—his mother will willingly do it for him. There is no need to learn to be kind and helpful—his mother will not demand it; she will extend these qualities without reciprocity.

In other words, the young man will grow up with an unrealistically catered-to and gorged id, and will not be prepared for real life, where the ability to give and take is a prerequisite for healthy and enduring human relationships. One could also describe this Momistically crippled individual as one whose innately selfish inclinations (the id forces) have gone unchallenged and unconditioned and whose superego development (the psychological processes whereby the members of society recognize and respect the norms and morals of their culture) has been truncated by the overpowering impulses of the free-running hedonistic forces.

This type of child raising tries to provide the child with everything he desires, so that, in a sense, he becomes "addicted" to the provider. The mother's "generosity," "love," and care are another effective way of conditioning him to adhere to Mom. Predictably, this type of upbringing deprives the victim of learning how to share or cooperate, and will render him greatly handicapped when the time comes for him to step into adult life. As in most other types of Momistic impairment, the shortcomings in the personality of the victim will not show up until later in life, when adult responsibleness is expected of him.

In American society we tend to condone children's egocentric and irresponsible behavior. Frequently we entirely overlook it, because we find it "natural"; or we think of it as behavior for which the child is not yet accountable. Our cultural permissiveness in regard to children allows the effects of the overindulgent Mom to go unnoticed for many years. It is not until the necessary assumption of serious responsibilities, such as a job, career, marriage, finances, etc., is expected that the victim of the overindulgent Mom is revealed and shows his emotional immaturity, which sometimes borders on psychopathy.

With the excuse of "making life easier for him" or "he mustn't suffer as I did," the overpermissive mother proceeds with subservience to the demands and the whims of the son, trying to meet his every wish. The case study of such a young man illustrates the process and the end result of being a victim of an overindulgent mother.[6] As a child, this son was exposed to the classic pampering of the overindulgent mother, without the counterforce of a strong father. He learned that his demands and temper tantrums got him everything he wanted. Instead of disciplining him and applying aversive reinforcement, his mother rewarded his unreasonable and egocentric fits by extending "love" and giving in to whatever he wanted. The first serious consequences of this type of conditioning showed up at school, when truancy became a chronic problem. Later, he again exhibited irresponsibility through absenteeism from jobs.

He had an extremely unstable career history and changed jobs frequently. After marriage, at age nineteen, he grossly neglected his wife and child, hardly understanding his obligation to support them. It was his mother who, again and again, willingly helped out. In a continual spectacle of financial irresponsibility, he would charge anything he wanted, always expecting that some "help would come." He treated his wife not as a spouse but as if she were an indulgent mother who "should understand," "support him," and "love him." Throughout the years his mother was a noncritical defender of his behavior, entirely ignoring the glaring maladjustment and immaturity of her son's actions.

His behavior eventually backfired: he got too deep into financial and other trouble, and his confusion and frustration grew—and at the age of twenty-five he committed suicide.

Another case study—incomplete since the child involved has not yet reached maturity and hence does not yet reveal the lasting effects—concerns the six-year-old son of a highly educated woman who had to raise the child and his one-year-old sister mostly alone, since her husband had been in prison for several years for refusing to be drafted into military service. This mother synchronized her emotional disposition of overpermissiveness with the idealistic philosophy that children should never be punished and, if possible, not restrained in their emotional outbursts and temper displays.

The little boy had free rein in the house; when he was frustrated or angry, he was permitted to smash any item that was available and smashable. Fixtures had to be replaced regularly. When he attacked his baby sister, which was an almost daily routine, he was not restrained; instead, the little girl was protected—as well as could be—against serious harm and injury. The usual mode of protection was the mother's holding a thick pillow over the head of the girl and letting her brother be-

Tuesday, October 26
11:00 a.m. - 4:45 p.m.
Alma College

Sponsored by Service Learning Program
For an appt, visit www.givelife.org, sponsor code alma.
Walk-ins Welcome!
Must have photo ID or donor card to donate.

Great Lakes Region
Blood Services

1-800-GIVE LIFE • www.redcross.org

campaignfall2003_paycheck

labor it with whatever he happened to have in his hands. (On one occasion, which the writer witnessed, this was a hammer.) Almost miraculously, the girl was never seriously injured. The reason for her exemption from an early death was the watchfulness of the mother, who never let the little boy out of sight and was always prepared to protect her daughter—by "nonviolent resistance," as it were.

The boy's moods, whims, and preferences were respected religiously. This was particularly notable at the dinner table, where roughly half of the dishes offered him were tossed against the wall or to the floor with impunity, except for a meek plea on the part of the mother to "please, be a nice boy."

Another study that traced the effects of permissive and indulgent mothers (mentioned earlier in the book) is Arnold W. Green's comparative study, where he found that it was not children who were brought up by authoritarian and punitive parents but those who were raised by permissive, punishment-shunning mothers who turned out to exhibit neurotic dispositions.[7] This was an astonishing finding because it contradicted every facet of popularized child psychology and commonly held definitions of parent-child love as reflected in middle-class women's magazines. It occurred to Green that perhaps the very existence of omnipresent mother-love might explain why these children suffered the neurotic symptoms that we are coming to recognize as common in the sons of middle-class parents in America.

Although the nonneurotic children grew up under harsh, often brutal conditions, the harshness and brutality were "external to the core of the self," Green explained. The authoritarian parents did not apply psychological techniques and did not have the time to "absorb the personality of the child." Rather their approach was direct, physical, and nonmanipulative.

On the other hand, the ostentatiously permissive

parents played a dangerous psychological game. First, the overpermissive upbringing deprived the children of the security and orientation that children acquire who learn self-discipline and have to cope with reality. Second, their discipline and learning were mediated through psychological manipulation, the conditional love technique, which tends to undermine children's self-esteem and causes lasting anxieties in them.

In essence, this study reminds us that there is a basic confusion in American life: indulgence and permissiveness are equated with love. It seems that "love" has been made the supreme issue in the mother-child relationship: the mother must "love" the child and the child must "love" the mother. This obsession has evolved partly because the love complex is part of the pathos of our time, exhibited particularly in the middle class, and partly because the mothers perceive themselves as having made many sacrifices for their children. Because of these "sacrifices," mothers expect their children to reward them with "love" and "good behavior."

This is what children are told, and they respond—neurotically.

The Martyr Mom

The martyr Mom is characterized by a specific manipulative inclination: she plays on the reaction of her child's superego. This is one way of saying that she manipulates his feelings of guilt, shame, and compassion for her own goals. The basic *purpose* for manipulating these emotions is usually the compulsive need to retain the loyalty of the son and keep him tied to her. The *means* for eliciting the pertinent emotional responses—the control emotions—can be found in a number of conditions, such as a disease or ailment, being lonely, feeling rejected, experiencing ingratitude, being burdened with too much work, getting old and feeling useless, being poor, and so on—*ad infinitum.*

A given condition, brought into the psychological battle to safeguard the loyalty of the offspring, may be actual, imagined, or pretended. In an interactional situation, the important implication lies not in how real the condition is in itself but how well it works. Many mothers have been surprisingly successful by using this approach, notwithstanding the crippling of their son's personality and making him forgo his personal dreams.

There are a number of maudlin variations of martyrdom through which a mother can play on the emotions of the child. One of them is the "ailing" mother who expects her son to take care of her, who instills a basic sentence in the mind of the child: *"Mother is always good; if she suffers, it is because I am bad."* Once internalized, this conviction provides the mother the "guilt leverage" to pull all sorts of tricks on the child.

For example, a team of New York social welfare workers discovered that the most formidable force preventing them from getting addicts off heroin was their possessive mothers, such as the mother who regularly developed an ear infection whenever her son decided to enter a clinic for treatment during the withdrawal period. The son was repeatedly prevented from carrying out his intention, for his mother persuaded him to stay home and nurse her. By keeping him addicted to heroin, which she financed indirectly by giving him almost $20 every day for a "hair cut," she also kept him "addicted" to herself. Once, when the young man succeeded in checking into a hospital for treatment, he withheld information of his action from his mother. However, she suspected as much and immediately began calling hospitals, until she located him, whereupon she rushed to him and pleaded that he return home and take care of "his sick mother." He did.[8]

The astonishing persuasiveness of the martyr type lies in her cunning ability to elicit guilt feelings in others.

Another theme of the martyr Mom has overtones of the reverse of the preceding description. Here the child suffers from some ailment (actual or imagined) and the mother insists on nursing him. She becomes the martyr of his suffering. And she lets it be known, loud and clear, that because of her dedication to her child she is forgoing a potential career, the cultivation of a talent, the leisure time she could otherwise enjoy, etc. The important points are two beliefs of the child: (1) what mother says is true and (2) he in fact needs mother for nursing him. This combination creates a convenient guilt lever for the mother: she presses the lever and her son reacts like a conditioned lab animal, salivating guilt, crouching with shame, rushing to do her dictates. While outsiders and detached persons may see her as maudlin and bizarrely manipulative, the son sees her beckoning with righteous demands.

This play on the offspring's control emotions must be seen in conjunction with the mother's conditional love technique. They form a powerful combination—perhaps the most forceful display of psychological weaponry in the arsenal of Momistic trickery. No wonder that some of the most grotesque cases of Momistic crippling—in the psychological and even the *physiological* sense—follow from it.

A striking illustration was a thirty-seven-year-old Wisconsin man whose mother took him everywhere in a wheel chair, allegedly because he suffered from paralysis derived from a childhood bout with polio. Welfare officials finally prevailed on the mother to have her son examined by physicians, who found nothing physiologically wrong with him. They thought him perfectly capable of walking. Further inquiry revealed that it was his *mother*, not polio, that had disabled him. Taking care of her son, as if he were completely helpless, fulfilled certain neurotic needs in the woman.

Psychiatrists then discovered that when the son was temporarily removed from the mother at age fifteen to attend school, he curled up in a fetal position and remained in this position for twenty-two years, spoon fed, diapered, and wheeled around by his mother, who insisted that she "liked him just the way he is." The mother reinforced the son's reaction. She did not allow him to attempt to get up on his legs, and in fact convinced him that he could not walk.[9]

We should hasten to add that this is an extreme, prototypal case of martyr Momism. The common occurrences seem vastly more harmless and plausible—such as the mother who simply complains about a severe headache caused by "worries" brought on by her noncompliant child. The migraine martyr may make the proverbial plea and charge: *"Look what you are doing to me—after all I have done for you."* She may actually believe it, and so may the child. It will etch the basic sentence more deeply in his mind: *"Mother is always good; if she suffers, it is because I am bad."*

The martyr Mom is particularly prevalent among mothers who have only their children to lean on, to share and communicate with, and from who to derive feelings of being worthwhile and useful. Thus widowed, divorced, unmarried, and deserted mothers are particularly inclined to resort to this version of Momism. Consciously or unconsciously, this type of mother uses her problems to engender pity and guilt and thus retain command over the child.

The combination of her "ailment" (or other salient problems), "devotion," and manipulation, on one side, and the child's anxiety about being an ingrate, on the

other side, is extremely powerful and makes it impossible
to extricate himself from his mother's grip. We may consider it axiomatic that a child who does not or cannot revolt against the martyr mother is a sick child—and usually stays sick and crippled for the rest of his life.

The Domineering Mom

Although the domineering Mom has overtones of the
overprotective mother—she also has an intimidating influence on the free unfolding of the ego processes (recognizing and coping with reality)—she differs in several
significant aspects and hence deserves separate categorization. Unlike the overprotective mother, the domineering mother reflects hostility and compulsiveness. She
makes constant and excessive demands on the child. In
fact, she is so overdemanding as to discourage the initiative of the child and nullify his incentive to think and act
independently. More specifically, the child finds insufficient opportunity to follow his thoughts independently
because his mother always dictates everything to him.
This is an effective way to establish absolute rule over
the young individual—he becomes too dependent on the
directions and commands of his mother.

Of course, all true Moms aim at the domination and
possession of their children; what differs is only their
strategy, whose selection is contingent on the mothers'
resources and emotional disposition. For example, one of
the motives of the domineering type—as well as the
seemingly opposite type, the overindulgent mother—is
the desire to enslave and possess. In the later case, however, this is done by ensnaring the child in incessantly
the desire to enslave and possess. In the latter case, how-
nurturant and unrealistically supportive mothering, which
establishes a dependency relationship in the captive.

The domineering mother does not tolerate self-
expression on the part of the child. She prevents per-

sonal assertion by stern discipline, punishment, and such ego-destroying techniques as revealing and ridiculing her son's mistakes and shortcomings in front of other people. An important additional condition is the child's inability to circumvent or avoid the parent and her constant supervision. Hence, the overwhelming expectations and ego-deflating demands act as an uninterrupted bombardment of personality-stifling episodes.

These experiences include a number of interesting factors:

1. The mother is highly *judgmental*, confronting the child with absolutist either/or, black-white, and good-bad propositions. He may not fail to live up to the norms defined for him, and must grace with success mother's endeavors to mold him into a model of perfection.

2. The mother is *punitive*. Rather than offering understanding and forgiveness, she punishes failures as if they are breaches of morality.

3. In the process of punishing, she turns *manipulative* and applies the conditional love technique: If you hurt-frustrate-disappoint mother, she won't love you anymore.

4. The mother *causes conflicts* in the child. She demands feelings and qualities from him that are inherently inconsistent and conflict with one another.

For example, she expects the child to express love, competence, and submissiveness—often at one and the same time. But a submissive child cannot show genuine love and affection because these qualities must spring from a free and unfettered mind. Likewise, a competent child cannot be submissive, because competence requires independent and imaginative personality processes.

5. The mother is basically (though possibly latently so) *rejective*. The very reason why this mother is domineering stems from her profound feelings of rejection and hostility for her son—which probably is nothing else

than a precipitation of her hostility toward men in general. Such animosity may have evolved either because of frustrating experiences with men (especially her father) earlier in her life or because she modeled herself on a domineering and hostile mother.

Because of complementary mate selection (choosing a spouse with opposite personality traits) by the mother, the boy ends up with a father who is weak and submissive (probably because the latter was raised by a domineering mother and an ineffectual father). The domineering Mom proceeds to belittle the worth and abilities of her husband and exhibits contempt and hostility for him. Then she transfers these attitudes to her son and includes him in the same category as his father. In the process, she deprives her son of the chance to identify meaningfully with his father (or any other adult male), precludes the development of a salient gender identity, and destroys his self-confidence. By having selected this type of husband, she has made certain that he will not stand in her way in taking the reins of child raising exclusively into her hands. She jealously guards her command of the offspring, and usually establishes uncontested monopoly over him. Instead of giving him a chance to make independent decisions, she commands the decisions, or makes a mockery of those he attempts to make, which results in confusion and anxiety in the child. Anxiety and diffidence evolve as prevailing personality traits, and probably color his interactional situations for the rest of his life. He will be inclined to bow uncritically to the commands of others—in fact, feel compelled to seek such subordination in order to achieve security, find a sense of direction, and think of his actions as meaningful.

Such an individual, whose natural aggressiveness and inquisitiveness have been broken through systematic defeats, will gravitate toward a powerful agent to vicariously experience the elation that the feeling of power engenders. In such an attachment, the individual relies entirely on the authority of the agent and does what he is asked to do without questioning its justification, logic, or humanity. The True Believer is born! To an objective observer, his actions may seem unenlightened and irrational; but to the Momistically crippled individual, the actions "feel" logical and legitimate because they imbue him with a sense of security and purpose. He has found his secure world—no matter how pathological its description by a behavioral scientist.

The basic sentence of the victim of this type of Momism goes like this: *"If I obey, if I am good, then mother will love me again."* He exhibits the typical traits of the authoritarian personality, visualizing a world that is ordered into superior and inferior, strong and weak, good and bad, those who give orders and those who must carry them out, etc. Woe to those who rely on his mercy, if for some reason they fall "below" him. He will be the perfect slave master, an unscrupulous guard in a concentration camp, or a pedantic bureaucrat.

But before we depict further consequences of Momism (which we defer to the next chapter), let's examine a few settings in which the transactions of the domineering Mom take place.

The case study of Peter[10] includes insights into the marital relationship of his parents that help us understand how his mother was able to enact her Momistic propensity. She was a woman of exceptional energy, intelligence, and competence, who liked to refer to herself as "top man, always." These qualities became noticeable during her school years, especially college, when she excelled in various leadership roles. As an adult, these proficiencies became even more visible through her successful involvement in civic, political, literary, and social groups. Although her appearance was flawlessly feminine, her demeanor in the home resembled what could be defined as traditional or assertive masculinity. The husband she chose, who was to become Peter's father, had been superbly preconditioned for her domineering style. He had grown up under domineering parents, had found life was easiest if he took the route of least resistance, had become a lawyer because of his parents' wish, and even in his profession selected activities that spared him personal assertiveness and direct confrontation. He specialized in legal research, leaving the fighting and sparring to the more aggressive colleagues of the law firm with which he was associated, and was generally known as an encyclopedia on two legs, able to save any colleague a trip to the library.

At home, "Yes, dear, but ... " was soon replaced by "Yes, mother" on the part of the male members of the household: father, Peter, and Peter's younger brother. The rules were laid down by a firm maternal hand. Yet it was not necessarily an unkind atmosphere; it was a benevolent despotism wherein they could not have their own way, but neither were they obliged to assume responsibility for themselves. Mother arranged everything, made decisions, gave orders; in other words, it was a rather smooth way of life—as long as everyone "cooperated." Failure to comply with the mother's desires and arrangements could result in unpleasant confrontations, which mother regularly won. It must have been realization of the utter futility of rebellion that caused the males to settle into a relatively secure, though eventless, living arrangement.

With the birth of Peter's younger brother, the security and tranquility were temporarily disturbed—particularly for Peter, who experienced the proverbial jealousy of the firstborn toward the younger sibling. The symptoms, however, were quickly dealt with—by decree of the mother. Peter was told to "be nice," "give in," etc.—and, on the face of it, he did. No overt problems boiled up. His natural assertiveness was replaced by unnatural sub-missiveness. Peter responded so submissively to his mother's dictates because the dispensation of security and "love" depended on his unconditional surrender and "good behavior." And it was his mother who defined the criteria of "good behavior." His father played a minor role in this respect; and his love did not matter much to Peter.

However, the outward show of acceptance and sub-mission was not an accurate gauge of Peter's real feel-ings. His younger brother remained a threat to him, en-dangered the exclusive attention he'd previously had, and reinforced his insecurity and anxiety—feelings that were predominant in Peter because of his mother's conditional love technique. These unresolved feelings of jealousy, in-security, and anxiety became general and diffused as-pects of his character; they were control emotions that made him comply with his parents, go through college with flawless grades, graduate from law school (chosen on account of his parents' wish), and become a lawyer.

And then came an atypical episode: as if making a last desperate effort to free himself from the maternal tyranny, he married over his parents' objection. The out-come was almost predictable. He could not handle the emotional demands of marriage, unravel the ensuing anxi-eties, and, least of all, withstand the interference of his mother. The marriage was dissolved as fast as it had been contracted—by annulment—and Peter's mother re-established her monopoly.

Peter continued to serve his apprenticeship in his father's law firm, and to all appearances was a person-able and promising young professional. His emotional deficiencies did not show when he did not have to live up to emotional involvements and responsibilities; he knew how to mask these character flaws—a skill he had ac-quired since childhood, when, under the strict regimen of his mother, he could never disclose his inner feelings. In fact, so suppressed were his real emotions and desires that he was not aware of their true nature. Hence his surface charm was not really a deception, it was sincere; but it was limited to certain facile situations. There simply was more to him than showed on the surface. His pleasant side was like the part of the iceberg above water, above a mass of hidden darkness. As events proved, in an emotional crisis these hidden forces—insecurity, extreme dependency, conflicts, and agonizing anxiety— could erupt and reveal the confused and hostile child underneath the thin veneer of upper-middle-class mannerisms. Peter was unable to establish a happy and secure life-style. Multiple marriages and divorces robbed him ever more of self-confidence, forcing him to rely more and more on the mask of his professional position—and on little else.

Perhaps the most fateful aspect of this case study is the effect Peter's Momistic impairment had on his children, in whom another generation's happiness and creativity were affected. Because of his neurotic disposition, Peter selected neurotic spouses, who, in turn, created neuroses in their offspring. Thus one case history ends and others immediately begin.

Another case history deals with what may be considered a minority type: mother-*daughter* Momism. The observations pivot on Irene, an attractive woman of twenty-five.[11] Curiously, it was not through problems or disasters of the victim that the case received attention. In fact, she appeared to be well adjusted and adequately functioning within the narrow life to which she had limited herself—encompassing her family and work situation and nothing else.

Indeed, the trouble could be defined precisely in terms of behaving *too* adjustedly. No normal human being in a diverse and problematic urban-industrial society like ours can evade the trials and tribulations that tax our ingenuity and confront us with difficult decision-making. If we observe in an individual the complete, or near-complete, *absence* of the decisionmaking, personal imagination, and natural dismays which a complicated society must elicit in its members, we may wonder about that person's sensibility and mental health.

As suggested above, it was not through Irene's doing that her situation became known but through her nineteen-year-old sister, Ellen, who bitterly complained about her mother's chronic and drastic attempts to control every aspect of Ellen's life. Unlike her older sister, Ellen had escaped the totalitarian influence of the mother by physically removing herself: she took up residence elsewhere, but in the process suffered considerable guilt, confusion, and anxiety. Irene, on the other hand, remained at home, enjoyed her mother's total care, and showed no signs of rebelliousness.

It is possible that the six years' difference in age between the daughters gave the mother enough time and opportunity to condition Irene, while Ellen experienced less than the mother's total concentration and found early contacts outside her family. Nevertheless, the pressures that the mother exerted to get Ellen back home weighed enormously on the young woman—to the point that she pondered moving again and keeping her address secret. Her mother incessantly checked at her apartment, called at her place of work, and questioned her friends to find out every detail of Ellen's activity, whereabouts, association, and the like. This was an immense embarrassment to Ellen—particularly the calls at work to ask her boss about her behavior, attendance, and whereabouts. Each time her mother found out that she had a date with a young man, she would complete a veritable dossier on him, then insidiously twist all sorts of information to present her daughter with a portrait which would presumably disqualify him from associating with Ellen. Her general dictum was "Children should stay home with the parents"; and she kept presenting Irene as a model to Ellen.

Indeed, Irene has never had a date! She has been content to stay home with her parents. Her mother would not let her date, or move from the parental home. She totally supervised Irene's college education, decided on a job for her (in a bank), and made all her plans and shaped all her dreams. Irene is so timid around people that she hardly talks, let alone indicates what she wants for herself.

As a stroke of irony, one day her mother decided that Irene's future should be a career with the United States Air Force, where she would be secure and have status and power. Why the mother saw status and power as important for her daughter is interesting, but at this time must remain a puzzling question. (Yet an explanation might be the mother's projection of her own desires, a compensatory dream, onto her daughter. Also, the mother, who fancied herself a woman's liberationist, thought such an aspiration timely and righteous.) Anyway, the diffident young woman dutifully obeyed and completed her application (including letters of reference from her college professors, who couldn't recall who this applicant was) for the deadliest force in today's world. Predictably, the Air Force could not be convinced of Irene's being an asset to its ranks. She has continued living contentedly at home, still totally dependent on her mother, and perhaps enjoying visions of commanding a supersonic jet with her mother as copilot.

The battle to subjugate, or resubjugate, Ellen and encloister her at home is still raging, and is unlikely to end in victory for her mother. The latest trick from the armory of Momism was an interesting sidestep to martyrdom. She again accused her younger daughter of causing her so much worry and grief as to make her ill and put her in the hospital. It was a convincing spectacle; she actually had herself admitted, examined, and a biopsy performed. The diagnosis was "valley fever," a common infection of the lungs by a regional (central Arizona) fungus. Notwithstanding the nonpsychosomatic diagnosis, the mother continued to blame her daughter for her suffering and for "putting her into the hospital."

The role the father played throughout all this was the classically weak and submissive husband who dared not stand in the way of Mom. He seemed kindly inclined toward his daughters, felt sorry for them, and frequently gave them spending money behind the back of his wife. (Money was among the items the mother controlled, absolutely so, and would allocate very sparingly.)

In summary, we see the almost total enslavement of the oldest child, the desperate struggle of the younger child to rid herself of external and internal persecution by her mother, and a passive father who could not check or balance the neurotic possessiveness of his wife.

The "Star" Mom

One of the less frequent variants of Mom is the "star." On the face of it, this type of mother appears quite harmless and even admirable—in fact, virtually adorable. She combines striking physical attractiveness with the status of a coveted socialite. Her husband is known as just that, "her husband," who demurely stands in her shadow and only occasionally reflects a bit of her fame and radiance. This mother's strategy may overlap with one or the other of the previously discussed Mom types, but her "stardom" provides her with a unique and effective resource in the battle for her child's body and soul.

Stardom becomes part of the leverage she is able to exert over the male child. She applies it to achieve personality-absorbing dominance over him and cow into submissive adoration not only her child but her husband and friends. The child is so profoundly impressed by the admiration lavished on his mother by all the people he knows that her conditional love manipulation operates on especially fertile ground. His basic interpretation of the world around him can be summed up by "Everybody loves mother; if I wouldn't love her, I would be odd." The fear of oddness, of being at odds with everybody and with something considered natural, works as a control mechanism and keeps the child in line with his mother's wishes and demands. This, of course, is the same control emotion operating in the other persons who belong to the star's entourage. This type of situation can evolve into a hollow pattern of interaction, a situation of pluralistic ignorance where each admirer is admiring only because he thinks all other persons are admiring. It is the old story of the naked king, parading to exhibit his gorgeous "clothes," with no one daring to point out their absence.

It is entirely possible, however, that this mother's charm is real to her friends and the public in general. It is then all the more difficult for the child to find a reason for dissent. "Hundreds of fans can't be wrong" becomes a reinforcing chant along the parade route of his docile servitude.

This mother commands a persuasive arsenal for "management of impression." It includes nothing less mundane than reliance on good old American commercialism, particularly the cosmetics industry. Her physical attractiveness is augmented by skillful makeup, effective clothes, and the latest hair style. Regular visits to the "spa," health club, or gym prolong her stardom and ensure the worshipful submission of others.

Under these conditions, the child grows afraid of

disobeying and rebelling against his glamorous mother. As a result, he can be manipulated easily—usually beyond the age at which such comprehensive maternal influence is necessary or conducive to the unfolding of an individual's independence.

A pertinent case study deals with a mother who enjoyed local fame as an amateur actress on the stages of a large metropolitan area. She also appeared (in addition to her stage performances) in numerous TV commercials, often promoting the cause of a worthy civic organization. She married at a relatively late age, in her thirties (a delay presumably brought about by her "being terribly involved in the fine arts of the community"), and had only one child, Antony. With her acting career waning, she shifted her concentration to her son and determined to raise him to become worthy of his namesake, the Shakespearean hero. She made up her mind to bless mankind by creating a superb actor out of her son.

Under the onslaught of his mother's domineering manipulation and awe-inspiring stardom, the boy grew up so lax in psychological stamina that his attempts at acting fell more than flat—they fell through. It was not that he was unwilling (what *wouldn't* he have done to please mother!) but that he simply could not express himself convincingly. It was like Linus trying to play the part of Zorba the Greek. The words came out all right (after all, they were interminably practiced under the direction of his mother), but something else—rather intangible—was missing. When, during his college years, it became obvious that a stage or movie career was not to be the fate of the young man, his parents reluctantly ordered a switch to business administration, and Antony (he was never called Tony at home) joined his father's business firm.

As if in search of a new cause, his mother began to show interest in the transactions of the business and started to make suggestions, and finally give firm orders, as to how the business should be run. Both the husband and son complied with deference. It was as if she had two sons, one younger than the other, except that she was married to the latter.

The case history shows that the business dealings became suspect, and finally were investigated by the authorities. Fraud and tax evasion were established. Against their better knowledge and business ethics, the father and son had followed the mother's instructions and engaged in dubious transactions. The judge, who obtained some insight into the psychological circumstances of the family, deemed the two men's childlike obedience an insufficient defense and levied heavy fines and back payments of taxes on the firm. In curious, roundabout sophistry, the mother nevertheless made the husband and son feel exclusive guilt for the fiasco. She called them "flagrantly ignorant" and declared that, *ipso facto*, she would have to supervise them more closely than before. She did just that. Her supervision included more than the business aspects; it also covered her son's "private" life. The last stage of the case history shows that Anthony got married. Or, more accurately, he was married off by his mother: she selected the girl for him.

It was not a complementary selection. The young wife, the exact female counterpart of Antony in passivity, in no way disturbed the established family pattern of superior mother and inferior everybody-else. It became a matriarchal and matrilocal arrangement, with the young couple living, securely stifled, in the mother's household.

The Pseudointellectual Mom

This mother, again, is a Mom in the minority, who is encountered less frequently than the first few types discussed in this chapter. It is not that this mother differs from the others in basic attitude and neurotic need, but she draws from a specific resource for making her Momistic influence stick. Her personal assets include vast knowledgeability, excellent memory, and exceptional language facility. In other words, she has the appearance of an expressive intellectual. Yet, unlike a true intellectual, she sees only one side to an issue—and a rather shallow one at that. She is more a dispenser of trivia than a pundit of profound insight. Her pseudointellectualism proceeds by expressing tidbits of information about virtually every subject that comes up, and she attaches an assertive opinion to each one. She tops off her style by garrulously criticizing the ideas of others.

Her verbal skill and never-ending criticism have a pervasive impact on her child's personality. He acquires a belief in the infallibility of his mother, grows intimidated by her, and ends up respecting all of her seemingly profound insights. He learns, through ego-deflating experiences, that no argument can be won against mother. She always seems to come forth with superior logic and knowledge.

All this proceeds in an atmosphere not, necessarily, of hostility but of "objective reasoning"—which on investigation turns out to be nothing but sly sophistry to prompt the child into doing what the mother wants him to do. In the end, he adopts a passive attitude and depends on his mother's knowledge and judgment. The basic sentence embedded in his mind is *"Mother knows everything and can do everything; if she would leave me, I would be lost."* While this is an understandable and normal attitude in an infant or small child, it becomes abnormal as the child grows older and, ultimately, is expected to assume adult responsibilities. So habitual will dependence on the mother become that his incentive to attain his own body of knowledge and understanding of life and the world around him is severely depressed.

Interestingly, this mother does not seem to notice his intellectual plight, and fails to give him a fair chance of thinking through his own problems and following up on his own notions. Here is the making of the perfect True Believer. His upbringing has not prepared him for critically examining dicta and credos—yet it has conditioned him to *need* them very badly, so that he grows up to be extremely vulnerable to some sort of presumably omniscient and omnipotent belief and commitment. Nothing less than a perfect substitute for an omniscient Mom will do.

Although the next chapter will present an extreme example of the consequences of this upbringing, a pertinent case study should be mentioned at this time.

Mrs. A visited a state agency concerned with mental retardation and expressed bewilderment about her nine-year-old son's chronically poor performance in school. She assured the director of the agency that she had always been very supportive of his learning and intellectual development. She let it be known that she was widely read, familiar with every aspect of the boy's academic curriculum, and capable of taking his education into her hands if it were necessary. She proudly reported that "he never needs to do his homework by himself; I sit down with him and help him." However, her "help" consisted of doing the homework *for* him. The support she gave her son in his intellectual development consisted not of dialogues but monologues, condemning the boy to passive listening. This "supportive" style became visible in the agency office during the interview with the child. During the evaluation session, the mother "helped" the child's performance with forceful verbal encouragement—even attempted to tell him what to say and how to say it.

It became obvious that the mother needed to lower her intellectual interference with the child's mental process, but it was no easy task to explain this to her. The agency psychologist saw it was necessary to demonstrate this requirement by showing the mother the differential outcome of the child's performance with and without her "help." Without the mother's interference, the child showed more age-appropriate orientation and ability, although in a somewhat slow manner. Under conditions of her assistance and encouragement, the boy seemed to switch off his independent thinking and let the outside agent take over. His comprehension and analytical ability rapidly fell below the normal age-appropriate range.

This case study, though incomplete because of the boy's age at this time, may demonstrate one of the luckier situations—where a potentially Momistic relationship was discovered just in time to introduce remedial measures.

The Child-Worshiping Mom

This mother is ostentatiously in line with good old Americana: the praise of motherhood. But at the risk of sounding platitudinous, we remind the reader that motherhood, by definition, has two sides: the mother and the offspring. The worshipful Mom, however, inscribes *both* sides of the ledger: the assets to her and the debits to the child.

This may sound contradictory, since the label suggests that she worships her child and hence ascribes true value to him. In reality, however, such a worshiper adores only herself and uses the child as a looking glass wherein she sees herself reflected in all her presumed worth and success. Her profuse praise of motherhood gives her the advantage of being able to practice her unwittingly harmful technique with impunity, appearing "to do what's best for the child." Not only is her obsessive and compulsive concern with the child condoned by the middle-class community (to which she belongs), it is applauded, envied, and emulated. In a sense, she serves as a model of perfect motherhood in the community.

165

Starting her child-raising practices on the simple premise of "being a good mother," she ends by pursuing it with such determination and fervor that "being a good mother" comes to be an end in itself, a status symbol that gives impetus to competition among her friends and acquaintances. In the course of her untiring endeavor to turn out a model son to the world, she forgets about his need for personalized nurture and, instead, uses him to convince herself and others of her outstanding performance in motherhood.

This, of course, is the mother who "most kindly" applies the insidious leverage of conditional love to make him conform to her wishes. And she has only "wishes," never orders or commands, since the latter are not consistent with the "good motherhood" she has read about.

The child is essentially reduced to functioning as an ornament in the family tree. The manipulation that is needed to have him acquire the suitable decor leaves him seriously impaired in respect to the growth of an independent and unique personality. He is the impeccable model child: glittering and shiny outside, hollow and boring inside.

This mother's motivation to have a "successful" child is based on deep needs. It is through their child's popularity that many parents compensate, through vicarious parasitism, for the lack of popularity they experienced during their own childhood.

Martha Lear has cited a number of examples of the child-worshiping Mom.[12] One mother was reported to be very concerned about her son's delay in starting dating, and was worried that perhaps, because of his small physical stature, he might be socially rejected. Eventually she found relief—her son succeeded in getting his first date, although he was only eleven. Other child worshipers gave testimony to their needs by preparing lavish birthday parties for two-year-olds, providing nine-year-old girls with training bras, inviting grade schoolers to "cocktail" parties (7-Up with fruit juice), and sensitizing eight-year-olds about "proper" wardrobes, styles of hair, and manicures.

Again, this type of Momism renders the child devoid of sufficient individuality and strength of personality to assume an independent outlook on life. In one form or other, they tend to remain Mom's little boy.

No doubt the array of types of Moms could be extended and include more and more esoteric and bizarre types, but the point has been made. While the underlying motivating force differs little among the various types, access to certain means and resources for implementing the basic propensity makes for colorful proliferation. All of them share the need to possess the child, to tie him to themselves, to live through him. But each is a different, unique formulation of Momism. It seems, however, that the more common expressions are the overprotective, overindulgent, domineering, and martyr types of Mom. The other classes—the "star" Mom, the pseudointellectual Mom, and the child-worshiping Mom—appear to be less common.

The stage is now set for a more detailed examination of the consequences of Momism. The next chapter will concern itself with those dismal aspects.

Chapter 6

*The American mother... she is the
unhappiest female that the primate world
has ever seen, and the most treasured
objective in her heart of hearts is the
psychological castration of husbands and
sons.*—Robert Ardrey

The Consequences
of Momism

This chapter concentrates more exclusively on the plight of the victim of Momism than the preceding chapter, in which we outlined Mom's nefarious approaches and only sketchily described the detriments wrought in the victim's contorted life.

The anguish derived from a childhood of Momistic manipulation may express itself in a wide variety of insidious ways. The major categories into which these pathetic consequences are ordered comprise the following.

1. *The True Believer.* Here is the individual who continues to be a slave to his overbearing need for the all-encompassing security that only an infant is entitled to demand from his mother. This victim embraces a mother surrogate in the form of a totalitarian belief or dogma.

2. *Sexual deviation.* Many victims of Momism turn out to be severely limited in their sexual responses.

Among them are the homosexuals, upon whom the mother has—as it were—cast a spell, preventing them from developing normal heterosexual interests.

3. *Drug problems.* This category deals with the victim who tries to alleviate his anguish through chemical alteration of his consciousness. In this connection, a major role is played by the illusion that drugs can provide "instant" gratification and problem solving. Again, this is an attitude more appropriate for the infant or small child than the adult, who is expected to realistically cope with reality.

4. *Mental problems.* This category includes the wide range of victims who suffer from excessive anxiety, confusion, and guilt. The range spans mild neurosis to complete inability to function, as in extreme schizophrenic withdrawal.

5. *Suicide.* Here we are dealing with the ultimate consequence, where the desperate victim of Momism is unable to find a viable solution for the accumulated anguish of Momism and decides on ending his life.

6. *The silent consequences.* It would be misleading to assume that all Momistic consequences express themselves in obvious dramas. Most victims are so broken in spirit that they are not capable of deviation or dramatic action. They are the silent victims; and it is this group which constitutes the majority of Momistic victims.

Again, it should be understood that the dreary consequences, as described above, are usually found in various combinations and degrees of intensity and compulsivity. Categories are introduced only for the sake of facilitating clear communication and offering devices for ordering the immensely variegated expressions of Momistic effects.

The True Believer

A common and often undetected outcome of Momistic conditioning is the type of individual who continues to rely upon a mother substitute who will "infallibly" make decisions for him. He may become a True Believer,[1] who exhibits fanatic adherence and loyalty to some supposedly universal and omnipotent ideology or charismatic leader and surrenders his whole being to this authority. Thus we witness the metamorphosis of Mom into an organization, religion, or movement. It is from these ranks that totalitarian movements recruit some of their most passionate campaigners and that charismatic rulers draw their most dedicated followers.

In a sense, it matters very little precisely *what* the "true belief" consists of as long as it serves as an effective Mom-in-disguise, who again pulls the strings and operates the victim's marionette-like personality.

Abraham H. Maslow has provided a framework which facilitates assessment of the Momistic situation and understanding of the psychological quandary of the victim.[2] The premise can be summed up by saying that the *Momistically impaired individual lacks adequate self-actualization.* He is strikingly deficient in a number of characteristics of the self-actualized person.

The following points describe the characteristics of the *Momistic person,* presenting the exact opposite points of the self-actualized individual.

1. A low degree of acceptance of himself, of others, and of the contingencies of human nature. He is ashamed of being what he is, and he is shocked and anguished to find foibles and shortcomings in himself or others.

2. He lacks spontaneity in thought, emotion, and behavior.

3. He constantly focuses on problems inside himself, is very self-conscious, and is a problem even to himself. Hence his ability to concentrate on problems outside himself, including tasks, duties, and the needs of others, is greatly diminished.

4. He cannot enjoy solitude. Apparently, he finds no use for privacy. Indeed, being alone frightens him.

5. He has little or no autonomy. He cannot remain true to an inner center or core of his conscience in the face of rejection or unpopularity. In the face of adversity, he cannot pursue interests, complete projects, or maintain integrity.

6. He is a joiner and, at best, an imitator. He is unable to create, invent, and innovate on his own in any sector of life.

7. He lacks the selfhood necessary for avoiding being "brainwashed" by his culture. His perspective is limited to the cultural dictates—or the demands of the powerful around him—and he follows them uncritically. Hence he remains unaware of the inconsistencies and acts of unfairness within his social environment.

This syndrome of attitudes, characteristic of the nonactualized person, leads swiftly to the perfect marriage of individual neurosis and social pathology. The consummation of this union is often seen in its most spectacular form in the effects of Momism.

And this brings us to a new vantage point from which to view the societal implications of Momism's effects: the fact that, to many, *personal freedom is a frightening monster!* It is apt to scare just about everyone, including the bravest, but particularly the Momistically conditioned individual.

Man is a creature who needs a structure—a familiar environment in which he can orient himself as to where he comes from and where he is going. This need appears on all levels of human life. It is to be understood in its most abstract form—*mentally*—in terms of internalized norms and values to think and live by; that is, in the form of a personal identity; *socially*, in order to relate meaningfully and consistently with others and thereby maintain a social equilibrium; that is, in the form of a social order; and *physically*, to assure bodily coordination and survival; that is, in the form of a tangible, physical environment.

Individual freedom, besides whatever positive functions it may have, tends to introduce equilibrium-upsetting elements into the structure of social life. This is anathema to the Momistically stifled individual, who frantically tries to preserve the security of an unchanging environment. As an infant seeks to cling to his mother for security, the growth-inhibited Momistic person desires to adhere to a nurturing and unchanging structure that guarantees total engulfment of the self. As the reciprocal to the structure, he becomes the True Believer.

It will be recalled that the reason why the Momistic personality experiences such a powerful compulsion to adhere to a structure lies in the conditional love manipulation to which he was exposed in early life. It was this manipulation, in conjunction with the absolutism of the power figure, Mom, that deprived the victim of the basic emotional grasp of what a democratic process is like and made development of self-confidence extremely difficult for him. This process has prepared him *to believe that he needs love and acceptance, although he does not feel worthy of receiving them.* And this sums up the fundamental psychological dilemma of the Momistic individual. This dilemma remains a perennial source of anxiety for him. Where does a person, driven so relentlessly by a combination of acute need and fear of rejection, turn to? It has to be a structure that accepts and "loves" him totally, despite his infirmities.

At this time the reader is invited to consider an interesting—some might say blasphemous—exercise. The introduction to a recent edition of the New Testament paraphrases what the editors believe to be the essential "facts" of the Bible.[3] They present these "facts" as the essence and meaning of the God-man relationship, and refer to specific verses to defend their conclusion. The "facts" are summed up in five logical steps:

1. We do not deserve God's love.
2. God loves us so much ...
3. We must accept God's love.
4. If we accept God's love, our life will be transformed and we will live forever.
5. We accept God's love by surrendering our lives to Him.

As an exercise for the more accurate understanding of the state of mind of the Momistically crippled individual, let us replace the words "God" and "Him" by "mother" and "her." The "facts" of life, then, read as follows:

1. We do not deserve mother's love.
2. Mother loves us so much ...
3. We must accept mother's love.
4. If we accept mother's love, our life will be transformed and we will live forever.
5. We accept mother's love by surrendering our lives to her.

Even for the majority of Momistic persons there comes the time when they must physically let go of mother. Then a transference of the attachment occurs, and the "facts" become attached to a mother substitute. In other words, the conditioned needs and ways of looking at the world remain; the changes lie in the transformation of the central agent, who metamorphoses from Mom to Church. An insidious remark might be that the expression "Mother Church" is all too apt to reflect more than just coincidental terminology.

Be this as it may (let psychohistorians worry about substantiation of a possible relationship between personality variables and historical variables), it appears quite plausible that Momistically impaired individuals would find a tailor-made psychological environment in the fundamentalist version of Christianity. However, we add *emphatically* that no insinuation is made here to the effect that Christians *in general* are drawn to their belief because of Momistic experiences. Such an inference would equal the facile conclusion and questionable logic of saying that people who suffer from appendicitis go to the hospital *and*, thus, all people who are in the hospital suffer from appendicitis. All that is implied here is that fundamentalist religion *may* serve as a sanctuary for Momistically crippled humanity.

And why shouldn't it serve in such a capacity? Has it not openly assumed the role of comforting, guiding, and "saving" the poor souls who are suffering? And do not Momistic souls need salvation very badly?

The attractiveness of fundamentalist religion is increased by its ability to provide for submittal of all problems to a higher power. Thus a Momistic individual can submit his problems, anxieties, and grievances to an always kind and forgiving deity, and decisions can be based upon "what the Lord [*Mom*] wants me to do," rather than on one's own ingenuity and effort to understand and come to grips with a situation.

Fundamentalist religion is not the only medium through which the Momistic sufferer can find solace and deliverance—to whatever degree this is possible. The transfiguration may involve other groups and movements with whom the victim of Momism can identify and in which he can find another Mom—as long as they offer totalitarian authority and security; that is, a structure that is as all-engulfing as the placenta. Hence the Momistic victim might experience a similar attraction to Nazism, Communism, racism, the occult, any form of save-our-country chauvinism, etc. The medium serves its purpose as long as it provides the victim of Momism with the opportunity to get absorbed into a "true belief," become part of it, obey with uncritical regularity, and hence derive personal security.

Unfortunately, however, such security is often acquired at the expense of the happiness and well-being of other human beings, who do not happen to be considered part of the in-group, the "elected," or the "superior."

For the victim of Momism, then, many of the traditional religions and totalitarian movements or organizations may be potentially attractive. For example, Communism offers powerful psychological attractions: the august cause, the prophets and "saints" of the movement, the "holy days," the sense of orientation and destiny, the universal fellowship, the promise of deliverance, and the demand for absolute obedience. In other words, many of the psychological elements of traditional religion can be found in the Communist Manifesto.

In return, the believer obtains satisfaction of his deep-seated needs for security, belonging, and dependency. In a Communist society, the party and the ideological dicta eliminate the follower's independent thinking and assume the responsibility for his actions. He attains a childlike sense of belonging and knows that a higher power is looking out for him. This orientation comes to mean what Erich Fromm calls "escape from freedom."

The True Believer syndrome can be applied, under certain circumstances, to the environment provided by the armed forces. As psychiatrist Edward A. Strecker noted in his classic investigation of enlisted men in the Second World War, "the Army is so structured that it could become a mom surrogate."[4] There is enough absolutist regimentation, division of life into superiors and inferiors, and dependency enforcement that it resembles the contingencies under which a Momistic child grows up. In return for his loyalty and obedience, the soldier is rewarded with total protection and care. Every detail of his life is ordered, prepared, and routinized for him, including his room and board, clothing, companionship, medical care, entertainment, and games. He is told how to perform such relatively minute tasks as grooming; what to wear, precisely how to wear it; where to walk, precisely how to walk; what to do, exactly how to do it; *ad infinitum.* This comes awfully close to infantilization.

He becomes dependent on authority and superiors in almost every sector of his life and keeps forfeiting personal decisionmaking. The "right kind of officer" (with the proper charisma) assumes the parental role and looks after his men as if they were children. Many of the soldiers like and desire this type of relationship; they want an officer to whom they can come for help and counsel when they experience problems—problems not only associated with Army life but also with personal affairs. This life-style maintains the immaturity of dependent personalities.

Strecker, however, feels that the armed forces provide a home for only a small minority of such immature soldiers and that most of the Momistic victims are screened out at the beginning of their military episode and returned to Mom's apron strings. Although Strecker's famous report is based on the rejects, one might conjecture that many Momistic cases slip through the screening tests, elude the eyes of the Army psychiatrists, achieve the transition from Mom to Army, and find a cozy Mom surrogate in the military setting.

The pivotal point for achieving this adjustment is the *transitional* period. If they are "washed out" before they sense the Army's resemblance to Mom, they will go back to their mother or go on searching for another, less-hard-to-get surrogate. If they endure the transition and feel the Momness of the military environment, they may adjust astonishingly well and come to love their new "Mom." It would be an interesting research project to discover how many of these soldiers become "lifers," making the military their career.

Perhaps we should reiterate that no assertion is made to the effect that *all* followers of a movement, party, or organization are, *ipso facto*, Momistic persons. Certainly many followers are motivated by healthy propensities and sane deliberations. Nevertheless, it is useful to identify the *potential* avenues that victims of Momism can travel throughout their lifetime. Without doubt, a "true belief"—the conviction of having found the eternal and absolute truth—has a strong attraction for a person whose security is chronically tied to an external (in contrast to his internal) authority. The more powerful the agent who makes the "infallible" decisions for him, the more attracted and dedicated he will become.

As Eric Hoffer pointed out, "faith in a holy cause is to a considerable extent a substitute for the lost faith in ourselves."[5] For the victim of Momism, it would be more accurate to say that he merely *transferred* his faith: from Mom to the holy substitute, whatever the latter may be. He had never lost faith—he always had it in his mother. Another thing is certain: he never had faith in himself—and that is the mark of the True Believer. In conjunction with the fellowship of believers, the "true belief" can fill the agonizing void in his life.

In sum, then, the Momistic victim is a non-self-actualized person whose uncertainty and insecurity cause him to gravitate toward an agent in whose shadow he finds deliverance from anxiety.

Psychotherapist Carl R. Rogers has found that many patients are deficient in being "authentic"—that is, true to themselves, to their potential. His concept applies to Momistic individuals, though it was aimed at a broader spectrum. Nevertheless, a person cannot be *fully functioning* if the following Momistic characteristics prevail.[6]

1. The person adheres to facades. He seeks to be a

person he is not, and tries to give the impression
that he is the imagined person.
2. The person adheres to "oughts." His conduct is
   constantly guided by what he feels he ought to
   do, ought to become.
3. He compulsively attempts to meet the expectations of others and assumes subservient and even
   slavish manners (but only toward his "superiors"). He feels constantly compelled to please
   others.
4. He is other-directed and chooses his behavior
   style in alignment with others' example. In the
   process, he cannot distinguish between a responsible and an irresponsible action.
5. He lacks self-acceptance.
6. He blots out thoughts, emotions, perceptions, and
   memories which touch him as unpleasant. In the
   process of doing this, he is not open to realistic
   experience.

It is no simple matter to find case histories to illustrate the Momistic True Believer. Curiously, the difficulty is not in finding enough cases but in finding cases
where the impairment is definable as a maladjustment
and a social problem. Most cases seem to be so adjusted
and "normal" that they would not make a clear point.

Why this "normal" appearance? The answer lies in
the reciprocity of personal and social pathologies, which
often "fit" one another so perfectly that they look
"natural."

For example, sometimes a government prolongs certain social injustices or engages in ill-advised foreign
policies without most members of the society speaking
out against the policies. They feel indifferent or even
comfortable with what is going on—and is being done in
their name. From any objective historical or scientific
point of view, the events would call for an outcry and for

counteraction, but nothing of the sort is forthcoming. Hence the goings-on are not defined as socially pathological. On the personality level, the pathology manifests itself through the fact that the people behave adjustedly and tolerantly in the face of societal pathology. Within the frame of their "true belief," the people are tolerant, if not supportive, of inhumanity, cruelty, and injustice committed with their tacit approval.

We must therefore select a case with such increased potency of Momistic pathology that it makes the point beyond ambiguity. It is comparable to the situation where a doctor intentionally nurtures bacteria to grow a visible culture of them. Under normal conditions, such concentration of the pernicious bacteria might be rare; under laboratory conditions, however, the amassment can be achieved easily.

Although life cannot be neatly divided into "normal" and "lab" conditions, some situations are so subject to the combination of peculiar variables that equally peculiar results become visible. One such situation, the outcome of severe Momistic conditioning and oppressive political circumstances, illustrates an extreme case of the Momistically induced True Believer.

The case of Jacques Vasseur was revealed in France in 1965.[7] The "stars" of the drama were Mme. Vasseur, approximately seventy years of age, and her son Jacques, forty-five. Jacques's childhood was a classic example of Momistic upbringing: father-absence from the socialization process, an overindulgent mother who catered to every whim of the child, and isolation from other children, neighbors, and potential male models. His mother kept him to herself, gave toys (particularly dolls) for him to play with, and provided only one companion for him—herself. Her son was her "cause" in life, and her dedication continued unabated after he had grown up.

However, a major interference threatened the "idyllic" life-style. With the Nazi conquest of France, adult males were subject to deportation to forced labor camps in Germany, and the mother prevailed on the son to choose any alternative other than separation from her. Choosing such an alternative, he became a fervent and dedicated collaborator of the occupation power—a power as absolute and all-engulfing as his mother's love had been. After the war ended and French sovereignty was reestablished, he was a hated and hunted criminal. There was only one problem blocking justice: he was nowhere to be found.

It was not until 1962 that he was discovered; his mother had hid him for seventeen years in a garret above her second-story apartment in a suburb of Lille—while the police had kept him on their "wanted" list. Mme. Vasseur took every precaution to keep her son's presence a secret. She shopped for two on her widow's pension by dividing her purchases among several stores. She knitted special house shoes with felt soles so that neighbors or visitors could not hear him moving about. In his tiny living quarters, Vasseur spent his time learning seven languages, in addition to French and German (his mother joined him in learning Latin). She invited him to her apartment to watch TV on quiet nights, cooked and shared all meals with him, and in general was his constant companion—duplicating his childhood years. All this came to an end when the police discovered him as they paid a routine call to Mme. Vasseur and found him hiding behind a curtain. It is remarkable that Vasseur could have found refuge outside France but preferred to stay with his mother. As he put it, "I was in perfect joy to stay with *Maman* [Mummy]."

His joy was disrupted by detention in prison and a widely publicized trial a few years later, in 1965. The State Security Court in Paris conducted the investigation and amassed formidable evidence against *"Maman's* boy," amounting to treason, murder, torture, and the deportation of his countrymen to labor camps in Germany. He was held accountable for 430 arrests, 310 deportations, and the death of 230 Frenchmen while he was a servant of the Gestapo. Approximately 200 witnesses recited the horrors they had suffered under "Vasseur the Terror," recounting how he beat them, tortured them, and condemned their relatives and fiancés to death. One witness said he had been bull-whipped for ten hours by Vasseur; a woman testified that he had burned her breasts with a cigarette; and others told of the mercilessness with which he handed over to the executioners their fathers, brothers, and sisters.

Jacques Vasseur did not deny these accusations but accepted them impassively, with an occasional "Yes, it's possible" or "It's plausible." The trial reached a dramatic climax when his mother took the witness stand and tried to take all the blame on herself. "I had a very strict mother," she said. "I wanted to spare my son. . . . It's not he who ought to be on trial. It's me. It's my fault. Punish me, but let him go."

The attending psychiatrist agreed with Mme. Vasseur and explained to the court that Jacques's subservience to the Gestapo was a transferred attachment from his mother to another powerful agent, that he embraced his grisly duties because he needed the approval of the Mom surrogate, and that his power over other humans gave him the opportunity to express his suppressed virility. The psychiatrist reminded the court that Vasseur still referred to his mother as "my Mummy" and that his greatest suffering during his imprisonment was caused by seeing "Mummy" only once a week.

After all the evidence and testimony were in, the court announced the sentence: death by firing squad.

This story supports Patricia Sexton's thesis that murders are committed more often by quiet and gentle men ("nice guys") than by ruffians and the overtly aggressive. Sirhan Sirhan and Lee Harvey Oswald, both reared by protective Moms, grew up as quiet and dutiful sons. They were alienated from their peers, father, and normal male associations. They were typical of a "rapidly growing breed—the 'feminized male'—whose normal male impulses are suppressed or misshapen by overexposure to feminine norms."[8]

Sexual Deviation

Applying the term *deviation* to sexual activities may arouse strong objection among many of today's liberated readers. What is deviation? Do we refer to a statistical oddity? Do we moralize? Or do we simply mean behavior that deviates from the culturally established way?

Since this book is not the place to thrash out the complexities of the question, it must suffice to indicate that we mean the term primarily in the latter sense: a deviation from the cultural norm. (Of course, if the cultural norm ceases to be compelling and distinct, deviation is no longer deviation for the simple reason that there's nothing to deviate from. But such a state of sexual liberation has not yet been achieved in American society; hence "deviation" still carries validity.)

One form of deviation is homosexuality. Among its numerous—and still poorly understood—causes is Momism. (We must immediately say that there cannot be talk of just one cause; real life always presents a constellation of causal conditions. But certain aspects of Momism seem to be highly significant ingredients and strong predictors of homosexuality.) In the Momistic situation, especially where infantilization is the mode of life, the boy's early experience with his mother is so overpowering that he grows up unable to step back, as it were, and look at females without the distorting effect of his domineering image of his mother. This image is somehow transferred to other females; he cannot view them as equals, as sex partners, or, least of all, as the traditionally submissive girl friend or spouse. The natural sensual desires toward girls are suppressed and experienced as unpleasant. In short, he does not develop a normal interest in the opposite sex.

Unwittingly, Mom has helped this process with the inculcation of aversion to girls; she systematically degrades them, finds endless faults with each girl her son would get to know, and channels his energy into different directions. In addition, she will inject poor sexual attitudes into her son, telling him that sex is impure, evil, dangerous, and a sign of weakness.

The result is the acquisition of attitudes that are inhibiting, if not hostile, to heterosexuality. This opens wide the gates to seeking satisfaction of sexual desires in other relationships—other than the normal man-woman relationship.

While it is nearly impossible to make accurate predictions about which type of Momistic influence will ripen into the True Believer syndrome, in homosexuality the determining factors are often quite visible. There is relatively widespread agreement among experts in the behavioral sciences that a certain constellation of conditions is highly conducive to the development of homosexuality in men. Within this group of determining factors, a number of Momistic conditions stand out, such as a passive, disinterested father and an overbearing mother. It is hardly possible to produce a male homosexual if the father is affectionate to his wife and son and supportive of the son's masculinity.

Characteristic of the growth of homosexuality is the mother's close relationship with her son, who usually is the only child or is preferred above her other (usually widely spaced) children and whose company she prefers even above that of her husband. Studies show that the mother acts in a seductive way (though unconsciously so) toward the young boy, interferes with his attempts as a child to assert himself, and undermines his ability to make personal decisions. She also blockades communication between the father and the son, and does this with minimum exertion since the father is usually detached from the family in general and from his son in particular, who is often his least favorite child.

Another feature of the victim's process of deviance shows up in notoriously poor peer relationships before he reaches puberty. Usually the Mom manages to isolate the child from the normal play activities of his peers and persuades him to take up atypical activities and hobbies (a surprisingly high proportion of this type of victim is characterized by an interest in grooming, fabrics, and fabric designs). In her cunning, she exposes the child to the rejection and ridicule of other children.

A typical case history of these features describes a high school boy whose mother succeeded in implanting in him two definitive sentences (in the sense of defining his identity and fate): (1) Mother is so pretty and worthy of you—she cannot be matched by any other girl. (2) Sexual intercourse is horrible and dangerous, and you should stay away from it—if for no other reason than not to hurt and shame your mother.

These beliefs became deeply anchored in the emotions and motivations of the young man. No girl could ever measure up to his mother; so he steered away from the companionship with girls that normally is part of a high school boy's life. On a summer vacation, a middle-aged relative seduced the boy and introduced him to the world of homosexual affection, which the boy found nonthreatening and gratifying. From then on, it became routine for the boy: he looked forward to homosexual encounters and, on occasion, let himself be "picked up" in public places he frequented for that purpose. Finally, he was introduced to the "gay" subculture, started to hang out with the gay crowd in gay night spots, and gradually assumed a homosexual identity.

(A more detailed homosexual case history—the case of Jed—was recounted in the previous chapter because of its valuable clues as to how the *overprotective Mom* exercises her destructive propensity.)

This is hardly an exciting story, one might think— this almost platitudinous development of a homosexual, which nowadays causes relatively few raised eyebrows. That Momism was the force behind the scenes might be overlooked or found to be of no particular significance. But that is just the point: Momism is a *silent* disease! It affects the victim without creating upheavals or overt tragedies until much later in life, when a limited and stifled life-style reveals itself.

A similar background emerges in studies of transsexuals who have performed the radical change of physical gender identity (in addition to the already established psychological change) from male to female. One of America's foremost experts on transsexualism, Dr. Robert J. Stoller, recorded the case histories of a number of boys who felt they were really females but unfortunately were endowed with the wrong physique, and wanted their bodies to match their female identities. It is interesting to note that they all grew up under very similar conditions, resembling those described under homosexuality. His research on problems of gender identity led Dr. Stoller to suggest the following factors as significant in determining male-to-female transsexualism.[9]

1. The boys grew up in an *intense relationship with their mothers* and had extremely close physical contact with them.

2. The boys had *little opportunity to witness normal*

male-female interaction; they were either exposed to a weak and nonmasculine father or to no father at all.

3. *The mothers feminized the boys,* often playfully dressing them as girls, and let them play with dolls and other feminine toys.

4. The boys were *rejected by their peers as sissies* upon entering school. (Prior to entering school they had very little, if any, interaction with other children.)

5. The boys were emotionally, as well as in all practical aspects of life, *extremely dependent on their mothers.*

6. They had *no involvement in the masculine subculture.*

7. They experienced *conflicts and difficulties in interaction with females.*

The first two items, extremely close relationship with the mother and a lack of normal male-female relationships, are also typical of suicides and victims of schizophrenia. However, to complete the etiological picture of the transsexual, the other five items are necessary.

Caution must be taken, however, to avoid oversimplification of the causative process: a number of factors can intercept the developmental process of the transsexual, in spite of exposure to the conditions listed above. These modifying conditions must be considered in making predictions about sexual deviance, particularly the transsexual version. They include the quality of peer-group interaction, the influence of teachers, the size and structure of the family, exposure in terms of quality and quantity to the mass media (especially TV), birth order (if there are siblings), and the timing of father-absence or father passivity (the most vulnerable time is the preschool years).

Although we have indications that these conditions make a difference as to whether a boy will develop into a sexual deviate, there unfortunately is not enough research to warrant a reliable statement as to precisely *how* they operate.

A plethora of case studies has emerged from the Gender Identity Research Treatment Program, a unique psychiatric clinic at the University of California in Los Angeles. Under the leadership of psychiatrist Richard Green, homosexual and potentially transsexual boys between the ages of four and ten are treated. All are visibly effeminate: they walk with a mince, talk with a falsetto and lisp, and invariably want to be girls. Without exception, they have experienced harassment and rejection. A seven-year-old had his shirt torn off by his peers at school, who wanted to see whether he had female breasts. All are ridiculed for not being able to keep up in physical play or games at school, for not being aggressive, and for talking "funny." At home, these children are often allowed to dress in female ways (in dresses) and play with dolls—and are found to be "cute."[10]

Over nearly ten years of research, Green tracked down the causative factors and found at least five relatively consistent background features that fall in the domain of Momistic mothering:

1. *Maternal overprotection,* which prevented real boyishness and rough-and-tumble play, during the preschool years.

2. *Excessive maternal attention and physical contact,* preventing the boy from forming a separate and individualistic identity.

3. *Lack of a male model during the preschool years.*

4. *Lack of male playmates.*

5. *Maternal dominance* of the family, with the father playing a powerless and passive role.[11]

Drug Problems

That it is the overindulgent and possessive mother who hides behind the props and pulls the strings of her marionette-addict son has been suspected by an impressive array of drug experts and social workers who have been watching the drug scene for many years.[12] There is evidence that many mothers unconsciously promote deviant behavior as a means of vicariously achieving their goals of significance and possession. For example, a two-year study on young male heroin addicts (in their twenties) by the Lower East Side Narcotic Center in New York showed that few of the mothers wanted their sons to be cured. These mothers, in fact, sabotaged the rehabilitation program. One was known to regularly flush her son's withdrawal medication down the toilet; another appealed to her son's guilt complex by asking him to stay home and nurse her ear infection, which reappeared whenever the son was ready to hospitalize himself for treatment of his addiction. Other mothers gladly gave their sons money "for a haircut," when they must have realized that the amount of money and the frequency with which they gave it signified less mundane purposes. One mother, ignoring her twenty-three-year-old son's addiction, was concerned only about his being late for meals, his getting home before midnight, and his reluctance to let her hug him.

Another study was completed by psychologist John Schwartzman of the Family Institute of Chicago, who looked into the lives of a sample of male heroin and/or barbiturate addicts, ranging in age from sixteen to thirty-six and averaging twenty-three. After interviewing the addicts and their immediate families intensively, a Momistic background emerged clearly and the stars of the tragic drama became visible: the ineffective father, the domineering-but-protective mother, and the helplessly dependent son. Because of the disinterest and, in many instances, drinking problem of the father, the mother turned her attention and affection to her son. In order to perpetuate his need for her, she saw to it that he remained addicted. Schwartzman reports of one mother who found pills and heroin kits and did not destroy them; of another who actually left money around for her addict son to steal and purchase drugs.

These observations have been corroborated by other researchers. David Laskowitz, for example, reported that a mother's neurotic needs are a crucial determinant of her son's addiction and that her overindulgent attitudes are highly correlated with his enslavement to drugs.[13] Underneath his assertive posture, the addict hides infantile needs and outlooks—which have been, and still are, nurtured by Mom with cunning and diligence. In essence, the son wants to be pampered by his mother and his mother wants to pamper her son. This is the perfect coalescence of two neurotic need complexes. (However, the situation ceases to be "perfect" when adult responsibilities and mature behavior are expected of the young man.)

Addicts who have been institutionalized or hospitalized are visited by mothers who inquire of their grown sons, "How is my baby?" and continue to lavish verbal endearments on them, such as "my dearie," "my lover boy," "darling," "my sweetiepie," and "my honeylamb." The mothers frequently refer to their sons by the same terms when they talk to social workers about them.

It has been found that addicts' mothers like their sons to be dependent; they want them to live and eat at home and they feel needed when their sons ask them for favors. In fact, many addicts' mothers prefer mothering to mating, and exhibit an uncanny talent for selecting mates who will be almost certain to leave them. For them, fulfillment of womanhood lies not in being a wife but in being a mother. Hence the idea of their children's leaving them is a direct threat to their womanhood and, in a sense, they feel that their lives will end when their children leave home. They need to be needed, and in the process they become demanding and overprotective of their children, as if they were still small infants.

However, these mothers very rarely make *direct* demands on their sons; they get what they want by manipulating their sons' guilt feelings, and strike the most sensitive nerve by declaring that they are "hurting mother." These mothers prolong not merely the psychological dependence of their sons but even their physical dependence. They sit at the sons' bedside, give them massages, lull them with gentle backscratching, help them in grooming, and sit cozily side by side watching TV for hours on end.

When we say that the male addict has a much more peculiar affinity for his mother than most other groups of deviants, we rely not on intuition or colorful sensationalism but on scientific studies and observations. For example, Dr. Sidney Cohen, director of the Division of Narcotics Addiction and Drug Abuse of the National Institute of Mental Health, has concluded that parental (especially maternal) overpermissiveness is a significant cause of drug abuse by American youth and that "most addicts have the word 'Mother,' with or without various designs, tattooed on one or both arms. It is psychologically significant that it is into this tattoo that the narcotic or other drug is injected."[14]

Another inquiry into the mother-son relationship of addicts systematically compared the addicts' characteristics with those of other deviant groups.[15] It was again found that the male addict is afflicted with a strange affinity to his mother. University of Colorado psychologists tested the hypothesis that the male narcotic addict first "gets hooked" on Mom, and identifies so closely with her that he becomes confused about his own identity.

A most interesting technique was applied to determine the degree of mother-son affinity, which consisted of human-figure drawing. The subject was asked to "draw a person"; then he was asked to draw a person of the opposite sex from the first. It was assumed that if the mother-affinity theory is true, the addict should consider the female figure more important and should draw it first—and larger than the subsequent male figure. The findings, based on several hundred institutionalized male addicts, verified these tendencies. Comparison groups were subjected to the same test, and included an array of different groups: noninstitutionalized nonaddicts, institutionalized male alcoholics, psychiatric cases, and pill poppers. None of these groups indicated as strong a tendency as the addicts to associate thought and activity with the mother figure.

The addict cultivates an idealized image of his mother. At the same time, he abuses her (as she abuses him). He does not plan on leaving her, though he has all sorts of complaints about home life—making sure, however, to exempt his mother's character from such criticisms. Studies have shown that over 50 percent of addicts have experienced a home life characterized by the absence of an effective father figure during their childhood.[16] This gives the mother free rein to direct her son's life and enables her to steer him (mostly unconsciously) in the direction of a life-style severely limited and stifled not only by drugs but also by various forms of sexual maladjustment and deviation.

Many addicts, who perform homosexual prostitution to get money for drugs, are attracted by women who will "go on the turf" (be prostitutes) for them and make no demands. This is a potential avenue for Mom substitution: playing the role of the pimp, who is totally supported and cared for by his prostitutes. Some may make an attempt at heterosexual involvement, but few are genuinely attracted by women, and very few establish a meaningful and intimate relationship with the opposite sex. Their sexual fantasies suffer under the heavy burden of guilt and shame that Mom has heaped on them.

One of the most telling obstacles to authorities' work

with addicts is their failure to confront the major insti-
gators of the problem: *the mothers.* Motherhood is protected by cultural tradition and it is taboo to openly
criticize it. Thus effects of motherhood which are destructive and evil can proceed with impunity and spin their
silent webs around innumerable victims, who are usually
equally silent, muted by the pernicious constrictions of
Mom's "love." It is in such fashion that the Silent Disease
prevails—rarely attacked and even more rarely cured.

For example, the Lower East Side Narcotic Center
has identified the source of the problem and made attempts to work with the mothers, but has failed to make
headway in its rehabilitation plans since certain sponsors
(who call the financial tune) insist that "mothers are in-
violate" and may not be maligned. Criticizing American
motherhood is like suggesting deicide.

As a consequence, many agencies are forced to stress
poverty and other sociological conditions when discussing
addiction. In the few instances where mothers were
drawn into the battle against addiction, it was almost impossible to make the mothers believe they had any part
in it and/or bore responsibility for their sons' drug problem. The cultural sanctity of exempting a mother from
blame had been conveniently internalized by these women.
"Mother love" was a shield against any attempt to make
them see their neurotic attitudes, and—by and large—no
advance could be made in controlling the most persuasive
force behind the drug habit.

Everyone and everything else was blamed by the
mothers—but not motherhood. There were "bad" children, drunken and "inept" husbands, "rude" and "not understanding" employers, "evil" peers, neighborhood med-
dlers, *ad infinitum*—but never a bad mother. The effort
to expose the Silent Disease was curbed.

Other drugs besides narcotics are associated with
the Mom complex. Alcohol, for example, has been called

"Mom in a bottle." Unlike narcotic addiction, however, there are very few data indicating how a mother uses alcohol to control her son and assure his retention. The reason for this lack of information is that the use of alcohol is usually legal and hence is not subject to as much scrutiny and evaluation as the prohibited narcotics (especially heroin). It is therefore quite possible that Moms use alcohol, just as they use narcotics, to keep their sons ensnared; but the practice does not become a visible piece in the mosaic of the Silent Disease.

A somewhat clearer picture emerges, however, if we focus on alcoholism as a Mom surrogate; that is, as a substitute for Mom *after* the son is no longer under her physical purview. Heavy drinking renders an amazing bundle of services to the insecure victim: the euphoria of the infant, escape from adult responsibilities, and the illusion of power and self-significance. Thus alcohol serves as a pseudoremedy for insecurity and immaturity. It is a pseudosolution because the sensation of well-being is very temporary and the disabilities ensuing from inebriation outweigh the ephemeral benefits and complicate life even further. Alcohol becomes the tricky lubricant to a swift and ever swifter downward slide in life.

Moms have not provided these losers with the emotional self-sufficiency for coping with life as it is, for making rational decisions, and for controlling one's behavior.

The seriousness of Momistic alcoholism is highlighted by the statement of psychiatrist Edward A. Strecker—who has investigated enough cases of alcoholism to carry authoritative credibility—when he says, "In about 80% of alcoholic cases I have studied, momism in childhood was the basic, underlying cause."[17]

The case histories that describe the plight of the Momistically induced alcoholic sound very much alike. The victims start out with emotional immaturity, grow extremely self-conscious, and finally find that alcohol alleviates their anxiety. The phase when anxiety becomes unbearable and alcohol an imperative usually starts when Mom is no longer available to tell them what to do, and the most traumatic cases begin to unfold at Mom's death. Grown men have been observed to fall completely to pieces, having lost all sense of direction, and frantically look for a Mom replacement. Intoxication helps them escape into the relaxing world of unreality and fantasy, and makes it easier for them to turn their back on the problems and responsibilities of life. Suddenly everything seems easier, and the alcoholic—not unlike the schizophrenic—enters a world of his own making. Viewed through a whisky bottle, the world looks more friendly: Mom is with him again, sheltering and pampering him.

There is still another chemical promise in the world of drugs from which Momistically conditioned individuals expect fulfillment of their unrealistic and infantile desires. We are talking about the *psychedelic drugs*, including mescaline, psilocybin, and of course LSD. What does an immature person expect from this type of drug? (We must, of course, allow for the possibility that mature persons also avail themselves of psychedelic "trips" for other than immature reasons.) It seems that wishful thinking in the Momistic individual has something to do with "instant" and "effortless" achievement, such as sudden insight into the riddles of the universe, immediate answers to one's puzzlements, instant beautification of an otherwise dull life, and fast relief from anxiety and confusion.

Yet, because of the way life works, these things *cannot* be obtained instantaneously. Only an infant seriously demands instant gratification and, in fact, gets it, because we extend special care and quick reaction to his needs and demands. Most of the infant's needs *can* be taken care of in an instant fashion, since they involve simple physical services such as "keeping the lower end dry and the upper end full" and providing physical warmth and affection.

Adult life and adult needs are considerably more complex. If an adult seriously expects instant gratification of complex social and psychological needs, he exhibits an infantile outlook on life and behaves like an infant. It is true, though, that we are all affected and tempted by the lures and promises of instant gratification and solution, so ubiquitous in American culture. Myriad vendors surround and persuasively address us with promises of immediacy—whether we like them or not, whether we are conscious of them or not. A study of the more tangible promises of "instantness" called attention to the significant role the psychopharmaceutical industry plays in this connection (from "instant breakfast" to "instant energy" to "instant sleep" and back again to the "instant breakfast").[18] This all-American concern with chemical manipulation can help us understand the surprisingly tenacious pursuit of psychedelic drugs among American youth. It is little wonder that so many young people believe in "instant" insight through chemicals— we have promised them "instantness" in virtually every other sector of life.

Expectations of instant solutions abound in American society and are at times observed in hilarious forms. For example, a high school sophomore stopped a psychiatrist, who had just given an assembly talk, and wanted to know the brand of "that pill that you can take to hypnotize yourself so you'll wake up knowing everything you need for the test without studying." College students were found to believe that they could take chemicals during exam week that would "clear their minds" so that they would perform superbly without having to study for the exams. One student declared that "psychology has proved that when you're really motivated, you learn instantly." Still another claimed that "if the professor can't make it interesting enough so that you know it without working, that's his fault, not yours." Another student dropped out of college because he placed greater trust in the instantaneous power of "intuition" than in the class-room process.[19]

The adamant fact of life, however, is that in mental achievement, learning, and coping there is no instant "answer" that magically drops from the skies. Hard work and effort—here on the ground, not in the skies— is the answer. Although our psychopharmaceutical revo-lution has made admirable advances, it cannot do every-thing for us, and especially cannot make us mentally mature and responsibly adult.

While sooner or later the experimenting American youth who has a normal preparation for life will abandon psychedelic magic as a means for gaining entry into the world of knowledge and wisdom (he may still enjoy it as an occasional recreation), the Momistically conditioned individual is tempted to take serious stock in the prom-ises of psychedelia. He engages in excessive and pro-longed use, and may mistake random neural impulses for magnificent formulations of eternal wisdom. LSD is a Mom to whom he can turn any time for quick advice, in-formation, and superior knowledge. What he does not realize is that through the psychedelic drug habit he perpetuates his illusion that a solution can be instant and is only as far away as a few milligrams of "acid." The psychological peril to the naive user of psychedelic drugs is the tendency to foster an unrealistic attitude toward life and its conditions and to reinforce the belief that instant solutions are possible in *all* areas of human ex-perience. The instant solution for him is "Mom in the sky"—the psychedelic surrogate for the agent who failed to prepare him for earth.

One of the hardest things for the Momistic individual is to learn that no one except himself, through disciplined effort and learning, can give him insight, knowledge, and skill. Unfortunately, systematic actualization of his potentials is one of the most alien concepts to the Momistically impaired person. The essence of his malaise, to put it bluntly, is "wanting something for nothing."

The psychedelic scene is more closely associated with middle-class college youth than with any other segment of American society. It is there that we have witnessed the proliferation of demands for "instantness" and shortcuts in life. While many of these demands, especially in modern technology, are entirely feasible and recommendable, there are limits and exceptions. The educational institution is one of these exceptions. Nevertheless, college youth have been furious at their frustrated demands for "instant education," often disguised under the cry for "relevance" and "social justice," and this institution has felt the brunt of modern youth's attack on tradition. As Bruno Bettelheim observed, "The expectation is that education can hand over knowledge and skill, and this nearly instantly."[20]

However, let us not carry the theme of Momistic craving for instantness too far: certainly not all college students who demand instant education or relevance do so because a Mom prepared them for that particular outcry. Many of their requests and suggestions are sound and have potential to save the institution from stagnation and rigidity. Our generalization concerning college youth pertains only to their common middle-class background, career-preoccupied fathers, educated mothers, and small families—all factors that facilitate the enactment of Momism. Hence when those who have been sent on their way by a Mom enter college, where they encounter psychedelia galore (if they have not already made that encounter during high school), they may find the lofty promises of such chemicals irresistible and may readily adopt them as their surrogate Mom.

It must be noted that research on the relationship between Momism and psychedelic drug abuse has not yet made a breakthrough and has left us largely with guesses and hypotheses, of which the above paragraphs are good examples. Once in a while we come across a striking case study that seems to support our hypotheses and, at the same time, reminds us that we should commence with more thorough testing of them. One of the most classic case histories that has come to the attention of this writer is recounted below.

The subject is a college student we shall call Francis, who was raised in a luxurious suburban New Jersey home by an overindulgent mother of Italian ethnicity. The college-educated mother had two miscarriages in her late twenties, before her only son was born, and upon his birth was informed that she could not have more children. Thus Francis became her cause in life; she focused all her affection and care on him, as if to make up for the children she could never have. She took the entire responsibility for raising him, though perhaps not voluntarily, since her husband took an extremely aloof stance from the child-raising process.

This man was of German descent, college educated, and somewhat atypical for the husband of a Mom inasmuch as he was a disciplinarian, authoritative, and infinitely stubborn (he completed military duty as an Army officer during World War II). He never showed affection or care, neither to his wife nor his son. In fact, he removed himself completely from the child-raising process, and was so indifferent to it that he and his son would not talk to each other for years at a time. He dedicated all his time to his career as a business executive with a large corporation.

The break in communication was so absolute that he

never inquired about his son nor asked the mother to inform him about the goings-on of his son. And when Francis phoned home and heard his father answer, he would hang up.

Mother was Francis's sole nurturing agent. She gave him money, "covered up" for him, and later, when he moved away to college, would act naive about his immature actions (involving drug problems, overspending, poor grades, etc.).

Francis's overt troubles did not begin until he was in college. (His high school record was quite good; he was an A student during the first three years and did not "make the drug scene" until his senior year.) Away from home and mother, at a college in the western United States, he entered the drug scene with total abandon. All his social relationships revolved around drugs; he would buy friends with it (or sometimes with money and financial favors, such as paying for dinners, entertainments, and trips), interact only with drug-oriented persons, and find ephemeral solace in a variety of drugs. His consumption grew phenomenally: in approximately two and one-half years he took 212 LSD trips (he kept a record), regularly smoked at least eight to ten "joints" a day (in addition to a pack of cigarettes), experienced over 1,000 "hits of speed," tried heroin a few times, and experimented with a number of other drugs.

The staple of his drug consumption was speed. Over a six-month period he systematically increased the dosage, taking twenty tablets a day for about a week at the peak, then systematically decreased the dosage to "normal," that is, "just a few, once in a while." (While a massive dosage of twenty "tabs" could possibly be fatal—something he knew—he survived because of his *systematic* control of the increase and decrease.) He fought sleeplessness with aspirin, Bufferin, and Sominex—or a combination of them. For example, he would take a handful of aspirin or Sominex in one gulp.

He attracted an entourage of unbelievable parasites —all, including himself, decked out in the classic decor of hippiedom and the jingling, bizarre paraphernalia of psychedelia. They sought his "friendship" for only one reason: to get free drugs and other material and financial benefits. He was known for his free and indiscriminate spending, made possible through the generous donations of his mother. His "friends" shared enthusiastically in the benefits of his playboy philosophy, while behind his back they were contemptuous and derisive of him. This led to some tragicomic situations, as when he financed a trip for about ten of his " friends," picked up the tab at the motel, and realized that they had incurred additional expenses (amounting to several hundred dollars) *after* their common trip had presumably ended. As usual, his mother's credit card took care of the bill. Francis had a crying spell, felt cheated and abused by his "friends," and swore to forsake them. But of course he did nothing of the sort; he was as much a parasite on them as they on him. He sucked psychological benefits from them (security and a feeling of having prestige and being liked) just as they sucked material benefits from him, in symbiotic fashion.

His naiveté in human relationships was well known (and laughed about). He could be duped into anything— although, it must be remembered, he was not unintelligent. His emotional need tricked him into being gullible and overindulgent. The same could be said about his mother, who was intelligent enough to see that Francis wasted and endangered his life, yet she did not *want* to see it. Her need to be overindulgent motivated her to give in to her son's every whim.

One year she sent him back to school with $8,000

spending money, a new Le Mans, and credit-card privileges. He was expected to continue college. However, he
had fooled his mother into believing he was still enrolled
in the state university, whereas during the preceding
year he had changed to a city college, signed up for a total of 36 hours, and ended up getting only 15 hours'
credit and a grade point average of 1.8. Again, this was
not a function of lack of intelligence but lack of concentration, work, and class attendance.

Francis was extremely restless and impulsive.
Within five months he put 23,000 miles on his new car,
mostly through joyrides. (Driving his car was a way of
life for him; he would not walk a block if he could drive.)
He would decide on the spur of the moment—or it would
be decided for him by one of his "friends"—to drive from
Arizona to New York, from there to Florida, and back
West.

He could change his mind about major plans within
a matter of hours. One hour he would declare a serious
intention to become a writer, then suddenly his mind
would take a turn and favor the idea of becoming a disk
jockey. Then he changed his mind again and wanted to
become a lawyer, which reminded him of several drug
busts and a conviction for shoplifting a can of clams
(just after Mom had given him $8,000), which prompted
him to decide on a still different career.

His ability to establish an intimate relationship with
the other sex was predictably poor; more precisely, it was
nonexistent. No one had ever known him to "go steady"
or have some sort of permanent relationship with a girl.
Notwithstanding this, Francis frequently talked about
his girl friends, especially one who went to school in
Colorado. He had not seen her in two years, when he
talked to her on the phone and there and then decided to
be engaged to her. He and the girl made plans to spend
the summer together in New York, and commenced to do

so, but again the result was predictable: the girl left him after a few days. On another occasion he answered an ad in a paper of a large West Coast metropolitan area through which "phone dates" could be arranged. With great excitement and anticipation he went out to meet his date, only to return, disappointed, with the knowledge that it was his billfold and not himself that had attracted the young lady.

He would frequently boast about his "exploits" with prostitutes in nearby Mexican border towns and on one occasion a number of his acquaintances accompanied him to one of the fabled places, only to find that Francis was totally unfamiliar with the town. Suspicion grew that he had never been there, nor frequented prostitutes, and that his boasting was merely a means of seeking status and prestige.

There was no record of homosexuality, though some of his "friends" wondered about this since he consistently urged them not to have girl friends. He exhibited symptoms of jealousy—which could be interpreted as wanting their total attention or as a sign of latent homosexual desires. No clear-cut diagnosis could be made.

Today, twenty years old, Francis continues to live the life-style of the stereotypical hippie, outwardly "liberated" and free from the traditional biases against which hippiedom presumably rebels. Yet he hates blacks and Mexicans, expresses himself with a high degree of male chauvinism about women, and loves money and expensive cars—and, of course, Mom. She keeps in touch with him by phoning or writing frequently. The letters can be classified only as love letters, with every other sentence assuring the son of her love and dedication. While one moment she will admonish him not to smoke "that naughty weed," the next moment she will give in to his request for $400 for "a week's food bill"—when every healthy impulse in her brain ought to tell her this is an absurd and fraudulent reason (he needed the money for marijuana). Yet she gives in. Only once has she tried to put her foot down. When Francis again phoned for an exorbitant sum for a "food bill," his mother refused, prompting him to break out in tears and beg for the money. He simply could not understand that his mother had said no to him, if only for a moment; but she relented and offered him the money to stop his crying.

At this time Francis has no direction staked out for his future. One short-lived illusion of grandeur vies with another in his rapid succession of impulsive moods. He is still *at*, not really *in*, college, using its environment and associated drug scene as his hangout. He has no stable human relationships whatsoever—except the neurotic mother-son relationship. (One wonders what would happen to him if for some reason, such as death, his mother should no longer be available to him.) He is a notorious procrastinator when it comes to serious work or important decisionmaking. He lives one day at a time, with drugs as his companion.

He has grown haggard; his body shakes constantly; most of his hair has fallen out of his head; he looks about ten years older than he is; and he gets ill very often (even a common cold could wreak havoc with his body and make him seriously sick).

Mom's "love," father's indifference, and psychedelia's promises have done their work.

Mental Problems: Infantilization, Psychopathy,
Retardation, Identity Foreclosure, Neurotic Anxiety,
Schizophrenia

The psychological scars of a Momistic man are manifold, ranging from relatively mild neurosis (recurrent minor anxiety that allows a person to function nearly adequately) to total withdrawal into schizophrenia (a psychic paralysis sometimes beyond retrieval). In between is a mental carnage ground littered with the confused, maimed, and anguished victims of misapplied parental love and care. These cripples of Momism are permanently wracked by at least four afflictions: insecurity, guilt, anxiety, and disorientation. But diagnosis of these reactions is not simple, for they tend to express themselves in an eerie array of permutations.

The reason for the variety of expression can be found in the many circumstances that surround the Momistic enactment, such as Mom's particular style, technique and degree of dominance (here, the possibly modifying role of the father enters the scene). While one mother may capitalize on the conditional love strategy and imbue her son with agonizing insecurity, another Mom may systematically block his personal decisionmaking to the extent of rendering him totally disoriented without her (or a surrogate's) continual guidance. Still another Mom may exert intellectual intimidation, leaving the child with a deep-seated inferiority complex or the appearance of retardation.

It is therefore difficult to devise exhaustive classifications that include all expressions of the Momistically affected individual. (As we saw in the preceding chapter, a classification of types of Moms may be somewhat easier.) Nevertheless, the following paragraphs should provide insights into some of the basic mental reactions to Mom's devious transactions.

Infantilization. This concept connotes a technique as much as a product. A mother who fails to stop treating her child as an infant infantilizes the victim's thoughts and actions. Such a mother is characterized by an abnormal craving for love and by making the child the target of her incessant outpouring of "love" and care. An extreme dependency neurosis may be the lasting result, with the victim growing older but arrested at the level of childlike apathy and irresponsibility. The trademark of his personality (except for the makeup of the puzzling psychopath) is pervasive passivity, a weak ego or sense of self, a weak superego or grasping of human values, failure to become interested in active aims or ambitions, inability to reason abstractly, indifference toward the feelings of others and, instead, a narcissistic preference for cultivating infantile dreams and egotistic desires.

These are the preponderant Momistic victims among the several hundred thousand men whom Dr. Strecker, a consultant to the Surgeon General of the Army and Navy, found unusable for military service.[21] They retreated into infantile attitudes and behavior (frequently involving serious psychoneuroses), often only a few days after induction, and were unable to face life, cope with social interaction, and think independently.

A similar psychiatric report originated with Dr. David Levy, who studied a sample of mothers who damaged their children to a pathological degree by overmothering. These mothers treated their children as if they were infants and overindulged and overprotected them. An example is a young teenager who threw infantile temper tantrums when his mother hesitated to butter his bread, who still expected her to help him every morning with getting dressed, and relied on her doing his homework with (for?) him. He summed up his expectations in life by saying "his mother would butter his bread for him until he married, after which his wife would do so."[22] The mothers showed no inclination to reeducate their sons to a more mature and independent outlook, and seemed pleased to utilize them for satisfying their obsessive need for love. These mothers exhibited a tendency to attract the sons by their feminine appearance; they freshened up, put new lipstick on when the sons were due home from school—just as a girl would do for her date or a wife for her husband. To these mothers, their sons were everything. Usually they had no husband or stable and creative career, and, as Mom types go, played the martyr with flair and drama. Both the mothers and the sons submitted to lengthy psychotherapy, which, it was hoped, would break the pathological cycle.

After a few years, reexamination showed very little improvement; the therapy had been largely unsuccessful and the overmothered sons were even more deeply enslaved. In the few cases where the sons had escaped psychological harm, the decisive factor seemed to have been the mothers' finding a new target (substitute) for their craving to attend to something or someone. These mothers had redirected their neurotic focus, acquired a stable interest or activity in their lives, and had lessened their unconscious demand to live through their children. In a few cases the children had almost miraculously liberated themselves from Mom, usually through circumstances involving the help of mature adults, and had staked out a realm of relative independence which excluded mother. But—discouragingly—therapy as such seemed completely ineffectual; whatever progress was made was made independently of the therapy program. (Some observations on the perils and ineffectualness of trying to cure Momistic individuals by the traditional therapy approach of emphasizing "helpfulness" will be discussed in the next chapter.)

The work of a college professor provides a good opportunity for observing infantilized young people, who usually can be recognized by their inability to be logical and consequent; that is, to understand essential cause-effect relationships and make decisions accordingly. One of the more comical examples along this line is the student (encountered once or twice every school year by this writer) who dismally fails examinations and then comes to "cry on the prof's shoulder." He always turns out to be a "nice" and apparently intelligent young man. Asked what he thinks might be the reason for his failure, he will assure you—with apparent sincerity—that he reads the books, is interested in the subject matter, and likes the lectures—but seldom goes to hear them. The puzzled instructor is then informed that the reason for the student's high absenteeism rate is the instructor's failure to take roll call at class time. "Why should I attend class if no one calls my name, checks up, and wants to know whether I am attending?" It is always difficult to make the student see the faulty logic for his attitude.

Psychopathy. The observation that the so-called psychopath will hardly manifest himself and become problematic apart from social interaction has also caused him to be labeled a sociopath. It is *in relation to* other human beings (and sometimes animals) that the psychopath's frightful lack of sympathy and compassion has been noticed. His conscience is vastly underdeveloped and deficient in those qualities that enable a person to be a sympathetic and compassionate human being. He is extremely egotistic, indifferent to the welfare of others, incapable of acquiring morals and shared feelings of his cultural environment, and fails to make normal emotions part of his motivation. He seeks gratification of his desires (mostly in impulsive spurts) whether or not it is injurious to others.

However, one must not confuse the psychopath's emotions with his intellect: in contrast to his emotional deficiency, he does not suffer from intellectual deficiency. While he seems unable to acquire the proper social sentiments, he is quite adroit in "watching" his actions so as to avoid suspicion, detection, and punishment. This watchfulness is usually not based on the insight that he is psychopathic, but on his unconscious censoring of his behavior. He has an intuitive knack of knowing "how to get away with things." In other words, he knows right from wrong perfectly well, and applies a rational check on his behavior in congruence with such cognition, but lacks the *emotional* motivation to differentiate between them.

Since a psychopath usually does not know he is a psychopath, he might consequently think—if he should pause to do so—that the manner in which he controls his actions is as normal as everybody else's. It is his reasoning power, not his feelings of guilt or shame, that keeps him from overt deviancy most of the time.

The psychopathic condition can be further clarified by contrasting it with the psychoneurotic condition, although both are on opposite sides of the normal. While the psychoneurotic suffers from profound inner conflict, the psychopath makes others suffer by his lack of inner conflict. The former feels too much guilt and remorse, the latter too little—he can commit the most appalling acts yet view their consequences wih indifference. The psychopath has a shallow capacity for love. His emotional relationships, if he has any, are superficial, fleeting, and designed to satisfy his own wishes. The two essential traits that mark the psychopath as different from other people are guiltlessness and lovelessness.

The psychopath is a great imitator. His mannerisms are often impeccable. His associates may admire him for efficiency, intelligence, and a certain charm. No one may suspect his psychopathic nature—until it is too late and his monstrous irresponsibility has done its work. Then woe to his victim: unveiled psychopathy knows no mercy or compassion! However, the psychopath's actions are rarely violent; they usually constitute coldly enacted egotisms within (or nearly within) the realm of legality. He may suddenly leave a "loved one" (spouse, children); simply stop working; squander a month's pay on a prostitute; knowingly transmit VD; refuse to help someone in distress; declare bankruptcy as a way out of mismanagement; fall into alcoholism or drug addiction; etc. Apart from such behavior, he may act normally and exhibit what has been called the "mask of sanity."[23]

Precisely how does a psychopath develop? No one knows for sure. His origin and development (as well as his cure) are largely *terra incognita*. Nevertheless, hints from a number of experts suggest that his background is often associated with (if not caused by) features that have the familiar face of Momism. For example, the pioneer studies of psychiatrist Robert Knight indicate a significant relationship between the psychopathic alcoholic and his mother's style of bringing him up. Knight goes as far as concluding a *causal* relationship between a weak, pampering mother (in combination with a fitful and inconsistent father) and development of the psychopathic disorder.[24]

Other researchers have found that mothers craftily used their children as pawns and unconsciously encouraged them in theft, arson, and sexual deviations in order to fulfill their unconscious need to engage in such conduct themselves. The child, even after he has become an adult, remains unaware of the parent's adverse influence and of the motives for his antisocial (psychopathic) actions. Frequently such victims, superficially classified as juvenile delinquents, come to the attention of the authorities and psychiatric case workers, whose most formidable obstacle to therapy is often parental unwillingness to give up their vicarious criminal satisfaction.[25]

Psychologist Eugene M. Fodor, who worked with adolescent psychopaths, reported that their backgrounds were characterized by fathers who failed to praise them as children, did not share significantly in the child-raising process, and were negligent in teaching the child activities and skills. Their mothers were overprotective or overindulgent and failed to demand responsible behavior.[26]

A pertinent case study centers on Paul, whose parents represented the classical twosome so often observed in Momistic homes: the overindulgent mother and the remote father who is more interested in his business than in his son. During childhood, Paul experienced the exclusive company of his mother, who was able to pamper him without limit or interference. Paul was virtually fatherless. When he got up in the morning, his father was already at his restaurant, serving breakfast; when he went to bed, his father was still at the restaurant, serving late dinners. Since his father ate his meals at the restaurant, Paul and his mother enjoyed private meals together at home—and this became the routine seven days a week for many years. The father's attitude reflected more than indifference, it manifested rejection of both his son and his wife. In short, Paul grew up as if he had no father at all. The few instances of father-son encounter were characterized by mutual alienation and rejection, and the mother maintained her pampering monopoly until Paul entered elementary school, when a significant change in the mother-son relationship took place. Paul found himself minus Mom for two reasons: he had to spend his days away from her at school, and his mother joined his father at the restaurant, getting quite involved in the business and gradually modifying her intense preoccupation with her son. This was a pivotal time in the life of Paul, and his unchecked hedonism ran head-on into difficulties at school. He could not find the unreserved catering to his egocentrism to which he was accustomed.

The first symptoms of his maladjustment to a Momless world came in the form of truancy—not the usual type of truancy but a shrewd, almost ingeniously staged operation. As far as the school authorities were concerned, Paul was at home, sick with dental problems that had required surgery. It said so quite clearly on the dentist's memo sheet, neatly typed, signed, and addressed to the school. As far as the parents were concerned, he was at school—since he left home in the morning and was not seen during the day. After several weeks of such "illness" he would reappear at school, but not for long; the dental problem would soon recur. The scheme was finally exposed when the school's nurse checked with the dentist's office and discovered that there were no dental complications of any sort, whereupon the school officials and Paul's parents unraveled the mystery. Paul had pocketed stationery when visiting the dentist's office, typed the excuses himself, and skillfully forged the signatures (which he copied from prescriptions the dentist issued to his mother).

He had spent the school days sleeping—not because he was lazy (Paul, in fact, was unusually alert and bright) but because he did not sleep much at night. In the evening, after his parents had gone to bed, he would get up, dress, and wander around in the streets, alleys, and along the canals. He would sneak back into bed just before his mother "woke him up" to have breakfast and get ready for school. He would eat breakfast, leave the house, and—as soon as his parents left for work—go back to his room and sleep *under* the bed.

Reprobation and entreaties were of short effect; he accomplished the same goal by different tricks, sometimes forging his parents' signatures.

Paul's demeanor in no way reflected his deviant and stealthy character; he was always polite—in fact, charming. He was intelligent, of quick comprehension, and in spite of frequent absenteeism was able to keep up with the academic progress of his peers. The typical judgment of his teachers was that he was a genius who, for some reason, could not be motivated to apply his full potential. Other character traits included incredible shows of unrestrained impulsivity and fearlessness, laced with unmitigated cruelty at times. On one occasion he took a huge bull snake to the high school lab and dissected it alive. On another occasion he tied up the neighbor's dog and threw it into a swimming pool to watch it drown. He was found to sexually experiment with children and with a retarded boy. From whatever insight could be obtained, Paul was absolutely amoral concerning sexuality, including bisexuality, sex play with animals, and "experimenting" with children.

Although, face to face, Paul was always polite, well-mannered, and verbally apologetic (quite eloquently, in fact), he never showed genuine remorse over the horrible consequences of his amoral experimentations. He was unpredictable; his impulsivity would show up in sudden switches from good manners to cruel actions. This gave his behavior an air of disorientation—probably a true reflection of his disoriented personality. He was not credible; lies and charming rhetoric were routine means to achieve his ends, and his words could rarely be trusted to reflect what he actually felt and wanted. He would often back up his eloquence with seemingly considerate, responsive, and obliging action. Casual acquaintances found it very difficult to believe that he was not highly endowed with gratitude and eagerness to please others.

Outward social graces came easy to Paul, and he learned quickly how to ingratiate himself with others, especially his peers, by manipulating the trivia of existence. In this way he would gain their admiration and alliance. In surface aspects he appeared to act with undesigning spontaneity and to be prompted by excellent motives. For example, he would buy a bag of candies on impulse and bring them to a sick neighbor lady or give a boy enough money so that he could buy a model plane he had wanted for a long time.

Notwithstanding his surface charm, Paul got into more and more serious trouble during his high school days: sexual deviations, stealing, forging, at least one "play act" torture of another boy, lethal experimentations with pets, and drug abuse. What finally brought the decisive action of the authorities was the discovery that Paul was not only "mainlining" heroin but was trying to turn other youngsters on to it. He was, in effect, peddling heroin. When he was brought before the juvenile court, his reaction was one of childlike innocence and astonishment. His attitude was "What's wrong with drugs? They are fun."

In concluding this discussion of the Momistic psychopath we should again point out that the etiology of the psychopath is obscure. There are many instances in which children turn into psychopaths without a Momistic experience, and, of course, there are numerous instances where children with Momistic backgrounds turn into everything *but* psychopaths. All we can say at this time is that background studies of psychopaths reveal that many of them had mothers with Momistic features.

Retardation. Momistically imposed retardation consists of oppression of the child's behavior to the infantile level, plus oppression of his mental processes to the pseudo-stupid level. Some social caseworkers call this form of retardation pseudostupidity to distinguish it from true retardation. While the latter involves persons who suffer from relatively irreversible biological defects, usually brought on by genetic factors or brain damage, the former involves persons who are products of conditioning that leaves them with a slow and limited learning capacity. These symptoms are often mistaken as *innate* limitations of a child's intellectual potential and thus beyond remedy. These unfortunate conclusions cast the child into a mold that, by strength of social consensus, forces him into playing the role of the retardate. The victims of this consensus usually do not know that they are role playing. They (as well as others around them) do not realize that under different environmental conditions they could change from an oppressed and retarded-appearing individual to one who is perfectly normal and capable of functioning intelligently.

While it is not always the mother who is the villain in pseudoretardation, increasing numbers of reports have disclosed that mothers are in a particularly powerful position to stunt the emotional and intellectual growth of the child. She can accomplish her unwitting atrocity by marshaling two insidious forces and enmeshing her helpless child in them: isolation and overprotection.

Isolation from peers and a variety of human beings can seriously delay maturity in children. Developmental psychologist Harold M. Skeels found he could dramatically improve the social and intellectual development of institutionalized infants by pairing them with adolescents who lived in the same facility.[27] The older children provided stimulation for the babies' development in every aspect: physical, emotional, intellectual, and social.

While the mother naturally provides a type of early association (a key factor to normal development), the situation becomes problematic if she is the *exclusive* associate, since no *one* human being can give what a variety of individuals offers. The situation becomes pathological if this mother is a Mom who exposes the child to her neurosis. Growth-fostering stimuli are so severely diminished and one-sided that the child's mind cannot unfold and develop. The result may be virtual nondevelopment.

Overprotection, as we have seen in earlier discussions, is the tendency to do everything for the child, not allowing him to experiment, and ultimately making him utterly dependent on Mom and later on others. The result is a stunting of the child's ability to try his potential genius on the problems around him.

In combination, the two results (which are really two sides of the same coin) may symptomize themselves in the form of severe pseudoretardation. An illustration of this type of affliction in real life is Carl, who at age fifteen was for all practical purposes considered a retarded youngster. Soon after he was born, his father had a fatal accident, leaving him, the only child, to the exclusive care of his mother. The ensuing style of child raising was typically Momistic, with the prevailing features of isolation and overprotection. Carl was given little opportunity to play with other children; and his mother, as if to compensate for the loss of her husband, compulsively lavished stifling affection on the boy. In essence, she tried to keep him an infant, afraid that when he grew up she might lose him too—the classical live-through-the-child theme.

At the time of Carl's entry into elementary school, a significant degree of retardation was determined. His passivity and slowness in learning and comprehending made him a candidate for "special education." Within this environment of diminished educational demands, Carl adjusted very well and functioned commensurate with his classification as an average retardate. For many years there were no changes or upheaval that necessitated reclassification. Carl remained "mother's baby" and continued to be passive and an extremely slow learner.

He was fifteen when his mother died of cancer and his custody was transferred to an aunt and uncle. His aunt always had reservations about the way the mother had raised Carl, talking to the teenager as if he had been an infant and preventing him from doing anything on his own. Kindly but firmly, the aunt started a reeducation program that reached into every aspect of Carl's life. For the first time in his life, age-appropriate demands were made of him. Although the initial phase was associated with traumas, Carl not only recovered but developed at a surprisingly rapid rate, was ultimately able to transfer to a regular high school and graduate with adequate grades and capabilities.

Identity foreclosure. Mom has a knack for thoroughly interfering with her son's development of a stable identity. This is the specialty of the domineering Mom, who is compulsive and harbors hostility and contempt for men. The process whereby she forecloses her son's identity comprises three main steps:

1. *Rejection of masculinity.* She exposes her son to a constant campaign in which she degrades masculinity. Whatever her personal reason for this negative attitude, in effect she makes her son the scapegoat. In many instances this depreciative attitude is shared by her husband, who has little esteem for his own masculinity, because he feels this is the only way he can retain his wife's love, which he fears he is in danger of losing. (This concern is a telling indication of the type of father we are dealing with: the passive, self-depreciative, weak man.) The mother rejects the son's sexuality to the point of often letting him know that she would be happier if he were a girl and that she finds him deficient and inferior to females.

2. *Possession of the child.* The mother is highly possessive of the child, wants to use him for her own goals, and denies him independent action and thought. Although he is not the girl she wanted, she nevertheless (or because of it) becomes very involved in him and insists on ruling his life for him, on "making something out of him."

3. *Absorption of personality.* The combination of these two processes results in a thorough undermining of the boy's self-esteem, self-reliance and, most importantly, his identity. He becomes the type of person who is very much dependent on other people to tell him what he

is. His mother, who has not respected ego boundaries, has failed to step back and let him grow into a separate entity.

This, then, adds up to the dismal situation of identity foreclosure. The ensuing problems for the boy can be of many kinds, the most conspicuous one being his poor masculine self-view. He may, indeed, be deeply afraid to assume a masculine role because he thereby fears losing his mother's love. In the long run, he may deem it safer to assume a weak masculine image, devoid of active, assertive, and aggressive characteristics. His susceptibility to becoming involved in homosexual relationships is great since he has no personal identity or point of departure from which he could successfully enter into meaningful relationships with the opposite sex. His identity is hung up with his mother. He cannot separate her world view from his, which means that there has not been a personal crystallization of convictions and attitudes.

Another glaring consequence, which is mingled with the one mentioned above, is the boy's deep-seated inferiority complex. His self-image is incredibly poor. This negative assessment of his worth and capability carries over into his daily activities and often functions as that most insidious of all self-defeating mechanisms: the self-fulfilling prophecy. In essence, it means that the self-concept of a person completes its confirmation in actual activities and aspirations—which means that if a person believes he is not acceptable or lovable to others, he will behave in ways to actually make himself unacceptable and unlovable. Or if a person feels he cannot accomplish a certain task, such as academic work, because he sees himself as too stupid, he may erect his own barricades against succeeding. The failure of his halfhearted attempt will then serve as the confirmation of his inability and deepen the conviction of his inferiority.

Hence, identity foreclosure can also be called foreclosure of self-trust. This may explain why the affected boy usually shows severe learning problems, sometimes to the point of appearing retarded. His chronic hesitation to be intellectually aggressive and competitive stems from the dual complex of, first, believing he is too unintelligent for the task at hand and, second, fearing to offend his mother by displaying masculine traits that she has belittled. Both his teacher and his schoolwork become objects of the boy's negativism.

The consequences of identity foreclosure can take many forms: homosexuality, delinquency, retardation, neurotic anxiety, and stagnation—and a life wasting away without creativity or much happiness.

Tony is a case in point. An eleven-year-old boy with normal intelligence, he was referred to a guidance clinic because he was having learning difficulties that seemed to become more pronounced as demands on him increased.[28] Inquiry by a social caseworker revealed the typical background features of hostile Momism. To his mother, boys were "monkeys and horrible creatures who are graded 'C' in conduct." She made few demands on her son, for she wished to think of him as a little girl. In fact, she had him sleep in the same room with his two sisters, aged seventeen and eighteen, who fondled him and treated him like a doll. The mother discouraged the girls from having boy friends and did her best to degrade males in the eyes of her children. She let them know she considered it a tragedy that little boys had to lose their curls and that she had to make a boy out of Tony.

His mother's disdain for everything masculine affected Tony; he internalized this attitude, and it showed its detrimental effects in his school career. It seemed, however, that more serious consequences were prevented by the intervention of the caseworker, who persuaded Tony, as well as his parents, to submit to counseling.

Neurotic Anxiety. Whereas a certain amount of anxiety is an unavoidable and nearly normal by-product of living in a complex society, neurotic anxiety exceeds this experience in frequency and intensity. The former can be called a "situation neurosis," where a normal person develops anxieties because he is confronted by an external situation full of conflicts and threats. For example, "battle neurosis" is such a situation, where the individual is compelled to face the horrors and perils of war without being prepared for—and often without being convinced of—the rightfulness of his compulsory action. The latter can be called a "character neurosis," where an individual is afflicted with more or less permanent personality defects. This true neurosis creates a severe amount of mental pain (that can also become physical in its psychosomatic extension) and has a crippling effect on the individual's functioning as an autonomous agent. In plain words, he has problems managing his life.

In order to elicit a neurotic anxiety reaction, two factors must coincide: a particular *self-attitude* and a *situation* that demands a certain competence. If, for example, a profound conviction of inadequacy prevails, a situation that calls for relatively modest and normal competence would generate a neurotic anxiety reaction. This means that a neurotic condition emerges when the self-attitude is unrealistic and when the competence for solving the problem potentially exists but cannot be enacted because of the self-imposed mental block. Neurotic anxiety may also result when the individual views his potential relatively realistically but has the habit of fearing the complexity of the task and, consequently, thinks he cannot complete it. Profound feelings of defeatism result from such attitudes.

We are dealing with a *neurotic person* when these depressing assessments continue on a *chronic* basis and become a *generalized* anxiety reaction, manifesting itself by a person's habitually declaring defeat before even trying. This individual tends to avoid direct confrontation in anxiety-provoking situations and engages in various defense mechanisms (e.g., scapegoating, repression, rationalization, reaction formation, etc.) which usually narrow the scope of possible adjustment and creative solution of a problem.

Mothers are in a uniquely powerful position to plant the seed for neurotic anxiety—and an extensive study, including eight New Jersey communities, lends credence to this statement. Columbia University's Bureau of Applied Research, funded by the U.S. Office of Education to investigate cheating in high schools, found that the typical cheater, usually a bright youngster, was characterized by exposure to maternal—not paternal—pressure. Only 35 percent of those students who were exposed to little or no maternal pressure cheated, whereas 54 percent of those who were exposed to definite maternal pressure cheated.[29]

Basic anxiety arises in children whose parents (usually because of their own neuroses) fail to endow them with self-confidence and a feeling of self-worth. The cornerstone of self-worth is the experience of *being wanted and appreciated for one's own sake.* To achieve this, parental love and care must be *unconditional.* However, what stands out as the central strategy in Momistic cases is *conditional* love. When unconditional love is denied, the environment comes to be dreaded as unreliable, unappreciative, and merciless. The afflicted person develops diffuse anxiety about life in general—a condition that reduces his free use of energy, initiative, and self-reliance.

Because of this character weakness, the individual longs to be protected and taken care of and to unload personal responsibility upon the shoulders of others. The conditional acceptance he experienced as a child makes him constantly afraid of being a failure and rejected.

And it is at this juncture that the individual tries to guard himself against anxiety by devising neurotic habits. Sometimes these habits succeed in controlling anxiety, the cost being some sort of neurosis or even monomania (obsession with one idea to the point of losing perspective on reality). Sometimes they do not succeed, and the individual goes on exhibiting free-floating anxiety. But somehow he needs to escape from anxiety, and in his frantic search he may solidify certain personality patterns to function as bulwarks against it. Psychiatrist Karen Horney describes the major escape routes in the following categories.[30]

1. *Neurotic need for affection.* While normal affection is a natural part of the give and take of love, the neurotic craving for affection is based on insecurity and a chronic need for reassurance. The excessive need for affection is a disguise for the excessive need for approval —a craving that can never be satisfied. This individual has a terrible fear of being disliked or disapproved, and will do everything possible to avoid such exposure. His guideline in life is "If they love me, they won't hurt me."

Sex serves as a means of securing affection—and thus approval. In his panicky determination to be approved, the neurotic individual tends to engage in sexual relationships compulsively and indiscriminately. He is in search of unconditional love and expects to be loved and accepted, irrespective of his failure to love in return and irrespective of his irresponsible behavior. This, of course, often nets him rejection—renewing his frenzy to seek approval elsewhere.

Even if he should find a person who extends sincere acceptance and love, the neurotic *could not* accept it because of his deep conviction of being unworthy of it. Most likely he would select from the spectrum of actions and remarks of the caring person those aspects which would confirm his belief in his personal unworthiness.

2. *Neurotic striving for power.* This individual tries to compensate for his basic anxiety and inferiority complex by seeking power and control over others. His motto is "If I am mightier than the other guy, he can't harm me." He has a need to be right at all times and have his own way. Anyone who is superior in skill or knowledge poses a threat. This, obviously, makes life a frightful arena, since he cannot be expert in all things. Often the wish to disparage others and see them harmed plays an important role in his motives and actions. As a consequence, his deep-seated need to be approved and loved, on one side, and his animosity toward others (particularly those who appear more competent to him) clash irreconcilably and create tearing conflicts in him.

3. *Neurotic withdrawal.* The motto of the person seeking escape from anxiety by withdrawal is "If I don't let people come close, they can't hurt me." This anxiety-haunted individual finds it difficult to maintain intimate human relationships. The emotional demands of such relationships frighten him; he feels vulnerable, open to abuse, and fears he may suffer rejection once he opens up to a relationship. Yet his deep desire to be independent of people runs into the opposing need to be approved and loved by them. Again, his life is raked by tormenting conflicts.

4. *Neurotic submissiveness.* The neurotic individual may try to beat anxiety by playing helpless, being subservient to the powerful, and expecting them to be protective in return. The "powerful" may be the leader of a movement, a religion, a tradition, or the opinion of the influential. The service he expects from the outside agent is total psychological sustenance, relieving him of the necessity of figuring out his own life and destiny. His motto is "If I submit, I will be liked and protected."

This individual is far from being as harmless and passive as he seems. In the hands of a powerful agent, the neurotic may be willing to do everything he is told, and so can become the tool and executor of incredible atrocity and irresponsibility (reminiscent of the True Believer!). This is typical of the individual who has the makings of the authoritarian personality: he obeys his "superior" as unquestioningly as he relentlessly commands (and if necessary destroys) his "inferior." His neurotic anxiety demands a simplistic solution to the complexity of life, and he invents a world view in which he finds rigid order and security. The rigidity of his world view often has dire consequences for many innocent and helpless people.

An important feature of these neurotic attempts at escaping from basic anxiety is their conflict-proneness. Although an individual may hasten along a particular escape route, he inevitably will become confused and uncertain as to its wisdom and switch to another. Before long, he again is plagued by conflict and uncertainty and decides to switch again and head down still another avenue that seems to promise assuagement. The neurotic usually chooses routes regardless of whether they are suitable to the circumstances.

It is precisely this confusion that confounds the basic anxiety and leads to the *basic conflict*, which is the beginning of new trouble. It grows into a neurosis in its own right, often overshadowing the basic anxiety that generated the conflict in the first place. The new conflict demands new remedies, and the neurotic is quickly lost in a tangle of self-created problems.

This, then, is the maze in which the Momistic neurotic is ensnared. It is a frightful existence, which should invite our compassion and understanding. It places heavy responsibility on being a parent.

One could spin out the theoretical categories and consider the possibility of matching type of Mom with type of neurotic pattern—that is, assume that particular anxiety types derive from particular Mom types. However, this would lead us too far out on the thin ice of theorizing. Suffice it to say that there are connections between the domineering and overprotective Mom and the neurotically submissive victim, between the martyr Mom and the withdrawing, guilt-ridden victim, and between the overindulgent Mom and the power-craving victim. Yet, depending on special circumstances, the outcome may be reversed, as when an overprotected child grows up and seeks compensation in the domination of others. Likewise, the product of a martyr Mom may be so guilt ridden that, instead of withdrawing, he seeks to attack and destroy what to him appears threatening and guilt provoking. The connections are too many and unpredictable to justify categorization at this time. However, this certainly presents a challenge to research and systematic evaluation of casework with Momistic individuals.

To present case studies to illustrate the foregoing types of anxiety-troubled neurotics would exceed the proper limits of this chaper. Moreover, it really is not necessary since all case studies throughout the book can be understood as describing neurotic conditions. In most cases the condition manifests itself as a specific problem, such as drugs, a fanatic belief, sexual aberration, or (as we shall see) suicide. It is through such forms that the neurosis becomes recognizable—there is no "formless" neurosis. Hence we have presented and classified many of them on the basis of their expression and problematic behavior.

For example, a severe case of neurotic withdrawal was cited under "The Overprotective Mom" in the preceding chapter, where a grown son let himself be pushed around in a wheel chair. Another extraordinary case was that of the Momistically induced authoritarian personality (classifiable as either neurotic striving for power or neurotic submissiveness, depending upon the side from which one looks at it)—the "True Believer"—under whom incredible atrocities were committed on the basis of "doing one's duty." The value, then, of presenting a typology of neuroses consists in allowing cross-classification of the various neurotic cases and shedding additional light on the background features responsible for the rise of a particular neurosis.

Schizophrenia. An extreme effect of Momism on the victim is his retreat into the private world of schizophrenia. This reality-evading technique is a rejection of our world, as we know it, and creation of an isolated reality that is not shared, or sharable, with anyone else. The most withdrawn type of schizophrenia, occasionally observed among victims of Momism, is absolute and all-inclusive rejection of reality where the individual maintains a rigid, curled-up body position, is insensitive to pain, refuses to eat, and is indifferent to toilet habits. This catatonic form, fortunately, is relatively rare compared to other forms, where the schizophrenic dwells in a different mental world but, at least, is still physically functioning.

Through the mentally lethal combination of isolation, unrealism, and anxiety, a Momistic individual may be so utterly unsuited for real life that, if forced to face it, the shock and confusion may prompt him to turn away and escape into schizophrenia—which psychiatrist Strecker saw functioning as "an unfailingly kind and lavish Mom."[31] Schizophrenia, acting as a Mom surrogate, was apparent to Dr. Strecker when he surveyed young draftees. He diagnosed this form of escape as immaturity "so great and complex that the only path open for the child is the retreat into the fantasy—of schizophrenia—to remain there forever enwombed."[32]

Psychiatric literature has increasingly dealt with the "schizogenic" mother (who causes schizophrenia in her offspring), who uses the child as a means to pursue her own sick motives and expresses hostility under the subterfuge of mother love.[33] It is interesting to note that the "symbiotic relationships" between disturbed mothers and their children differ, depending on whether they are boys or girls. Usually the mothers were overprotective of their sons and surprisingly permissive with their daughters. This practice failed to prepare the sons for meeting the challenges of life, and encouraged their daughters to meet these challenges prematurely.[34] Hence, there is justification to believe that the disturbed mothers harbor greater schizogenic potential for boys than for girls.

One of the determinants of the schizophrenic retreat has to do with the breakdown of the differentiating boundaries between mother and son—that is, between *her* self and *his* self. In a normal situation the mother takes the initiative to wean the child from his dependence on her and begins to foster a sense of autonomy. Between the ages of two and four, the child should be encouraged to leave the tight mother-child relationship and become a member of the family beyond the mother-child unit. This is precisely what does *not* happen in the schizogenic family. The interdependent relationship of mother-son grows into a compact symbiosis that prevents the son from growing up. In essence, the mother fails to promote in the child the necessary self-assurance to move out, and creates in him the feeling that it is his function to complete the parent's life.

In a figurative sense, this leads to situations where the child is given a laxative if the mother feels constipated. She cannot grasp the idea that the child is to see the world differently than she does. While the sickness of the mother is connected with her extreme and destructive egocentrism in trying to "own" the child, the sickness of the child is far worse since he lacks egocentrism and has a completely mother-centered orientation. This means that he has no personal center of gravity, no roots in personal projects, and depends on the parental goals and projects. The moment the latter are shaken or removed, he suffers a complete loss of orientation. As a result, he can be thrown into the paralyzing *confusion* of the schizophrenic.

It seems that the human mind cannot bear basic confusion for long; direction and clarity are a *must*. If the real world does not yield clarification and order in time, retreat into a "clarified" world *of his own* can be the result. This world has its own language, characters, events, laws and principles, places, and time. If a psychiatrist wants to fully understand a schizophrenic, he has to submerge himself in a completely new world. Traditional psychiatric practice, however, attempts to do the opposite: to pull the schizophrenic out of *his* world and reintegrate him into *our* world— a practice that has come under attack by a new psychiatric approach, "radical therapy."

The Ultimate: Suicide

The most dramatic outcome of Momistic conditioning is suicide. The frequency with which this finality strikes victims of Momism is not known by any precise statistics; there are no death certificates marked "Momistic suicide." Its incidence can only be surmised.

Reliable indication that Mom is able to prepare the stage for this tragedy has come to us through an international study. The National Institute of Mental Health funded Dr. Herbert Hendin, a psychiatric instructor at Columbia University, to complete a four-year study of suicide in the Scandinavian countries.[35] One of the main goals of the research was to determine the reasons for the puzzling difference in suicide rates between Denmark and Sweden, on one hand, and Norway on the other.

While Denmark has one of the world's highest suicide rates (over 20 per 100,000 population), Norway has one of the lowest (about 7 per 100,000 population). Sweden is second after Denmark (with about 17 suicides per 100,000 population). Since in the more obvious areas of public life—religion, tradition, language, economy, politics, racial stock, etc.—the three countries very closely resemble each other, the reason for the difference in the suicide rates had been an enigma to behavioral scientists.

Dr. Hendin, after analyzing decisive elements responsible for differences in Norwegian, Swedish, and Danish character, cited the following elements: child-rearing practices, with particular attention to the ways dependency is encouraged or discouraged; methods of family discussion; relations between the sexes; attitudes toward work and success; and styles of channeling aggression. The data from the different countries were then compared and a striking discovery was made.

The Danish child-rearing style resembled Momistic conditioning to a far greater extent than that of Norway. The Danes predisposed children to self-aggression by creating guilt-conscious, aggression-inhibited, and dependent personalities. Manipulating a sense of guilt in the child was the principal disciplinary tool in Danish homes. When a child disobeyed, the mother would admonish him that he was "hurting mama," was making her unhappy. The natural aggressiveness of the child, the drive to explore and master his environment, was severely curbed thereby.

Similarly, Swedish child-rearing practices also burdened the child with guilt and shame. Swedish parents discouraged their children from showing emotions and taught them to be "reasonable," regardless of how disturbing a situation might be to the child. This traditional dictum applied particularly to boys, who were emphatically discouraged from crying.

Also, the elements of competition and success were highly stressed in Denmark and Sweden. The child was expected to excel, and he endangered his "lovability" unless he scored high in achievement. Here again, we recognize the element of *conditional love*.

In Norway, on the other hand, the study discovered greater permissiveness for emotional expression. The children were allowed to exhibit aggression, in the positive as well as the negative sense, including a show of hostility at times. Also, the child was far less supervised and much less emotionally tied to the mother than his Danish and Swedish cousins. Young Norwegians were free to direct their aggression outward. Competition was not the high command it was to children in their neighbor countries, and they did not have to be first and best to be acceptable to their parents.

The imprint of these different child-rearing climates became obvious by comparing the children of these countries. On the whole, Danish and Swedish children appeared noticeably "better behaved" than most of their Norwegian peers. They exhibited more passive dependent, and obedient manners. These are typical traits of Momistically conditioned children.

In sum, then, the Scandinavian enigma—the puzzling question as to the reason for the age-old difference of suicide rates among their countries—seems to be solved. The main reason appears to rest with the *different child-rearing styles* among the three countries. Since there is no competing scientific theory or plausible argument, the credibility of this explanation is enhanced.

It is tempting to contemplate the findings if one could divide the United States population into two categories, the Momistic and the "normal" households, and compute the suicide rate for each. (The suicide rate for the total United States population is approximately 11 per 100,000 population.) Would the statisticians corroborate the Scandinavian finding? We probably won't know for certain since such a large-scale study is not in the offing.

At this time, then, we are limited in our interpretation of suicide in the United States and must rely on isolated studies. (A pertinent case history was recounted in "The Overindulgent Mom" in the preceding chapter.) We know, however, that male suicides outnumber female. (Women, however, make up approximately 70 percent of the unsuccessful attempts, many of which were never seriously intended.) White middle-class males appear to be particularly vulnerable, with nonwhite males apparently finding other outlets for their violent impulses. It has been found that males who are hospitalized for attempted suicide tend to have strong attachments to their mother, weak relationships with their father, and poor masculine identification.[36]

The "Silent Majority"

The various examples and case histories of Momism in the preceding sections represent extreme consequences and might be grossly misleading without the following commentary. These accounts illustrated the exceptions—the minority—among the possible outcomes of Momistic situations. Most situations result in far less conspicuous and sensational consequences; in fact, they are relatively "silent" and unnoticed. These overlooked cases probably number several hundred to each of the extreme cases recited. They are overlooked because they symptomize themselves as problems relatively noninjurious to others and, therefore, go unreported and unchallenged. But they may be injurious to the victim. The silent tribute he pays to Mom is the loss of a creative and free life. He is broken in spirit from the beginning to the end.

The typical Momistic boy is usually too inanimate to be found among the juvenile delinquents, who engage in violent offenses. In fact, violent crime is rarely in the repository of Momistic consequences, unless it is associated with the True Believer syndrome, where it usually sails under the flag of dutiful behavior and collective legitimation—at least as long as the regime retains enough power to enforce the definitions. Possibly, drug addiction is also a Momistic symptom that may be associated with criminal activities—not because of the illegality of drug use *per se* but because of the side activities (such as stealing, prostituting, pimping, etc.) which serve the purpose of continued drug use.

Another reason why the typical Momistic boy is not a juvenile delinquent is the rejection he encounters on the part of his peers. Most juvenile delinquency is a collective phenomenon that springs from an *esprit de corps*, from the momentum of a sense of solidarity, and from the bravado of the masculine subculture. The Momistic boy is ostracized from these dynamics and is defined as a sissy. His mother isolates him, supervising him too closely to allow him opportunity to adventure into delinquent—or even nondelinquent—explorations.

In other words, the true victim of Momism is not the robbed, beaten, raped, slain, or mugged citizen but the broken-spirited, squelched child himself. And these factors are not as easily visible or assessable as overt acts of violence. Whatever the victim of Momism does, he usually hurts himself more than others—except in those situations where others put emotional stock in his presumed maturity. But maturity or immaturity is not defined by law, and immature persons are not necessarily criminals just because of their emotional retardation. One can inflict severe emotional hurt on other people and in no way be classified as having engaged in an illegal act. What it boils down to is that a certain range of emotional maturity is not covered by legal prescriptions or proscriptions. It is in this area, the twilight zone between legality and morality, that the Momistically handicapped individual moves and is prone to spread the hurt he carries in his psyche to others around him.

Actually, we still have insufficient knowledge about the Momistic character. We have a good idea concerning some of his core habits, such as extreme dependency parasitism, unreliability, and anxiety, but deeper and more extensive exploration is needed to identify him more fully. For example, while we have consistently talked about the harmful effects of Momism, it is only fair to mention (as was done very briefly in Chapter 4, "The Vulnerability of the Boy") that Momism can have some *positive* consequences. Sometimes children who grow up with maternal overconcern exhibit superior verbal skill and do exceptionally well in pursuing academic interests. Also, some types of Momistic children succeed in putting their anxiety to constructive use, develop a strong achievement orientation (to please others or to keep proving their self-worth), and in this way make contributions to their community.

Again, whether they are good or bad, most Momistic consequences appear to be seminormal and to remain silent. The point where the silence is broken is invisible (if we may mix metaphors) ; it is in the individual's mind where tormented self-rejection speaks loudly and clearly. Unless a conscious effort is made to detect the passivity and overdependence in situations where a young person fails to make his own decision or at least express his own opinion, the fact that he suffers from Momism may be unsuspected.

Precisely how does one catch a glimpse of "silent" consequences? Most likely through coincidence, since no caseworker would witness or bother to write up a "nonproblematic" observation. Below is an example of the "respectful," well-behaved, and opinionless behavior of a nineteen-year-old draftee who exhibited this type of personality absorption by Mom.[37]

After Kenneth was drafted, his mother, who believed in racial segregation with religious fervor, swore to petition the President of the United States to have her son guaranteed all-white military duty. Mrs. G. stormed out of a draft board hearing and said her son Kenneth, nineteen, would appear to take his physical, as ordered, but under protest if blacks were present. She assured everyone that if Kenneth was forced to integrate against his religious conviction, that meant the First Amendment was void. The mother then sent a wire to the President to inquire whether he was aware that this amendment was being violated. She declared that America, unlike Nazi Germany or Communist countries, is in line with God's will and hence Kenneth must obey *her* under God and the law. She threatened Lt. Col. P., the draft board adviser, with quotations from the Bible which indicated atrocious punishment for him if he should disobey God's word. She referred to Matthew 18:6:

> But whoever shall offend one of these little ones which believe in Me, it were better for him that a millstone were hanged around his neck, and that he were drowned in the depth of the sea.

Throughout her protestations, Kenneth stayed close to her side, declining comment. He did, however, say he preferred that his mother do the talking. It is interesting that the mother selected a scriptural passage that referred to "little ones"—as if it were applicable to her nineteen-year-old son.

It does not appear that Kenneth will do anyone any harm—ever. But that is not the point. He is so child-like, passive, and overdependent that he must be considered a casualty in the arena of personal freedom and imagination. And that is what the Silent Disease is all about.

Another "normal" case study comes to mind, which was described in detail under "The Domineering Mom" in the preceding chapter. Peter had a "normal" career and "normal" divorces—like hundreds of thousands of other Americans. There was nothing extraordinary about his experiences, since the personal tragedies of unrewarding human relationships are commonplace. What is noteworthy, however, is that in his case these relatively common experiences were evidently brought on by a Mom. This should make us pause and consider how many "normal" divorces are actually the product of a Mom who pulled the strings so decisively in her son's life that he goes through the same marionette motions for the rest of his life, never finding a sense of self-determination.

We are finally coming to the end of a long chapter, and a few comments of summary, modification, and caution are in order.

If hard pressed for a one-sentence summary of the typical consequences of Momism, we could say that it is a person whose center of gravity—whose core or orientation and organization—is not anchored in himself. From this lack of true selfhood arise a number of telling characteristics: (1) inability to make decisions, (2) chronic feelings of inferiority, (3) frequent and easily aroused anxieties, (4) irresponsible actions, and (5) a general parasitism, manifesting unchecked narcissism and immature egocentrism.

The product of Momism is rarely seen by one clear-cut symptom but usually as a conglomeration of immature neurotic symptoms. Mom's spell adds up to a complex curse, possibly including—at one and the same time —servile dependence, sadistic inclinations, sexual inhibitions, antisocial or oversocialized behavior, drug addiction, and other forms of addiction to Mom substitutes.

Some of the symptoms appear paradoxical or contradictory, but it must be remembered that persons who rely on a center of orientation that is not truly their own behave unpredictably, illogically, and inconsistently with an overall premise. The permutations of Momistic symptoms are literally endless.

How long do such symptoms persist in the life of a victim? Such impairment differs from person to person. In some cases the crippling effect may last a lifetime; in other cases it may disappear soon after a mother and son are separated. In a situation of relatively simple overdependency, where the influence has not been too severe or constant, the apron strings can be cut as soon as the son leaves home. The Army often has a way of speeding this up since the duration of separation and the distance involved force the son to stand on his own legs and start making his own decisons. However, there are many exceptions, and mother dependency continues although she is no longer physically present. Servicemen have been known to go AWOL, break down, and exhibit extreme emotional disturbance upon receiving letters from their mother, criticizing them for leaving home or begging them to return home. Even with her death, dependency on a Mom may not cease. Men in their fifties have become disoriented upon the death of their mother and have never regained normal contact with reality.

Now a point of caution—and possibly consolation. Many a reader's progress through these chapters may have been accompanied by increasing levels of discomfort and trepidation. He may have become aware of various personal features whose origin he is able to trace to his mother's influence. It would not be surprising to identify numerous "made-by-mother" traits if one bothers to search for them. But these consequences must be distinguished from the "made-by-Mom" attributes.

It is only natural that we reflect the impressions

our mothers have left in our thinking and behaving. In normal cases there is absolutely nothing wrong with such influences; and the discovery of the relationship between certain aspects of our being and our mother's way of raising us is to be expected. The fact that a mother is our earliest and most intimate socializer leaves indelible female-created orientations and impressions in the personality of the male. Thus no pathological connotation should *ipso facto* be attached to a mother's influence becoming manifest in our lives. "Hypochondria" about mother influence is unnecessary and would ultimately be in vain, since such female-induced features are deep-seated and pervasive. Pathological consequences should be suspected only when *Momistic conditioning* has corrupted normal mothering.

Finally, it must be realized that diagnosis of a personality disturbance as an outcome of Momistic child rearing is often extremely difficult and should be attempted only after careful, professionally competent scrutiny of the life history and family circumstances of a given person.

This should remind us that the disturbance with which Momistically crippled individuals end up can be arrived at by other than Momistic avenues. This means that when we talk about drug addicts, sexual deviants, neurotics, schizophrenics, suicides, etc., we must be aware that only a *portion* of the victims trace their problems to Momistic experiences. The problems of the other victims must be traced to different origins.

In the next chapter we shall give thought to a most difficult and perplexing question: *What can be done about the Momistic problem?*

Chapter 7

No equation can divine the quality of life,
no instrument record,
no computer conceive it—
only bit by bit can feeling man
lovingly retrieve it.—Jerome B. Wiesner

Prevention, Cure— and Other Optimisms

This book is intended as an exposé, not a panacea. While the search for solutions and remedies is natural and necessary, such an endeavor usually becomes fruitless and extremely frustrating if it is not preceded by diagnosis. Blind groping to soothe a pain whose cause or nature is obscure would result in confusion, selection of the wrong medicine, and further pain-inflicting injury. The primary purpose of the book, then, is to analyze and diagnose Momism. It is hoped that the preceding chapters have met this need.

To leave off at this point without sharing at least some modest ideas about the possibilities of prevention and cure would end the book on an almost painfully incomplete note. Likewise, to assume to offer a complete preventive and remedial program would be pretentious and far beyond the framework of this book. Therefore let this diagnosis be exposed to scrutiny, further research, and corrective modifications before a definite cure is suggested. In other words, let verification, as part of the scientific method, intervene between this analysis and its remedial implementation.

This chapter is therefore meant to give the reader a bit of comfort rather than a serious outline of a program of remedy that, somehow miraculously, will make Momism vanish from the American scene. Any pretense to be in possession of an effective plan for abolishing Momism would be chimerical at this time; it is too complex and firmly established to give way to an intellectual or merely literary exorcism. It is a symptom of a whole system. Its roots draw nourishment from virtually every nook and niche of the American civilization. To visualize a Momless America is to dream of some Utopian country —one that has little resemblance to America as we know it. There is no immediate solution in sight for the problem, and the future will probably see not less but more of it.

Notwithstanding this pessimism, things can turn out worse if they are approached unpreparedly. Hence some remarks systematically assessing the avenues to the problem's prevention and cure may contribute to a better approach. This influence, hopefully, will do two things: (1) have a limiting and controlling influence on the worst transactions of Mom and (2) blunt the worst pain once the injury has been done. The first aspect deals with prevention; the second with cure.

In order to open up avenues to the above goals, the components that play the major roles in the Momistic syndrome must be examined as to their modifiability. (The thrust of certain changes can result in the control of Momism.) These components can be broken down into four main variables, the most concrete of which is the *individual* as he or she enacts the role of father, mother, son, or daughter. Previous discussions have looked at these roles and identified their corruption as generating or reflecting Momistic tendencies. We will discuss how the "scripts" of these roles can be safeguarded to bring about a lesser Momistic effect.

A second component deals with the *family* as a unit. We will discuss how a modified family arrangement might stem the surge of pathologic motherhood. Questions as to how a different structure for child rearing can reduce or eliminate Momistic consequences will be examined.

A third focus for change deals with the larger social environment, the *society*. The questions involved center around human interaction, conditions of work, education, economic opportunities, and other important factors that influence the mode of bringing up the young in our society.

The fourth focus of change for reducing Momism has to do with the *cultural images* that pattern our thinking and viewing of social reality. Here we are dealing with tradition—the cultural prescriptions and proscriptions defining what is right and wrong.

These four foci for change will now be examined in detail.

The Individual as Focus for Change

Social science makes the assumption that the human organism in itself is meaningless unless defined within a role. *Homo sapiens*, that peculiar social creature, has a profound need for order, clarity, and predictable relations. To meet this demand for orientation, the organism is integrated into a pattern of social roles. It is within the social roles that we "become" and "are." Our identities are intimately associated—if not coterminous —with status and role. In ideal instances, the role pattern is useful for the individual as well as for society at large. For example, the roles embedded in the family situation—mother, father, son, and daughter—have the potential to work for the good of all involved. They also have the potential to work for the detriment of all, or some, involved. And it is at this point that the scripts of the roles are corrupted and misused. This is what Momism is all about.

It is the composite of the perverted roles of mother, father, son, and daughter that engenders the Silent Disease and fosters it. To avert the tragedy of Momism, the scripts that these actors and actresses follow in their respective roles must be purged of the Momistic slant. For the play they are called upon to perform was not meant to be a tragedy but an adventure story—the adventure of a creative and exciting life for each family member.

In the following sections we are concerned with the guidelines that should guard the scripts of these players against infection by the Silent Disease.

The Script of the Mother. The star of the Momism drama is, of course, the Mom. Her role carries the highest prestige—so high, in fact, that her actual performance does not seem to cloud the respectability of her status. Anyone who enters the stage with the motherhood script in hand is by nature a star, and virtually protected against criticism. It is therefore frequently overlooked that she reads her script with the compulsivity of a monomaniac, under the guise of the Motherhood Myth, and intones it as a biological calling, while it actually echoes a psychological malaise. Under the mask of respectable mothering, she proceeds to usurp her child's life-style. In American society, she has done so not merely with impunity but with gratitude and reward for a job well done. Society has a way of going on and on despite harmful arrangements, and culture lacks an organ to rid itself of anachronistic waste, as, in this case, medieval and idolatrous reverence for Moms.

What are some of the changes that should be written into the motherhood script to prevent her from slipping into Momism? Spelling out a healthy mother role is best approached by identifying the non-Momistic elements that must be substituted for the destructive features of Momhood. The wholesome script for the mother must therefore emphasize:

1. *Unconditional love,* not conditional love. Love based on conditions of compliance is the most vicious tool in Mom's arsenal. It destroys self-confidence and self-reliance, and it creates crippling anxieties. Healthy motherhood reaches out and offers unconditional love that supports the child's sense of self-worth.

2. *Strong selfhood* instead of parasitic needs. The higher the strength of self in a mother, the less self-centered she is. Secure selfhood frees her from making overly selfish demands on others and enables her to help without ulterior motives.

3. *Freely chosen motherhood,* not the motherhood compulsion that is a product of the Motherhood Myth. Such women play the role and read the script because they believe they *have* to. No wonder their voices are shrill, their acting insensitive and self-centered: they never liked the script. What is badly needed is full awakening to the fact that motherhood is just *one* alternative among a number of different life-styles. Mothering is a life-style that must be chosen voluntarily and deliberately, not automatically. In other words, not all women should think of motherhood—for that matter, even marriage—as their "natural" destiny. The assumption that having children is the essence of a woman's life is as myopic as it is dangerous. Motherhood as a way of life has been oversold to American women.

4. *The child as an end,* not as a means. The typical Mom fails to visualize the uniqueness of the child and constantly compares him with others. This comparison is extended to careers generally, and she feels that for the sake of motherhood she has bypassed other worthwhile careers. This creates a feeling of deprivation in her, a need to compensate for it, and the tendency to use the child as a success symbol. The healthy script must discourage this. Motherhood either comes from the heart, and is truly a loving experience, or the role should not be played at all.

5. *Discipline,* not overindulgence. While the overindulgent mother pampers an egocentric and selfish personality, the mother who puts a normal emphasis on discipline will help her child grow up to be a responsible and well-oriented human being.

6. *Care and concern,* not overprotection. The child must have the benefit of feeling cared for and knowing he can approach the parent with his problems. Otherwise he will feel lonely, rejected, and insecure. On the other hand, overprotection is a perversion of care. It exceeds normal needs for protection; it denies the child exploration of reality on his own; and it prevents him from becoming a self-reliant and mature individual.

7. *Guidance,* not domination. Domination does not allow the unfolding of the child's maturity and sense of responsibility. He gets accustomed to accept outside agents as authority for each and every action, and does not develop a sense of evaluation based on his personal judgment and knowledge. On the other hand, normal guidance and instruction are a *must* for the child's welfare. Without such attention, he will not develop a sane sense for assessing reality.

8. *Knowledge and information,* not pseudointellectualism. The responsible mother is eager to learn to be a

good parent and, in the process, is open to professional advice and counseling. The pseudointellectual mother tries to impress. Her goal (mostly unconscious) is to enslave the child—and everybody else who falls for her facade of learnedness. An expert on relatively insignificant details, she has lost sight of basic purposes of the child-rearing process, such as true maturity for the child She persuades the child to learn intellectual trivia, but fails to give him the emotional strength to integrate the details and apply them to some fruitful goal.

The Script of the Father. While the mother-turned-Mom is guilty of acts of commission, the father in the Momistic situation is guilty of acts of omission. This means he does nothing to balance the scales of child nurturing. Fathers, being so busy elsewhere and refusing to share their lives with their sons, indirectly teach these boys to retreat from their responsibilities. The masculine script, as we know it today, omits the necessary encouragement for the male to be a child raiser, as demonstrated by the fact that our vocabulary provides us with the word "mothering" but not "fathering" for the job of bringing up the child.

This one-sidedness is even reflected by authorities who should know better. For example, the National Association for Mental Health publishes pamphlets under the motto "What every child needs for good mental health," trying to reach parents and educate them to raise emotionally healthy children. However, the vast majority of the literature addresses itself exclusively to the mother, not to the father. This is particularly obvious in pamphlet 525, presumably directed toward "parents." In actuality, the pictures and drawings accompanying the text reveal it to be exclusively oriented toward the mother-child relationship. The role of the father goes unmentioned.

In sum, then, the script for the father makes no provision for checking or balancing a mother's overmanaging. When the mother is left alone with the inumerable task and problems of raising the child, maternal overexertion is not only easy to fall into, it is almost inevitable. As Margaret Mead warned long ago, maybe we burden women with too much, expect too much of them, and are too quick in blaming them.[1] Unlike the bygone days of old-style farm living, when father shared in the upbringing of the boy by taking him along to work in the barn, stable, and fields, today's mother is expected to accomplish the extremely demanding job of raising him without the aid of the father.

The results of fatherless child raising were discussed in Chapter 4, where it was shown that the effects on children exposed to only the mother include (1) greater immaturity, (2) poor age-mate adjustment, (3) insecure identification, (4) lack of self-confidence, and (5) a general stifling of personality development.

One should not lose sight, however, of the fact that within the larger picture of this unbalanced child raising (call it Momism or whatever) the mother emerges as much a victim as the child whose life she warps. While the child is the victim of the maternal neurosis, she is the victim of an arrangement that causes her neurosis. She is the victim of a society that writes one-sided scripts and coerces her to play her role without the assistance and modifying influence of "fathering."

This point must be clearly understood, since blaming the mother for her Momistic transactions would amount to "blaming the victim."[2] We must beware of the tendency to narrowly focus on a problem or problem person, trying to "change" it/him/her, eradicating the "difference" between it/him/her and the "normal" society—and all the while forgetting the *systemic* nature of the issue at hand. We must learn to view the process of victimization as part of the larger societal picture.

It is with this thought in mind that we examine some of the other scripts that are intimately coordinated with the mother's role. Only then can we recognize the intricate nature of the constellation of circumstances from which Momism evolves. The script of the father is an ominous aspect of this constellation. (Of course, many other aspects are involved. "Cultural images," for example, are elements of great significance in the overall picture of Momism and must be carefully examined if we want to avoid "blaming the victim." Such aspects will be discussed later in this chapter.)

Learning the fatherhood script is hampered from the very beginning by three unique drawbacks. First, the paternal role is not structured by a biological capability. Unlike young women, young men cannot look forward to *having* babies—only to caring for them. This condition tends to narrow their parental experience and often makes it look diminutive or almost irrelevant. They do not get the full grasp of parenthood the way the female does. As Bruno Bettelheim put it, "for boys, fatherhood is added like an afterthought as part of their self-image as mature men."[3]

The second disadvantage is that the father role has been changing radically, while that of the mother has remained essentially the same throughout the ages. The mother has always been the nurturing figure for the children and has remained deeply involved in their upbringing. The script of the modern father, however, is inconsistent with that of his forefathers. He now works away from the homesite, often traveling a considerable distance; his responsibilities are largely invisible to his children; and his presence in the home is not sufficiently felt. For him to fulfill an adequate parental function, modification of his career and closer integration into the home scene will be necessary. (Many modern women undergo just the reverse orientation.)

The third hindrance preventing the male from assuming a fuller share in parenthood is the fact that American society is changing from a patriarchy to equalitarianism. This change has spread confusion in all relationships, including the wife-husband and the father-child relationships.

There has been growing uneasiness about the dormancy of the paternal role in American society. A suspicion has arisen that it is not right that millions of children are constantly surrounded and commanded by women: in the home, at nursery school, kindergarten, and elementary school. The role of the father as the exclusive breadwinner and that of the mother as his domestic bursar are under attack.

The fathering role has become acutely desirable today for a number of reasons. One of them is the insistence of women who want and expect help in child raising. They have been goaded to demand this because of increased career opportunities outside the home and by the reams of literature they have read in the area of child psychology. Thus modern technology and psychology have had an intimidating influence on modern women. They have become unspontaneous and afraid to proceed on their own initiative with their children. In short, increasing numbers of them step into the same technical and nonfamilial careers as men and deem it only fair that the home responsibilities, including child raising, be shared by the male.

Behavioral scientists, who woke up to the fact that a study of fathering was long overdue, encouraged a new look at this parental function and concluded that a variety of individuals can successfully nurture an infant. Among the pertinent studies have been experiments with primates showing that paternal care can be substituted for maternal care without stunting the emotional or intellectual development of the offspring.[4] The parental potential of the human male has gone largely unused in modern societies (although trends in Scandinavian countries indicate increasing activation of this human resource).

What specific recommendations can be offered for reshaping the father's script to bring about a more balanced and equitable performance of the parental function? It is felt that the creative and Mom-resistant paternal role can be safeguarded by:

1. *Genuine willingness to extend fathering.* Many males have ambivalent, if not aversive, feelings about fathering, yet they go ahead with it. Just as there is a Motherhood Myth there is an equivalent, though less emphatic, Fatherhood Myth. It propels the male toward the *biological* act of fathering without being fully willing to accept the responsibilities to continue with *social* fathering. By excluding ambivalent and unwilling males from fatherhood, a giant step toward the improvement of child raising could be made. Obviously, this suggestion will run into the same difficulty as the attack on indiscriminate motherhood by stirring up the old excuse and defensiveness about "parenthood as a natural right for anybody." This "free choice" of the father script should be curbed (at least by educational means) by setting a different emotional tenor for fatherhood by emphasizing (and enforcing) the everyday chores and responsibilities to be shared with the mother.

2. *The flexible father script.* The new script should allow respectability in a man's choosing to be a "homebody" and wanting to take care of a household and the child raising. The choice of being a "househusband" should not have derogatory connotations.

3. *The diffused breadwinner role.* Occupational career functions should be distributed according to likes and proficiencies. The masculine role is not to be seen

as diminished because the wife pursues a career and shares in the breadwinning for the family.

4. *Active involvement in home chores.* Balanced child raising calls for balanced investment of time and energy between the mother and father. It is important for the child to see different personalities at work and to escape the overbearing influence of one and the same person, thereby possibly avoiding the harm that could come to him through overexposure to a disturbed parent.

5. *Educational preparation for the father script.* The prematernal courses for young wives, which have been encouraged in some communities, should be redefined and include men as well. Such preparental education should focus equally on men and women and help them bring out their potential for raising their children sanely. Preparatory courses should introduce them to the various aspects connected with bringing up the child: rudimentary child psychology, physical care and health, hygiene, nutrition, clothes, budgeting, shopping, etc.

6. *The expanded male script.* In order to balance the female influence, males must expand their occupational interest into careers hitherto relatively shunned by males, especially as they apply to teaching in nurseries, kindergartens, and elementary schools.

7. *Reshaping cultural images.* None of the above suggestions can be implemented without considering the traditional definitions of masculinity and femininity. These definitions must be loosened and rewritten. Interaction between the parents and between the parents and their children must proceed on a more individualistic (rather than culturally ossified) basis. This, without doubt, touches on the most controversial and complex aspect of the entire book. A separate discussion is necessary to do justice to it, and we propose to do so in the section "Cultural Images as Focus for Change."

In sum, then, the proposed modifications of the father's script aim at bringing into our vocabulary the word "fathering" as representing a definite and mandatory aspect of parenthood. As an enthusiastic mother, who experimented gratifyingly with shared parenthood, exclaimed: "It's just the greatest for the kids to have two parents. In our society children don't have two parents; the fathers are too busy working and getting ahead and can't spend the time they should with their families. It's so much easier for a woman to raise children when she has someone to help her."[5]

The Script of the Son. The role of the son poignantly illustrates how strongly interdependent the players of the drama of Momism are. If the mother follows a Momistic script, her son will almost automatically assume a perverted script himself. The interplay among the actors does not allow him the freedom to follow some ideal script; rather, his script must be aligned to the roles played opposite him. He must respond to the cues offered and cannot help but integrate himself into the unfolding plot. In this way the boy becomes the victim of a distorted plot. Hence prevention of the Momistic role lies, for the boy, largely outside his personal power. Prevention will have to begin with two other roles: the roles of the mother (the "star") and the father. The boy can only react, not act.

It depends, therefore, largely on the wholesomeness of the roles of the parents whether a number of Mom-resistant qualities can be preserved in the script of the son. The *ideal* script for the son, then, should safeguard his:

1. *Freedom to improvise.* This means that he should feel free to respond with spontaneity and creative impulse, without fear of being cut down and reduced to a "reactor" or robot responding to manipulation by an

"actress" or "actor." The play of life consists of constant improvisations within flexible rules that respect the creative notion.

2. *Feeling of basic welcome.* The boy must sense that he is accepted and respected as a total person, appreciated as one of the major actors in the play of life and as a delight to the rest of the cast. Only if the sensation of "being of pleasure to others" is allowed to grow is it possible for the boy to evolve a sense of self-value. One of the basic truisms on which virtually all counselors, psychologists, and psychiatrists agree is that a feeling of self-worth is a necessary condition for a positively functioning human being.[6] *The boy who grows up knowing he is a source of joy to his parents will develop a healthy self-image,* which is the foundation of success in any future endeavor. (This is a one-sentence explanation of what makes for mental health and a happy life!)

3. *Nonisolationism.* The boy must be allowed normal mixing with his peers and, if possible, with a variety of adult models, such as relatives, neighbors, and family friends. It is playing, communicating, and sparring with age-mates that enables normal development of gregarious sentiments and a sense of social morality.

4. *Interaction with the father.* We do not live in a society of unisex, and probably never will, and therefore must provide the boy with a real and visible model of identification. Anything short of this is bound to create problems of insecure identity.

But what happens if the qualities suggested in the four points above are not respected by the other main actors? What if a Mom imposes her sick script on the defenseless son? Obviously, we are then too late with prevention. We must talk about *cure.*

There can rarely be a question of cure while the boy is associated with Mom. Cure for the Momistically impaired male is the most vexing aspect of the entire Momistic picture. The last thing a true Mom allows is intrusion into her dominion and abrogation of her domination. And even if a therapist should succeed in whacking his way into the Momistic jungle, his effort would probably have a short-lived effect because the rapacious growth of stifling Momistic vines would quickly reengulf the therapeutic clearing he had hacked open. The very nature of the cure calls for rewriting the boy's inadequate script— but how can this be done if his role playing depends on the quality of the roles played opposite him? Even if his script should be modified in the therapy session, the moment the boy reenters interaction with his mother he snaps back into the Momistic interaction.

This, simply, is the nature of the social drama; roles cannot be enacted in isolation from one another; if they were, we would be dealing with a cast of schizophrenic actors and actresses who, as if in a blind stupor, pursue their isolated plots. Therefore the only time for effective cure comes after the Momistically impaired individual is physically removed from his mother. In most cases this means later in life, when he is older and no longer under her direct supervision. The rather platitudinous conclusion derived from this situation is the same as in other diseases: An ounce of prevention counts more than a pound of cure.

However, the Silent Disease is not unconquerable altogether. There are two possibilities. One *can* happen while the boy is young and still with his mother. However, cure at that time is usually a result of events other than the formal therapy program in which the boy may be involved. Cure may result from relatives' taking the initiative and assuming a redirecting role in raising the child. This is especially effective if a strong male model enters the scene. In other cases of rehabilitation, a Mom may find an equally absorbing and rewarding substitute for domination over the child, which results in her relaxing her influence.

For example, an overprotective Mom was encouraged and guided to rechannel her Momistic drive from stifling her son to helping and teaching retarded children. The project was a double success: the son had a chance to grow and the retardates benefited from the woman's new dedication.

Whatever specific dynamics may be involved in the victim's recovery, all of them most likely include the restructuring of personal relationships to liberate the enslaved child.

The second curative possibility refers to the situation later in life when the Momistic patient enters a formal therapy program. However, not just any therapy approach will do—certainly not the run-of-the-mill approach that Robert W. Resnick calls "chicken soup."[7] By that he means the traditional "helpful" attitude of the therapist who "feeds" the patient tasty psychological chicken broth, perfect to the palate of the sick person but unable to reveal or treat his serious problems. The effective uncovering of problems is never palatable; rather, it is painful and demands rethinking and reorienting— it's *not* "chicken soup."

Many therapists, Resnick fears, consider themselves members of the "helpful profession," engaged in the "helping relationship." This is a dangerous attitude, that may not lead to the improvement of the patient but to his continued dependency and immaturity.

There is a significant difference between truly furthering mental health and "chicken soup" help. The latter consists of *doing for the other what he is capable of doing for himself.* This "help" ensures his not becoming aware that he can stand on his own feet. In the case of the Momistic victim, this seals his victimization forever.

The prevention of slipping into such finality is difficult and requires constant vigil on the part of the therapist. This is particularly tricky since the Momistic patient is looking for precisely this type of "help" in order to pamper and protect his apathy, narcissistic attitudes, and irresponsible habits.

Thus the Momistic patient requires a carefully fitted therapy approach, and Gestalt therapy may be among the most indicated therapeutic answers. Its basic goal is the substitution of self-support for environment support. And Momism is crippling precisely because it violates this principle: it relies on other-support and disregards self-support. Gestalt therapy is designed to reverse this process, but it is no easy reversal since the patient *wants* to remain infantile.

This may lead to a therapeutic impasse, where the patient tries to manipulate the environment, specifically the therapist, to support his pathologies. The Momistic victim will attempt manipulation by putting on a spectacle (often astonishingly convincing) of being helpless, having misunderstood, being misunderstood, crying, insisting on special favors, being depressed and mentally deranged, etc. The danger at this junction is that the "helpful" therapist lets himself be fooled and falls into the trap. If he (or anyone else with influence over the patient) is duped by this manipulation and decides to be "nice" and "supportive," he will succeed in keeping the patient as infantile as ever.

Fritz Perls, a renowned proponent of Gestalt therapy, used earthy prose when he suggested that such manipulation attempts *must* be frustrated, Gestalt therapy's goal *must* be achieved, and the patient *must* discover that he can "wipe his own ass."[8]

The effectiveness of the therapist's refusing to appeal to the spoiled and self-pitying elements in the Momistic patient has been documented by Edward A. Strecker in his classic treatise *Their Mothers' Sons.*[9] The case recounted dealt with Walter, a difficult case of Momistic alcoholism. Walter, as a grown man, was surprised and frustrated to discover that the physician who functioned as his counselor declined to play the role of Mom. From the very beginning, the doctor insisted on appealing only to the mature segment of the alcoholic's personality, however small it happened to be. Since the determining factors in this type of alcoholism were immaturity and indecision, planted during childhood, the effective treatment called for psychological reeducation to encourage more maturity and personal decisionmaking. Frustrating as it may have been at the start, Walter had to learn to make his own decisions and gradually grow up and act his age.

An alternative to Gestalt therapy, promising to be equally effective against the malaise of Momism, is reality therapy. This approach was originally suggested by psychiatrist William Glasser, who wrote the definitive work on it.[10] Like many Gestalt therapists, reality therapists are suspicious that the permissive, "understanding," and "helpful" attitude toward patients (and also juvenile delinquents) may defeat the goal of rehabilitation and only reward and reinforce the immature pattern. A realistic approach must insist on the patient's understanding reality, facing it squarely, and acting maturely—regardless of the "understandable" harm that has been done to him in the past. The Momistic patient must be held responsible for adjusting his actions to the actual world and not to the stifled and narcissistic reality to which he has attached himself.

There may be other therapy frameworks in addition to the two mentioned above which can be of benefit to the Momistic patient. Gestalt and reality therapy were singled out because they seem to be finely tuned to the shrill pitch of Momism. In the final analysis, however, success will depend very much on the individual therapist and his demeanor toward the patient. "Chicken soup" can be dished out under many labels, and it is the job of the therapist to guard against "helpful" reinforcement of the Silent Disease.

The Script of the Daughter. Ignoring the way the daughter's personality is shaping up would mean ignoring a potential Trojan horse that is being rolled onto the stage, ready and waiting for the drama of Momism to begin. It is surprisingly easy to lose sight of the most obvious and logical sequence: daughters become mothers, and mothers *can* become Moms.

But how do they become Moms? This is of course a most difficult question to answer, since there is an endless variety of reasons. (We discussed this at the beginning of Chapter 5.) Often a woman suffers emotional upheavals or deprivations after her childhood years that push her toward Momistic attitudes. Such events can occur relatively independently of the daughter script she followed as a child and are therefore not under discussion at this moment.

During childhood the girl can be exposed to several types of experiences that tend to prepare her attitudes for the Mom role. One determining influence can be a mother (who possibly, but not necessarily, is a Mom herself) who consistently indoctrinates her daughter with negative opinions about. males. The father (if present) may be the target of her "slander campaign." He, in fact, may serve for the girl's acid test of her negative assessment. If he meets the negative expectations—that is, confirms the girl's suspicion that he is "useless," "unwise," "vicious," "weak," etc.—a basic and pervasive negative attitude toward males generally can be derived. Of course, such suspicion and negative attitudes often are not based on the blind prejudice or emotional hangups of the biased person but on association with one or several male figures who *are* inferior and weak. Most often, however, a girl acquires the basic Momistic character from simple imitation of what she sees in her mother's behavior. Imitation is the cradle of many Moms.

Again, this is a reminder of how intimately the various roles of the family drama are meshed into one another. There can hardly be a sane script for the daughter if the mother enacts a sick role—especially if the perverted mother role is not checked or otherwise deflected by saner and stronger roles played by others in or close to the family.

What does a sane script for the girl consist of—that is, one free of the seeds of Momistic attitudes? Three fundamental principles of safeguarding against Momhood include the following.

1. *Equality.* She should learn to look at males as being neither inferior nor superior but as equal, yet different.

2. *Mutual helpfulness.* She should learn that human beings can help and complement each other. She should learn that such reciprocity is particularly beautiful if she chooses associates wisely, on the basis of compatible temperament and skill. Whether such association should proceed on the basis of masculine and feminine role definitions is, of course, debatable in light of the social and cultural changes in modern society, for these old definitions include connotations of superior and inferior elements. It would therefore be wiser to deemphasize the traditional, rigid roles and emphasize a common humaneness that all can share regardless of gender or any other biological or social characteristic.

3. *Respect for individuality.* Overlapping the previous points, the girl should learn that biological differences do not make for differences in the respect and dignity with which to bestow other human beings.

If the girl is raised with a sense of equality, encouraged to observe mutual helpfulness and kindness, and consistently reminded to be respectful to others, she will naturally be drawn to sound motherhood, rather than pathological Momhood.

The Family as Focus for Change

The Myth of Motherhood has throughout the ages functioned to keep women relatively calm and "in their place." Their place was the family (the golden cage), which they accepted as their natural environment—up till now. It was within this environment, and its mythical atmosphere, that Momism had a chance to evolve. But vital changes are under way, and the pertinent question arises whether or how the changes in American family life are going to affect Momism. A related and most important question is how changes can be "engineered" to diminish the threat of Momism. The following points are addressed to these questions.

1. *Family therapy.* The role and the personality of the individual family member cannot be understood, least of all treated or modified, without considering the family as a unit. This has been realized by progressive counselors, therapists, and social workers. In a situation of Momism, it would be virtually useless to single out one infected member without extensively treating the others. "Family therapy" has come to be accepted as a new counseling practice.

Psychiatrist Theodore Lidz is one of increasing numbers of counselors who emphasize that family therapy can stop parents from using the child as a pawn.[11] Lidz suggests that in many instances it would be better if the child left the home environment and went to a boarding school. Naturally, it is hard to convince most parents of such measures, and the psychiatrist reports that it often took him a year or more to bring parents around to see his point.

2. *Restructuring relationships.* "Restructuring" means to change arrangements and relationships to effect different patterns of human interaction. This is a necessary condition to stop or reduce a Momistic relationship. How can this be done? The answer seems to lie in taking advantage of various arrangements, institutions, and groups for rendering *auxiliary services* to the family —in other words, expanding the narrow, confining boundaries of the small modern family. Sociologist Patricia Cayo Sexton, in her challenging book *The Feminized Male,* urges that as many people as possible become involved in teaching and in deciding what to teach our children.[12]

The public has increasingly called upon the involvement of teachers, ministers, social workers, and professional people (such as architects, lawyers, computer experts, stockbrokers, veterinarians, etc.) to open up the world, with its ceaseless achievements and wonders, to the child. The emphasis is on expansion of the child's emotional as well as intellectual horizon. The process of not only intellectually learning from such a variety of persons but also having the opportunity of interacting with them as human beings goes a long way to prevent or diminish the Silent Disease of Momism.

Sexton assigns particularly beneficial functions to physical education, sports, and outdoor adventures for boys. She deplores that some 90 percent of elementary schools in the nation do not have gyms, only 2 percent of high school students have physical education five times a week, and athletics has become so overspecialized that it now belongs to experts and stars. What really must be remedied is the need of the physically *unfit,* who require coaching and a chance to play and exercise. (Imagine a boy, in danger of Momistic engulfment, being encouraged and drawn into sports! What would this do to him? Through patient coaxing and guiding, he could achieve a sense of identification with others—team members, coaches, sports heroes. It would mean building up stamina against Momistic encroachment.) New outlets must be opened for the endangered children, including better recreation facilities, in both the city and the suburb, permitting more male activity and creative targets for aggression.

The experience of group life among peers is most important for the child from the small, isolated family since the latter often fails to provide the necessary breadth and exuberance of experience needed for healthy personality expression and non-Momistic development. Such auxiliary services, augmenting a family's diminished resources, especially in cases of fatherless boys (as in divorce situations), often save a boy from exclusive supervision and domination by his mother. Rather than protectively keep the son at home, the mother should allow the boy associations which provide him with father substitutes in male relatives and friends. Letting him join a boys' group, where he will find an adult leader and also leaders among the older boys, may be the wisest decision a mother without an effective male partner can make for the child.

3. *Sex education.* Sexuality is another focus for change. In school and elsewhere, the child should be encouraged to frankly and openly approach the intimate subject matter. Many educators realize that sexual prudishness often represses normal heterosexuality, stimulates inversion (homosexuality, etc.), and generally perverts natural impulses. Such perversion is the trademark of the typical Mom. Preventive steps and countermeasures should be taken outside the family to preclude the unhealthy influence of a mother-turning-Mom.

4. *Child-care centers and mother employment.* Women liberationists avidly advance the idea of public child-care centers.[13] However, the idea has fallen far short

of implementation in real life. Such care centers are still run on a limited basis, costing mothers unduly because they are not yet the free public institution liberated women would like them to be. The traditional notion that children require twenty-four-hour-a-day care by their biological mothers to have a normal development has cut women off from a large number of educational, professional, political, and social options. This belief is now under attack. Researchers are not at all certain whether such extensive maternal care is good for the child.

In fact, one study found that women who discontinued employment because they considered it their duty to stay home with the children had greater child-rearing problems than working mothers. These "dutiful" mothers were less satisfied with their relationships with their children, had more problems controlling them, and felt more insecure in their role as mothers.[14] Another study found that if other conditions are equal, the children of mothers who worked because they *wanted* to work are less likely to be disturbed, have problems in school, or suffer from a lack of personal worth than the typical housewife's children.[15] Additional studies have supported these findings, showing that employed mothers generally had more favorable attitudes toward children and motherhood, *unless* they had more than three children.[16]

(We must be careful, however, not to oversimplify the relationship between maternal employment or nonemployment and the children's personality, because family situations involve too many intervening and modifying circumstances.)

In general, we may conclude that a mother's employment prevents her from exerting continuous power and influence over the child, and hence protects the child from her possibly neurotic tendencies and conflicts. In addition, the child is free to explore other human relationships. He learns to adjust to peers and is able to choose among various adult models. Generally he experiences a richer scope of intellectual and emotional stimulation.

In short, the idea of well-run child-care centers counters the Momistic trend. However, this is a goal not yet reached. The operation of a center that is efficient, well staffed, operates twenty-four hours a day, and is equipped to take care of infants and even newborn or sick children is a rather expensive proposition. But it is necessary. Progressive women insist: "Cost . . . has not stopped the establishment of elementary schools and should not stop the establishment of a sufficient number of child care centers."[17] And: "A longer-range solution to the problem of child care will involve the establishment of a network of child care centers . . . on a full-time, year-round schedule."[18]

Child-care centers are no panacea against Momism, however. One of their major "limitations" is that most mothers who seek employment outside the home, and therefore need child-care programs, are not the ones who are likely to turn into Moms. It may be that the Moms are those who, in spite of the availability of child-care centers, refuse to work because of either their traditional ideas about motherhood or their emotional dependency on the child.

5. *Alternative and experimental family groups.* Unlike most modifications of family life discussed above, other ideas have not yet reached the mainstream of society. These innovations are drastic and experimental and largely are still on the "drafting boards" of writers, educators, liberationists, counterculture people, and Utopians. What they have in common is the desire to radically change traditional ways, willingness to experiment with new forms, and the goal of liberating humans (or certain segments thereof) from oppressive norms and values. An interesting aspect of these innovative efforts

is the liberating effect they have on children threatened
by Momism. This is a preventive aspect that probably
was not deliberately planned; it is a by-product of a certain life-style.

Communal living appears to be in its heyday in
America. It is an experimentation with an alternative to
modern family life, which the communards despise, and
has interesting implications for child rearing. The communards think of the children in their midst as "our
children," provide a variety and multiplicity of adult
models, freely exhibit affection and love, and grant the
children a great deal of freedom of the obvious sort—no
"uptight" insistence on naps, cleanliness, order, regular
feeding, etc. In short, they abhor the restrictions, instructions, and goals of the stereotyped middle class, feeling strongly that no adult should "lay his trip on kids."

Generally, children are left to work out their problems among themselves. Parents encourage each child to
be assertive, yet gently so. Women are reluctant to serve
as models for girls because they fear they are not yet
liberated enough to present a nonstereotypical model, and
men abstain from teaching boys the chauvinistic male
role.

While this life-style may limit the growth of Momism, no assurance can be given that it does not foster
other malaises. For example, many counterculture people
refuse to distinguish the children's needs from their own,
failing to realize that their particular life-style is a *reaction* to the "Establishment," which the young children do
not know and thus have had no choice to accept or reject.
And to that extent the children's communal parents do
"lay their trips" on them.[19]

Some social scientists, nevertheless, believe that the
style of child rearing in the Age of Aquarius augurs new
directions in the mainstream flow of American society,[20]
although it may still be too soon to make this prediction.

In the meantime, communal living and child rearing remains experimental and capricious.

For the time being, this alternative-experimental family living will have a limited impact on Momism-prone situations, since each arrangement attracts different types of personalities. This means that mothers with Momistic needs will not join communes or similar experimental groups. One can only hope that, in generations to come, the need for Momistic relationships will be "bred out" of the females growing up in healthier and more liberated families or alternative groups.

6. *The Future: Psychological vs. biological parenthood.* It would be presumptuous to let on that one "knows" the future, and such best sellers as Alvin Toffler's *Future Shock* must be understood as purely speculative.[21] Similarly, B. F. Skinner's *Walden Two*[22] or Robert Rimmer's *The Harrad Experiment*,[23] two works that project man's intimate group arrangements, must be seen in a more novelistic than scientific light. Even George Orwell's *1984*[24] has lost quite a bit of its impressive and believable aura as we move closer to that year. In fact, it looks as if "1984" will have to be postponed. In short, the future is up for grabs: anyone with a good pen and lively style will be able to claim an awed audience.

Our purpose here is less pervasive but more somber. It is limited to extrapolating a few reliable signs that seem to indicate an important change in the future: a shift of emphasis from the biological to the psychological parent. What is at stake here is the welfare of the child. More and more voices question the wisdom of granting a man or a woman, or both combined, the privilege of more or less total determination over the life of a young human being solely on the grounds of being his/her progenitor. Sociologist Barrington Moore, a caustic critic of the modern family, feels that such automatic authority, based on nothing else than biological relatedness, is an obsolete and barbaric feature inviting the rebellion of the young.[25]

Moore condemns the obligation to give affection to a particular set of people as a "natural duty" merely because of the accident of birth. He calls it "exploitation" when parents insist on gratitude and affection when the social situation may not generate genuine feelings of warmth.

The critic looks to the future and anticipates a time when society will distinguish between the intimate relationship of two (or several) adults, on one side, and the child-rearing process on the other. (The two processes may well become separate.) It is better, many behavioral scientists believe, for the child to grow up in a warm and healthy institutional environment than in a family torn by obligations its members resent. And this resentment may grow at an unprecedented rate, for broad segments of the population are moving more and more toward a secular and nonsacred perception of the family. This means they no longer view the family as a divinely instituted arrangement but as a man-made institution that can and should be changed to meet new needs and new outlooks. The strong emphasis in modern society on individualism (vs. familism) that puts a premium on the individual's goals and desires, and not on those of the family as a unit, is additional pressure for a possible restructuring of the family as we know it today.

The same conclusion, or even recommendation, has been arrived at by a number of experts in various disciplines who feel that custody should not be settled by the rigid traditional custom but by what is psychologically beneficial to the child. For example, a team of authors made up of Yale law professor Joseph Goldstein, psychoanalyst Anna Freud (Sigmund Freud's granddaughter), and the director of Yale's Child Study Center, Albert J. Solnit, insist in their book *Beyond the Best Interests of the Child* that a child's relationship with his *psycholog-*

ical parent, whether or not he or she is the child's natural parent, should never be disrupted.²⁶ The main criterion in defining the "beneficial" parent depends on the degree to which the child is attached to him/her and feels wanted and appreciated; appreciated for himself—not for financial advantage, not for scoring against a feuding spouse in a divorce, and not for fulfilling an adult's fantasy. In other words, the attachment process must be mature as well as bilateral. Goldstein, Freud, and Solnit suggest child placement according to the best chances for the child's being raised to the greatest degree of self-actualization.

7. *Legal reorientation.* This obviously raises legal issues. As the law is *enacted* (not necessarily *written*) today, child custody is handled with sexist bias favoring the mother, who usually may retain the children if she chooses. (Which should remind us that in many instances of Momism, made possible by father-absence, such absence is not by the choice or default of the male, as being apathetic, disinterested, preoccupied with his career, etc., but by an arbitrary and indifferent court decision.) Many lawyers feel that such automatic court orders must stop.

For example, law professors H. Foster and D. J. Freed make the point that "it takes little familiarity with current literature in psychiatry, psychology, and the behavioral sciences to realize that the shibboleth that 'blood runs thicker than water' is untrue."²⁷ They recommend that established bonds, not theoretical ties of affection and love, should determine custody. A number of states, notably Michigan, reflect this sentiment in their statutes.

But what is the current *reality* of custody battles? (The daily press is so replete with stories of predictable court decisions that we spare the reader the repetition of an example.) Almost predictably, the child is handed over to the biological parents if they claim him, regardless of years of attachment to a foster parent, relative, or friend. Situations are created thereby that are not only heartbreaking for an adult but may prove to be of lasting Momistic detriment to the surrendered child.

But as ominous forces pool their resources and converge on the modern family, demanding its surrender to a new structure and more humane relationships, it would be most interesting to speculate on the nature of the new structure. Will it be along the lines of a modified commune environment, similar to the Israeli kibbutz, where children are raised in a community nursery independent of their biological parents? Will it be strictly on the lines of urban-industrial living, anonymous and lacking community spirit, where children are partly, or wholly, brought up by professional personnel in public child-raising centers? These are futuristic questions. Their speculative answers will not be discussed since they would go beyond the framework of this book.

What we can say with some assurance at this time, however, is that the future will see accentuation of psychological parents, respected before the law, and decline in the prerogatives of biological parents.[28] The special structural form that will implement this new idea is yet uncertain. Perhaps the form doesn't really matter that much anyway since it is only an instrument to render the necessary service. In any case, its full implementation is most likely in the *distant* future.

In summary, the focus on the family for changing the conditions of Momism includes a number of possibilities: (1) family-centered therapy, (2) restructuring relationships by seeking auxiliary services, (3) sex education, (4) child-care centers and mother employment, (5) alternative and experimental family groups, (6) shifting emphasis from biological to psychological parenthood, and (7) legal reorientation.

The important question now is, Will these possibilities deliver? The realistic answer, we are afraid, sounds like a paradox: Many of them will, but they won't reduce Momism in American life in the near future. First, it is quite conceivable that increased use of family-centered therapy, recourse to auxiliary services, sex education, and other commendable efforts will diminish Momism in *some* families. Second, it appears that many more families will drift toward a Momistic life-style, outnumbering those that benefit from the therapeutic and auxiliary services. In sum total, the American scene will not see less but *more* Momism in the *near* future. (A discussion elaborating the reasons for more Mom-prone families follows in the last section of this chapter.)

The *distant* future looks more optimistic. Many of the possible changes will take a long time, perhaps several generations, to be implemented and integrated in family and societal life, and a *gradual* development for the better may be expected in time. In the long run, we may witness the acceptance of diverse family groups (alternative forms of what sociologists call the "primary group") and toleration of various experimental approaches that attempt to carry out the vital functions needed for the emotional well-being of *Homo sapiens*. Likewise, the idea of public child-care centers may find its way into social reality. And new laws, or the unbiased observance of existing ones, will abrogate the powers of Mom.

Hopefully, the convergence of insight and new practices will radically reduce the operating space of the Mom a couple of generations hence.

Society as Focus for Change

Changes at the individual and family level to protect against Momism would be ineffectual unless they are protected and enforced by the larger social system. (This again reminds us of the systemic nature of Momism—or, for that matter, any other social malaise.) What, then, are the changes that must be built into the larger arena of social life to effect the protection of such Mom-resistant modifications as indicated in the first two sections of this chapter? In other words, how can society be instrumental in implementing Mom-resistant safeguards? The main preventive measures can be summed up in the following six points.

1. *Preventing unfit and unwanted parenthood.* The simplest method of preventing disastrous motherhood would be not to become a mother in the first place. A mother who doesn't really want to be a mother may well raise a boy who doesn't really want to be a boy—or, in extreme cases, even be alive. If society would insist on educating its youth about the realities of parenthood, it would go a long way toward preventing unfit and unwanted parenthood, and mothers from becoming Moms. Education for parenthood should be incorporated into the regular curriculum of elementary and high schools. Most colleges have courses to that effect, but they should be made part of the *required* curriculum each graduate has to pass.

On a limited scale, the U.S. Office of Child Development and the Office of Education carried out programs of exposing teenagers to small children and the responsibilities that go with taking care of them.[29] In 1973 these agencies sponsored projects in which teenage boys and girls from 234 school districts were taken into day-care and nursery centers to learn how to be parents. The goal was to enable young people to get a realistic idea of what child care is all about and to provide practical, helpful information for making wise decisions about becoming or not becoming parents.

The question remains, however, whether mothering and fathering can really be learned outside the intimate family environment. Genuine preparation for parenthood takes place through intimate, intense, and prolonged interaction within one's family, and the points made earlier concerning the safeguarding of sound "scripts" for family members must be reemphasized. Formal parenthood education and information projects for young individuals with a normal and relatively healthy family background must be considered as merely supplemental; and for youngsters with a defective family background, such formal programs would be both supplemental and remedial. But, in all cases, such programs are limited in what they can achieve. At best, they can only acquaint the individual with his own potential or nonpotential and assist him in making a wise decision.

Among a number of important aspects, at least three serious sides of parenthood should be elucidated in such educational programs for young Americans.

One side of the problem deals with the psychological preparedness of the woman for motherhood. It is truly amazing to realize that an important function—perhaps the *most* important function—of society, raising children and preparing them for an extremely complex society, is still in the hands of total amateurs. This is anachronistic, if one realizes that nearly every other important function in society is covered by conditions and demands for proficiency. The privilege of selling hamburgers is contingent on proof of sufficient knowledge, proper facilities, and a license; driving an automobile requires passing examinations and obtaining a license; flying an airplane requires training, passing tests, and receiving a license; becoming a lawyer demands preparation, passing stringent expectations, and acquiring a license; practicing medicine depends on schooling, examinations, and issuance of a license. Amazingly, however, becoming a parent depends on no established requirement or license whatever.

To protect the children, and the parents, against

themselves, the public has to be impressed with the fact that "parenting" is probably the most crucial and challenging job engaging an adult's attention. The demands and subtleties of motherhood must be made absolutely clear before an unsuspecting woman blunders into them and makes her child a Momistic substitution for frustrations and deprivations.

The second aspect concerns the forgotten partner: the man-turned-father. Precisely the same exposure to preparatory education must be asked of him.

The third aspect deals with birth control. All members of society who do not wish to become parents should be afforded the best medical means of prevention. Again, this applies to both male and female. (While it is true that some women become Moms after *unplanned* motherhood, most Mom types *plan* motherhood because they want a child for the very purpose of fulfilling their success needs. The point on birth control applies, therefore, only peripherally to the issue of Momism. As long as birth control is not legally imposable, Mom types will go on having children and making them part of their pathologies.)

The crucial question, of course, is how to impress the public with these new standards. Increasingly, voices are being raised with radical suggestions.

For example, Roger W. McIntire, under the telling title "Parenthood Training or Mandatory Birth Control: Take Your Choice," expressed hope that the progress of the technology of contraception and better insight into child-rearing principles will lead to a reevaluation of the sacred "right to parenthood."[30] Probably the most outspoken view was offered by biologist H. Bentley Glass, who recommended that parenthood will be allowed in the future only after a married couple obtains a "child license," which would be contingent on satisfactory completion of a parent education program. The punishment (and preventive measure) for violations would be sterilization.[31] Others, such as sociologist Kingsley Davis, recommend a number of sanctions, mostly economic in nature, to check thoughtless parenthood: charging higher fees for marriage licenses, levying a "child tax," eliminating higher taxation for single persons vis-à-vis married persons, abolishing tax exemptions for children, and legalizing sterilization.[32] Such measures, he hopes, would deter impulsive and immature parenthood and increase the ratio of mature, prepared, and non-Momistic parents.

Among those recommending a more decisive government role in the prevention of unfit and unwanted parenthood is a specialist in child development and family relations at the University of North Carolina, Dr. Vincent M. Rue, who urges the formation of a cabinet-level Department of Marriage and the Family (DMF).[33] The DMF would coordinate existing (but fragmented) family services and provide premarital, sexual, child development, and family-life education and counseling. Divorce proceedings, child welfare, and juvenile court issues would be transferred from courts of law to the special jurisdiction of a DMF Marriage and Family Arbitration Board. The board would be composed of social scientists and staffed by referee-investigators, social workers, accountants, and attorneys. Rue believes that the DMF, rather than leading to unnecessary restrictions and totalitarianism, would safeguard the happiness of children and parents and enhance the opportunities for education, counseling, recreation, and home management.

2. *Safeguarding parental employment.* The *active parent,* customarily the mother, should be absolutely free to pursue a full-fledged career outside the home. It might well add to a fuller, more creative, and freer life-style— for both the parent and the child. While great strides have been made in achieving equal employment opportunities between the sexes, the parent who is active in child rearing is still in need of special consideration. As long

as public child-care centers are largely Utopian, parents should receive special privileges that would enable them to enjoy both parenthood and the pursuit of a meaningful job. And this should be worked out to apply to both the mother and the father, who may want to share equally in the child-rearing process. Such choice should be open to women and men without penalty to their career and professional advancement. Being able to make an unencumbered choice of this sort would free the mother from conflict, unconscious resentments, and the temptation to substitute the child for career success.

Sociologist Safilios-Rothschild is concerned about this issue. Paraphrased below are some of her main points, which she feels would safeguard such choice and freedom.[34]

a) A new employment policy should be introduced, permitting *a man or a woman* to stay home and take care of a sick child for a number of days per year. A total of ten days after a year's employment and twenty days after two years' should be granted to *each* parent. This policy would make possible the care of sick children at home and relieve society of the expense of equipping child-care centers with medical facilities.

b) While their children are young, fathers and mothers should be able to work shorter hours without losing fringe benefits, seniority, and promotion.

c) Instead of narrowly defining a parent's temporary full-time dedication to an infant as *maternity* leave, it should be redefined as *parental* leave, giving the mother *and/or* father the opportunity to stay home and care for the child without losing their job and its benefits. (A specific recommendation is the Swedish model of providing a paid six-month leave, dividable between mother and father.)

In short, what we need today is a more creative lifestyle for *both* men and women. The old myth, sexistly stereotyped by some misguided female liberationists, that the male's world of work is so "creative" and "adventuresome," should be exploded once and for all. What's so exciting about assembly lines, greasy mechanics' work, selling insurance, or laying bricks? Caring for a child and taking care of a home is a thousand times more creative and entertaining. And if we talk about "human liberation," it may be high time to give the oppressed and job-dulled male a brighter day—a day at home with children, housework, shopping, and gossiping with the neighbors. (We may avoid Momism in the process but possibly introduce a new malaise: Dadism.)

3. *Modifying the educational system.* There is no more tenacious breeding ground for Momism than the American school system. Patricia Cayo Sexton calls it "l'Académie Féminine," observing that in elementary schools between 80 and 90 percent of the teachers are women. When one takes all public schools together, women amount to nearly 70 percent of the total.[35] On the other hand, women make up a small minority of teachers on the college and university level. It seems, then, that the younger the student, the more feminine and female dominated his experience. This serves as a natural strengthening of the Momistic exposure a child may have at home.

What is badly needed, if we want to attain liberation from Mom, is breaking the sex line so that both men and women are free to choose occupations without being limited by traditional bias or senseless routine. An important battle arena is the public school, where the decisive factor will be the hiring of more male teachers.

Another educational reorientation is needed in respect to opening up career preparation for women (in sectors other than elementary and high schools) and enabling them to pursue careers in such hitherto male bastions as law, medicine, engineering, architecture, government, etc. It is usually this type of intellectually inclined woman who, if frustrated in the materialization of high career aspirations, will seek proof of her acumen in the motherhood career, becoming a Mom and trying to live through the child.

As Sexton suggested, "what we must do is masculinize the schools and feminize the power structure of the society—balancing out the sexes so they don't corrode any one spot where they concentrate."[36]

The structure of higher education must therefore be loosened to provide more balanced opportunity for the sexes. In practical terms, this means that vocational and professional schools must put aside any bias they may have against either the male or the female candidate. Also, increased emphasis on evening school is necessary in order to provide education for working adults. Society should not allow financial problems to stand in the way.

Betty Friedan suggested that a national educational program be introduced, similar to the GI bill, for women who seriously desire to continue their education or training. In return, they would be expected to commit themselves and use their acquired skill and knowledge in a profession. This "women's vocational bill" would provide qualified women with funds for tuition, books, laboratory fees, travel and, if necessary, household help.[37]

4. *Providing a rite of passage for adolescents.* Humans are ritualistic creatures; their emotions can be profoundly influenced and patterned by participation in rituals and ceremonies. This psychological power could be used to reduce or counteract the influence of Mom.

Many societies have a ritual indicating the adolescent's passage into adult status and encouraging adult feelings and behavior in the candidate on that occasion. The young men and women henceforth have a clearer idea of where they stand in life. The lack of such an identity-strengthening ritual in American society plays into the hand of Mom ... who, unchallenged, can go on squelching the identity of the child.

It would be overoptimistic to believe that American society will inaugurate an effective rite of passage in the near future. Nevertheless, in the frame of sound social policy thought should be given to this partial solution.

Some societies have built the rite of passage into a prolonged instruction in the ways of adults by having young people spend an entire season in seclusion with selected elders of the tribe. Could we not learn from this example? How would American society benefit from a federal program that gathers youth in post–high school work/instruction projects—not dissimilar to the Civil Conservation Corps (CCC) of two generations ago, when part of the nation's youth were rescued from economic and social limbo by a work program?

The small-scale current equivalents (VISTA, the Peace Corps, the Youth Conservation Corps, etc.) should be expanded and made mandatory for every able-bodied high school graduate for at least one year, with a second year optional. The benefits from such institutions' gathering up all the eighteen-year-olds would solve various problems. It would reduce economic ills (such as unemployment of young people) and provide relatively inexpensive labor for vital public works, such as erosion control, slum clearance, rescue missions, paramedical service, clean-up projects, recycling programs (millions of cans and bottles could be cleaned up and put to good use), firefighting, etc. It most likely would also reduce juvenile delinquency, crime, and the disasters growing out of too-early marriages. Most importantly, in the context of this book, it would provide an opportunity to break with parental domination and take a step toward rehabilitating those who have suffered under Momism.

5. *Full equality for women.* It goes without saying that society's endeavor to grant full equality to women

underlies the success of all the previous points. As stated earlier, only the free are able to make wise and healthy decisions for themselves and for others. Momism will lose most of its venom once women are able to decide on motherhood freely as the project they really want to select from various options. There would hardly be any need to substitute the child for a frustrated career outside the home.

6. *Legal implementation.* It is society's obligation to see to it that the various steps for curbing Momism are legally implemented. In many instances the existing law is adequate but has not been enforced. In such cases, society must move from theoretical to *de facto* standards.

Cultural Images as Focus for Change

It would be nice if human beings would make sense. Sadly, however, their ability to make rational and practical decisions is severely limited. They are up against their own prejudices, irrational habits, fears and conflicts. Many of these irrationalities come to them through their cultural heritage, which continuously infuses them with massive doses of compelling images. We are all victimized by them.

Some of these cultural images stand in the way of modifying Momism and they become, therefore, a focus for change. Probably the most difficult and controversial cultural image that has a bearing on Momism deals with masculinity and femininity. Currently, these two images are the topic of heated arguments between the "liberationists" and the "conservationists". The core of the issue poses the question whether being "truly human" is obfuscated or enhanced by adhering to them. Anyone who can fully answer this question undoubtedly deserves the Nobel Prize for Peace between the Sexes. The issue is extremely complicated and no presumption is made to fully discuss, let alone solve, the problem here. Our discussion will cover only those aspects that appear to be pertinent to Momism.

One of the negative aspects of the cultural image of femininity was the connotation of inferiority, or at least submissiveness, to the male. This has motivated many women to make the resolution, unconsciously as it may have been, to prove themselves in the motherhood career and use their offspring as a success symbol—a pernicious form of Momism. The resultant frustrations paved the way to a variety of Momistic ills, among them substituting the child for deprivations, generating hostility against males in general, creating confusion and uncertainty that paralyzed effective parenthood, and fostering corruption of the power a mother possesses as the sole tutor of the child.

Understandably, a rejecting and resentful mood on the part of progressive women about the traditional status has germinated over the years. But this militancy has not helped to abate Momism. Their overt or latent antagonism against the male world tends to tinge their style of child rearing and often inflicts self-rejective complexes on their sons. It is difficult for the boy to learn a role if his tutor resents it and does not believe in it. This resentment may express itself in the form of domination or rejection of the male child—additional forms of crippling Momism.

Another argument holds that imposing roles on human beings obscures their true personality and natural talents. The argument can be focused on the feminine as well as masculine role. It could be argued that child rearing should not *necessarily* be the function of a mother just because she was able to give birth to the child. Her femininity may not be as pervasive as the traditional image would suggest, and the ability of being a *biological* parent is not necessarily coterminous with being a good *social* parent. The male may be just as qualified to carry out the functions of child care. In other words, rigid role definitions may obscure the truth about who is really the better parent in a given family situation. Momism might be prevented if the emotionally more stable and more truly qualified parent, regardless of gender, would take over the main chores of child rearing.

The Motherhood Myth is largely contingent on the Feminine Mystique. When the unrealities and pitfalls of cultural rhetoric are revealed and the Feminine Myth is corrected, it might have an immediate effect on the Motherhood Myth. When the attractiveness of motherhood is no longer upheld by fanciful cultural images, there might be fewer followers of it. Women might think and do more about development of themselves, their individual resources, and alternative life-styles. Far from being narrowly selfish, such development would give rise to hope for better motherhood. Its greater selectivity would make for happier mothers, children, husbands, and people in general.

Another Momism-furthering aspect of role playing is the limiting emotional expression that the masculine role allows. Would it not be healthier if the boy were allowed to cry as freely as the girl? Certainly, his emotional health is not enhanced by emotional repression.

These problems make it clear that saner arrangements can come only through saner cultural images. Our world has become too small and complex for the narrow-gauge male and female roles. We need men who chuck their repressions and have the courage to show their true emotions. We need women who show their intelligence and initiative. In other words, we need human beings vibrant with their true capacities, who accept their biological differences and meet each other on the basis of true individuality instead of on an artificial stage to play puppets labeled "masculine" and "feminine." As Myron Brenton reminds us, the American male need not feel threatened by the modern female's development of her talents. He should not interpret her new competence and adventurousness as "role reversal." Rather than feel he is "feminized" by becoming less "hard and rough," he should realize that males and females alike are becoming more civilized.[38]

These reconsiderations, however, do not negate an honest complementarity (attraction based on opposite emotional inclinations) between the partners to parenthood. It may serve couples well to pool their emotional resources in such a way as to achieve parental completeness together. Partner X, with aggressive and outgoing inclinations, may feel more comfortable with Partner Y, who is characterized by a more passive, nurturing, and "nest building" instinct than Partner Z, who is as aggressive and effervescent as X. In other words, considerable benefit may accrue to the couple which is well matched by polarities of personality characteristics. *But—* and this is the significant difference today—this polarity does not have to coincide with female-male categories, as in the traditional role images. They are now open human potentials that can be found in persons regardless of biological classification.

The time is coming when masculinity and femininity will be looked upon as *personality traits* and not as *sex differences.*

It cannot be emphasized enough that child rearing benefits from a polarity in the personality makeup of parents. The show of gentleness versus evidence of firmness, the pensive and passive inclination versus the outgoing, aggressive impulse—all are traits well capable of functioning as effective modes of coping and problem solving. A child should witness both approaches, for which at least two individuals are needed. But *which* parent typifies *which* approach no longer depends so much on sex identity as it once did. A set of parents, matched on mutually balanced traits, is of great importance to the emotional and intellectual growth of the child. Only then is he protected against the overbearance of one parent's idiosyncrasies and emotional shortcomings.

The importance of more than a "one party" system for bringing up the child can be illustrated by historical, cross-cultural, and political events. Disastrous results may follow the attempt to deprive the child of witnessing the natural tug-of-war of two parents trying to make the right decisions, solve problems, and get along with each other. In other words, "one party" parenthood cuts the child off from realizing that two people may disagree but still respect one another and cooperate to work out an arrangement that is acceptable to both.

For example, in the 1920s the Soviets tried to restructure the child-rearing process, believing the traditional marriage and mother-father family were bourgeois and outworn institutions that should be replaced. They quickly learned—despite their ideology, which would have gladly supported a different position—that no alternative structure could produce responsible human beings who would grow up and marry and also have children. Another example deals with the traditional German family, whose rigid masculinity dictated "one party" reign by the father. The children who grow up in a minisystem of this sort, relatively free from overt conflict and dissent, will naturally adjust to the larger societal system that also reflects totalitarian rule and dogmatism. Such children never learn the democratic way of life by seeing their mother and father have disagreements, honestly discuss them, try to sort them out, and arrive at intelligent and viable compromises. A "two party" family system (the "parties" can conceivably be extended to more than two), alive with the constant effort to understand each other and come to grips with differences in their likes and dislikes, will prepare the child for a society that also tries to thrash out problems and differences. This highlights the importance of the relationship between the type of family life, the personality makeup of the individual growing up in it, and the ensuing quality of citizenship.

We said earlier that human relationships patterned strictly on gender identity have declined or been modified. It appears that the vicissitudes of history have begun to erode the sharp contours of masculine and feminine role distinctions. While this is true to some extent, it would be chimerical to believe that it has reached any stage of completion. There *have* been modifications of the traditional sex-role behavior, but the social fact is that profound distinctions are still with us and, most likely, will stay with us for a long, long time to come. (Consider the male-entrenched governmental structure, the myriad sex-stereotyped images daily emanating from TV and movie screens, the rigidity with which religious and linguistic rules maintain ancient sex-role differences, *ad infinitum.*) For example, traditional sex roles still prevailed in a 1974 polling: only 29 percent of a national sample of Americans eighteen years old and over (sampled by Daniel Yankelovich, Inc.) disagreed with the idea that "men in our society have certain responsibilities and women have others. This is the way it should be." (Forty-four percent agreed with the statement and 27 percent had no strong opinion.) [39]

All we can do at this time is understand the tenacity with which cultural images enchain society, their extremely slow changeability, and the patience needed to work toward gradual alleviation of their harmful aspects.

We come now to a summary of the four foci for change—the individual (mother, father, son, daughter), the family as a unit, society, and cultural images.

Our understanding should be (1) obvious and not-so-obvious Mom-fostering elements lurk in all four in-

stances; (2) the foci and their Momistic elements overlap considerably, illustrating the systemic nature of the
Momistic malaise; (3) a number of changes in each area
are indicated—changes necessary to combat Momism
(the discussion aimed at stimulating the formulation of
social policy to liberate children, and humankind in general, from Mom); and (4) many of the suggestions and
hopes for change are frankly optimistic, if not Utopian.

The Future of Momism

The future can be divided conveniently into *near* and
distant—the former being well within the life of the
present generations, the latter being beyond the life span
of most contemporaries, referring to phenomena that
won't happen for another fifty to sixty years. Momism,
to put it simply, will increase during the near future but
decrease in the distant future.

The reason for long-term optimism is contained in
many points made during the discussion on foci for
change. Ultimately, we may speculate, social policy will
have a chance to grow on the accumulated evidence about
the Momistic drama. Its effects will be made more visible, and eventually it will outwear the patience and
tolerance of insightful individuals in all walks of life—
parents, teachers, politicians, lawmakers, therapists, behavioral scientists, etc. Yet most changes will be effected
not by *directly* focusing on the Silent Disease and administering therapy but by the side effects of changes in
various sectors of social life, such as the family, work
conditions, and technology.[32]

The biological family of the past will change toward
an *intentional group*, with hereditary engineering playing an important role. Work conditions will change toward full equality for the sexes, reshaping the style of
bringing up children at home or in child-care centers.
Technological innovations will speed the training and

schooling of children, entirely removing the educational function from the parents. The contingencies of the continuous energy crisis and reorientation toward new energy sources may call for a more rational pooling of child rearing to save time, effort, and natural resources, as could be accomplished more effectively by energy-saving care centers than by the isolated individual-family situations. All these changes and innovations will have a profound impact on Momism, mostly in reducing it.

But, obviously, the distant future is open to any speculation, and it makes more sense to examine and speculate about the *near* future of Momism.

The primary reason why Momism is a growing phenomenon in American society, despite the increasing recognition and preventive attention paid to it by middle-class people, lies in an interesting shift in the life-style of the middle class, on one side, and the working class on the other. While the former shows symptoms of attempting to break out from a number of the pathological conditions of urban-industrial life (through part-time farming, the commune experience of the young, outdoor emphasis, ecological concerns, innovative social policy, etc.), the latter shows all the symptoms of trying to emulate the customary middle-class life-style. It is yearning to get where the pathological action is: to adopt—unadulterated—the urban-industrial middle-class life-style, which all too frequently is characterized by Momism. Since many more blue-collar parents will enter the Momism-prone middle-class life-style and fewer white-collar parents will leave it, *more* Momism will occur over the next two generations in American society. It seems to be a historical truism that when a *nouveau* class ascends to a coveted social stratum, its imitation of the newly acquired social status is thorough and indiscriminate. In the case of the working-class ascent to a middle-class life-style, we may thus expect, among other things, its acquisition of the typical Momistic *ménage à trois:* the domineering mother, the passive father, and the stifled son.

Momism for the *nouveau* middle class will be a by-product of the dubious blessings of technocracy, the father's absorption in an away-from-home career, and the mother's feeling of deprivation, blind following of pseudoscientific prescriptions for child rearing, and her use of her child as a success symbol. In short, all the conditions of Momism, as discussed throughout this work, will be renewed and fortified by new waves of eager Moms. They are already in the wings, waiting to enter the stage and continue the drama of the Silent Disease. For two or three generations to come, there will be no end to the production of America's Moms.

The star of the Momistic drama of the *nouveau* middle class will be the young working-class woman (wife of the blue-collar worker), who numbers 40 million —almost 60 percent of all U.S. adult females. Customarily, her life centered around husband, children, and home. Now she is stirring restlessly, indicating dissatisfaction with her traditional life-style and the limited fate of being a housekeeper. She has received the message of liberation, although vaguely and indirectly. To her, liberation means a career or job outside the home, only one or two children, a comfortable home with modern appliances, more "say" in family matters, and an enhanced sense of self-worth. This sense of self-worth is extremely touchy since it is new, not yet tested, and thus demands verification. Reassurance may be obtained through producing a "top" offspring—and again we enter the vicious cycle of Momism: the child becomes the means for Mom's goals, particularly in situations where she has forgone or postponed a rewarding career away from home.

While she is elated to be liberated from yesterday's household drudgery and confinement, she is somewhat confused. In a sense, she finds herself in a position of semiretirement and, like retired individuals in general, looks for new goals and purposes to establish meaning for her life.

Also, the traditional middle-class sensitivity to keeping up with the Joneses has entered her world. Her envy is no longer aimed at the classy neighborhood across town, where wealth and status reside, but at the family next door. Her working-class life-style, neighborhood, income level, and expectations have changed. She now enjoys a new array of products and services, and greater independence. While her geographic residence may not have changed, her outlook and life expectations have, and their expressions have become the criteria of comparison and competition among the neighbors.

She is a delight to America's big business, developing confidence and shopping aggressiveness at a time when the middle-class woman is more and more alienated. She is less critical, more optimistic, and actively involved in improving her family's position. Her remarkable success in doing all this is a constant reinforcement for further pursuing the goods and services of our technocratic society. In the process, she is liberating herself from poverty, inadequate housing, shoddy furniture, mediocre clothes, and poor-quality food.

Most importantly, she is also liberating herself from the remnants of the extended family, in which her parents, grandparents, in-laws, or other relatives may have shared the household with her. With her mother or mother-in-law packing up and leaving, she has lost the live-in baby-sitter and is facing a new child-rearing pattern. She may decide to have fewer children (following "scientific" child-rearing advice) and stay home—at least temporarily—to launch her "motherhood career." These are the conditions that are all too often encountered along the familiar avenues of Momism.

And so the drama of Momism will continue.

This book may, at best, hasten the dawn of a social policy that will interrupt the drama and creatively rewrite the scripts. At worst, it will have little bearing on the drama and will merely provide a master script for following the infamous play more closely.

Epilogue

Children Learn What They Live

If a child lives with criticism,
   He learns to condemn.
If a child lives with hostility,
   He learns to fight.
If a child lives with ridicule,
   He learns to be shy.
If a child lives with shame,
   He learns to feel guilty.
If a child lives with tolerance,
   He learns to be patient.
If a child lives with encouragement,
   He learns confidence.
If a child lives with praise,
   He learns to appreciate.
If a child lives with fairness,
   He learns justice.
If a child lives with security,
   He learns to have faith.
If a child lives with approval,
   He learns to like himself.
If a child lives with acceptance and friendship,
   He learns to find love in the world.

—Dorothy Law Nolte

Reprinted by permission of John Philip Co., 1070 Florence Way, Campbell, Calif. 95008. (Silk-screened wall hangings available from this company.)

Notes

NOTES TO CHAPTER 1

1. Philip Wylie, *Generation of Vipers* (New York: Rinehart, 1942); Philip Roth, *Portnoy's Complaint* (New York: Random House, 1967).

2. Stanton Peele and Archie Brodsky, "Interpersonal Heroin: Love Can Be an Addiction," *Psychology Today* 8 (August 1974): 22–26; and *Love Addiction* (New York: Taplinger, 1975).

3. Sidney C. Howard, *The Silver Cord: A Comedy-Satire in Three Acts* (New York: Scribner's, 1928).

4. Among the earliest to come forth with a more scientific and systematic approach were psychiatrists David M. Levy, *Maternal Overprotection* (New York: Columbia University Press, 1943), and Edward A. Strecker, *Their Mothers' Sons: The Psychiatrist Examines an American Problem* (Philadelphia: Lippincott, 1946). Various aspects of these works will be examined in subsequent chapters.

5. Betty Friedan, *The Feminine Mystique* (New York: Norton, 1963).

6. Noel F. McGinn, "Marriage and Family in Middle-Class Mexico," *Journal of Marriage and the Family* 38 (August 1966): 305–313.

7. George De Vos, "The Relation of Guilt toward Parents to Achievement and Arranged Marriage among the Japanese," *Psychiatry* 23 (August 1960): 287–301.

Notes

NOTES TO CHAPTER 2

1. William J. Goode, *World Revolution and Family Patterns* (New York: The Free Press, 1963), pp. 15–16.

2. *Historical Statistics of the United States: Colonial Times to 1957* (Washington, D.C.: Bureau of the Census with the cooperation of the Social Science Research Council, 1960), p. 14, and *Statistical Abstract of the United States: 1966* (Washington, D.C.: Bureau of the Census, 1966), p. 616.

3. Adapted from *Historical Statistics of the United States: Colonial Times to 1957*, p. 16, and *Historical Statistics of the United States: Continuation to 1962 and Revisions* (Washington, D.C.: Bureau of the Census, 1965), p. 4.

4. David Cooper, *The Death of the Family* (New York: Vintage Books, 1970).

5. Margaret Mead, "What Is Happening to the American Family?" *Journal of Social Casework* 28 (November 1947): 326.

6. Barrington Moore, "Thoughts on the Future of the Family," in Maurice R. Stein et al., eds., *Identity and Anxiety* (Glencoe, Ill.: The Free Press, 1960), pp. 393–394.

7. Betty Rollin, "Motherhood—Who Needs It?" *Look*, September 22, 1970, pp. 15–16.

8. Pitirim Sorokin, *Social and Cultural Dynamics* (New York: Harper, 1937), 4: 776.

9. Alvin Toffler, *Future Shock* (New York: Bantam Books, 1971).

10. Talcott Parsons and Robert F. Bales, *Family, Socialization and Interaction Process* (Chicago: The Free Press of Glencoe, 1955).

11. Max Lerner, *America as a Civilization* (New York: Simon & Schuster, 1957), pp. 694–697.

12. Bernard Farber, *Family: Organization and Interaction* (San Francisco: Chandler Publishing Co., 1964), p. 461.

13. John B. Watson, *Psychological Care of Infant and Child* (New York: Norton, 1928), pp. 81–82.

14. Arnold Gesell and Frances L. Ilg, *Infant and Child in the Culture of Today* (New York: Harper, 1943), p. 57.

15. Haim Ginott's books include *Group Psychotherapy with Children: The Theory and Practice of Play-Therapy* (New York: McGraw-Hill, 1961); *Between Parent and Child: New Solutions to Old Problems* (New York: Macmillan, 1965); *Between Parent and Teenager* (New York: Macmillan,

292

1969) ; *Teacher and Child: A Book for Parents and Teachers* (New York: Macmillan, 1972).

16. Benjamin Spock, *Dr. Spock Talks with Mothers: Growth and Guidance* (Boston: Houghton Mifflin, 1961), p. 107. Another, even better-known work by Dr. Spock is *Baby and Child Care* (London: Head Press, 1955).

17. Helen De Rosis, *Parent Power/Child: A New Tested Method for Parenting Without Guilt* (New York: Bobbs-Merrill, 1974), p. 116.

18. "Young Suicide," *Society* 9 (June 1972): 12.

NOTES TO CHAPTER 3

1. Walter B. Miller, "Lower-Class Culture as a Generating Milieu of Gang Delinquency," *Journal of Social Issues* 14 (1958): 5–19.

2. Betty Rollin, "Motherhood—Who Needs It?" *Look,* September 22, 1970, pp. 15–17.

3. "Attitudes," *Psychology Today* 7 (May 1974): 102.

4. Graham Staines et al., "The Queen Bee Syndrome," *Psychology Today* 7 (January 1974): 55–60.

5. "Roundup of Current Research: Working Women," *Society* 11 (March–April 1974): 6.

6. Howard E. Wylie and Ralph A. Degado, "A Pattern of Mother-Son Relationship Involving the Absence of the Father," *American Journal of Orthopsychiatry* 29 (July 1959): 644–649.

7. Erik H. Erikson, *Childhood and Society* (New York: Norton, 1963): 291.

8. Noel F. McGinn, "Marriage and Family in Middle-Class Mexico," *Journal of Marriage and the Family* 28 (August 1966): 305–313.

9. Evelyn P. Stevens, "Machismo and Marianismo," *Society* 10 (September–October 1973): 57–63.

10. William H. Whyte, Jr., *The Organization Man* (Garden City, N.Y.: Doubleday, 1956).

11. American Management Association, "The Changing Success Ethic," *Research Report* (New York, 1973).

12. Bronislaw Malinowski, *Sex and Repression in Savage Society* (New York: Humanities Press, 1927).

13. George Bach and G. Bremer, "Projective Father Fantasies and Father Typing in Father Separated Children," *Child Development* 24 (March 1946): 63–68; J. W. Santrock,

Notes

"Influence of Onset and Type of Paternal Absence of the First Four Eriksonian Developmental Crises," *Developmental Psychology* 2 (1970): 264–272; Lois H. Stolz, *Father Relations of War Born Children* (Stanford: Stanford University Press, 1954); Pauline S. Sears, "Doll-Play Aggression in Normal Young Children: Influence of Sex, Age, Sibling Status, Father's Absence," *Psychological Monographs* 65 (1951).

14. Henry B. Biller, "Father Absence, Maternal Encouragement, and Sex-Role Development in Kindergarten Age Boys," *Child Development* 40 (June 1969): 539–546, and *Paternal Deprivation* (Lexington, Mass.: Lexingston Books, 1974).

15. David B. Lynn, *Parental and Sex-Role Identification* (Berkeley, Calif.: McCutchan, 1969); Alfred B. Heilbrum, Jr., and Donald K. Fromme, "Parental Identification of Late Adolescents and Level of Adjustment: The Importance of Parent-Model Attributes, Ordinal Position and Sex of Child," *Journal of Genetic Psychology* 107 (September 1965): 49–59.

16. Aaron T. Beck et al., "Childhood Bereavement and Adult Depression," *Archives of General Psychiatry* 9 (September 1963): 295–302; O. W. Hill and J. S. Price, "Childhood Bereavement and Adult Depression," *British Journal of Psychiatry* 113 (July 1967): 743–751.

17. Norman Q. Brill and Edward H. Liston, Jr., "Parental Loss in Adults with Emotional Disorders," *Archives of General Psychiatry* 14 (March 1966): 307–314; G. DaSilva, "The Role of the Father with Chronic Schizophrenic Patients," *Journal of Canadian Psychiatric Association* 8 (1963): 190–203.

18. Lorna M. Anderson, "Personality Characteristics of Parents of Neurotic, Aggressive, and Normal Preadolescent Boys," *Journal of Consulting and Clinical Psychology* 33 (October 1969): 575–581; Armand Alkire, "Social Power and Communication within Families of Disturbed and Nondisturbed Preadolescents," *Journal of Personality and Social Psychology* 13 (December 1969): 335–349; David M. Levy, *Maternal Overprotection* (New York: Columbia University Press, 1943).

19. Robert J. Stoller, *Sex and Gender* (New York: Science House, 1968).

20. Elliot G. Mishler and Nancy E. Waxler, *Interaction in Families* (New York: Wiley, 1968); Anthony J. Schuman, "Power Relations in Emotionally Disturbed and Normal Fam-

ily Triads," *Journal of Abnormal Psychology* 75 (February 1970): 30–37.

21. William D. Altus, "The Broken Home and Factors of Adjustment," *Psychological Report* 4 (September 1958): 447; Joan Aldous, "Children's Perceptions of Adult Roles as Affected by Class, Father Absence and Race," *DARCEE Papers and Reports*, vol. 4, no. 3 (1969).

22. Joan McCord, William McCord, and Emily Thurber, "Some Effects of Parental Absence on Male Children," *Journal of Abnormal and Social Psychology* 64 (May 1962): 361–369.

23. B. Miller, "Effects of Father Absence and Mother's Evaluation of Father on the Socialization of Adolescent Boys," unpublished Ph.D. dissertation, Columbia University, 1961.

24. Alice M. Propper, "The Relationship of Maternal Employment to Adolescent Roles, Activities, and Parental Relationships," *Journal of Marriage and the Family* 34 (August 1972): 417–421. Similar sentiments, on a broader theoretical level, have been expressed in Alice S. Rossi, "Equality between the Sexes," *Daedalus* 93 (Spring 1964): 607–652.

25. Arnold W. Green, "The Middle-Class Male Child and Neurosis," *American Sociological Review* 11 (February 1946): 31–41.

26. Ibid., p. 39 (italics added).

27. R. R. Sears, E. E. Maccoby, and H. Levin, *Patterns of Child-Rearing* (Evanston, Ill.: Row & Peterson, 1957).

28. "Parents Show Off Kids," *Arizona Republic* (Phoenix), March 1, 1970, p. 14.

29. From Sidney Howard's play *The Silver Cord*, as described in Sidney M. Jourard's *Personal Adjustment* (New York: Macmillan, 1967), p. 332.

30. See the discussion and case studies on the emotional stress of children of divorcing parents in J. Louise Despert, *Children of Divorce* (Garden City, N.Y.: Doubleday, 1962). Also see an interesting anthropological theory of why children in Western societies tend to engage in the "inflation of the parentage image," in Abraham Kardiner, *The Individual and His Society* (New York: Columbia University Press, 1939).

31. Roger Burton and John Whiting, "The Absent Father and Cross-Sex Identity," *Merrill-Palmer Quarterly* 7 (April 1961): 85–95.

32. See the references in Hans Sebald, *Adolescence: A Sociological Analysis* (Englewood Cliffs, N.J.: Prentice-Hall, 1968; sec. ed. 1977).

Notes

NOTES TO CHAPTER 4

1. Rosemary R. Ruether, *Religion and Sexism* (New York: Simon and Schuster, 1974).

2. Many behavioral scientists support this assumption, for example, Josef E. Garai and Amram Scheinfeld, "Sex Differences in Mental and Behavioral Traits," *Genetic Psychology Monographs* 77 (May 1968): 169–199; Jerome Kagan, "Acquisition and Significance of Sex Typing and Sex-Role Identity," *Review of Child Development Research* 1 (1964): 137–167; Susan Goldberg and Michael Lewis, "Play Behavior in the Year-old Infant: Early Sex Difference," *Child Development* 40 (March 1969): 21–31. However, a recent study concluded that the *majority* of girls go through a tomboy period during their childhood, which could support the theory that "feminine" behavior is *culturally learned*. See a review of Janet Hyde and Benjamin Rosenberg's research in *Psychology Today* 8 (August 1974): 43.

3. John Money, "Psychosexual Differentiation," in J. Money, ed., *Sex Research* (New York: Holt, Rinehart and Winston, 1965), pp 2–23; J. L. Hampson, "Determinants of Psychosexual Orientation," in F. A. Beach, ed., *Sex and Behavior* (New York: Wiley, 1965), pp. 108–132.

4. Ruth E. Hartley and F. P. Hardesty, "Children's Perception of Sex-Roles in Childhood," *Journal of Genetic Psychology* 105 (1964): 43–51.

5. Lewis M. Terman and Catherine C. Miles, *Sex and Personality* (New York: McGraw-Hill, 1936).

6. Hans Sebald, "Parent-Peer Control and Masculine-Marital Role Perceptions of Adolescent Boys," unpublished Ph.D. dissertation, Ohio State University (1963).

7. "Women's Action Alliance Breaks New Ground in Child Care," *Spokeswoman* 4 (November 1973): 4.

8. Stan Berenstain and Jan Berenstain, *He Bear, She Bear* (New York: Random House, 1974).

9. Ruth E. Hartley, "Children's Concepts of Male and Female Roles," *Merrill-Palmer Quarterly* 6 (January 1960): 83–91.

10. Albert Angrilli, "The Psychosexual Identification of Preschool Boys," *Journal of Genetic Psychology* 97 (December 1960): 329–340; Paul H. Mussen and Eldred Rutherford, "Parent-Child Relationships and Parental Personality in Relation of Young Children's Sex-Role Preferences," *Child Development* 34 (September 1963): 589–607.

11. Irving Bieber et al., *Homosexuality: A Psychoanalytic Study* (New York: Basic Books, 1962); Robert J. Stoller, *Sex and Gender* (New York: Science House, 1968).

12. Donald E. Payne and Paul H. Mussen, "Parent-Child Relations and Father-Identification among Adolescent Boys," *Journal of Abnormal and Social Psychology* 52 (May 1956): 358–362.

13. Myron Brenton, *The American Male* (New York: Coward-McCann, 1966).

14. Robin Lakoff, "Language and Women's Place," *Psychology Today* 6 (August 1972): 16.

15. David B. Lynn, *Parental and Sex-Role Identification* (Berkeley, Calif.: McCutchan, 1969); and *The Father: His Role in Child Development* (Monterey, Calif.: Brooks-Cole, 1974).

16. Saul Feinman, "Approval of Cross-Sex-Role Behavior," *Psychological Reports* 35 (August 1974): 643–648.

17. Ruth E. Hartley, "Sex-Role Pressures and the Socialization o fthe Male Child," *Psychological Reports* 5 (September 1959): 457–468.

18. David B. Lynn, "The Process of Learning Parental and Sex-Role Identification," *Journal of Marriage and the Family* 28 (November 1966): 466–470.

19. Susan W. Gray, "Masculinity and Femininity in Relation to Anxiety and Social Acceptance," *Child Development* 28 (March 1957): 203–214; Lionel M. Lasowick, "On the Nature of Identification," *Journal of Abnormal and Social Psychology* 51 (September 1955): 175–183; Hartley, "Sex-Role Pressures," *op. cit.* Thomas R. DuHamel and Henry B. Biller, "Parental Imitation and Nonimitation in Young Children," *Developmental Psychology* 1 (December 1969): 722.

20. A. G. Barclay and D. Cusumano, "Father-Absence, Cross-Sex Identity, and Field-Dependent Behavior in Male Adolescents," *Child Development* 38 (March 1967): 243–250; James Bieri, "Parental Identification, Acceptance of Authority and within Sex-Differences in Cognitive Behavior," *Journal of Abnormal and Social Psychology* 60 (January 1960): 76–79.

21. L. Carlsmith, "Effect of Early Father-Absence on Scholastic Aptitude," *Harvard Educational Review* 34 (1964): 3–21; Josephine R. Hilgard, Martha F. Newman, and Fern Fisk, "Strength of Adult Ego Following Childhood Bereavement," *American Journal of Orthopsychiatry* 30 (October 1960): 788–798; E. A. Nelson and E. E. Maccoby, "The Rela-

tionship between Social Development and Differential Ability on Scholastic Aptitude Tests," *Merrill-Palmer Quarterly* 12 (1966): 269–289.

22. Two excellent reviews, listing important research references on the innateness of masculine and feminine expressions, are "Male and Female: Differences between Them," *Time*, March 20, 1972, and Derek Wright, "A Sociological Portrait: Sex Differences," *New Society* 18 (October 1971): 825–828. Also see, in defense of innateness, Benjamin Spock, *Decent and Indecent: Our Personal and Political Behavior* (New York: McCall, 1970). Further notable research findings on biological and psychological differences are presented in C. Brindley et al., *Human Behavior*, no. 8 (June 1973).

23. G. Stanley Hall, *Adolescence* (New York: Appleton-Century-Crofts, 1916), vols. 1, 2.

24. Sebald, "Parent-Peer Control."

25. Donald Peterson et al., "Parental Attitudes and Child Adjustment," *Child Development* 30 (March 1959): 119–130.

26. Marvin Siegelman, "Parent Behavior Correlates," *Journal of Consulting and Clinical Psychology* 40 (February 1973): 43–46.

27. E. Mavis Hetherington, "Girls without Fathers," *Psychology Today* 6 (February 1973): 47–52.

28. Lois W. Hoffman, "The Father's Role in the Family and the Child's Peer-Group Adjustment," *Merrill-Palmer Quarterly* 7 (April 1961): 97–105.

29. Mussen and Rutherford, "Parent-Child Relationships."

30. For intriguing thoughts see Thomas D. Boslooper and Marcia Hayes, *The Femininity Game* (New York: Stein and Day, 1973).

NOTES TO CHAPTER 5

1. Benjamin Spock, *Dr. Spock Talks with Mothers: Growth and Guidance* (Boston: Houghton Mifflin, 1961), p. 107.

2. David M. Levy, *Maternal Overprotection* (New York: Columbia University Press, 1943).

3. An interesting treatment of this topic is anthropologist Anthony Storr's *Human Aggression* (New York: Bantam Books, 1970).

4. Interesting and perceptive discussions on "vicarious

living" and related symptoms are offered by Andras Angyal, M.D., "Evasion of Growth," *American Journal of Psychiatry* 118 (November 1953): 358–361; Erich Fromm, *Escape from Freedom* (New York: Rinehart, 1941); and Eric Hoffer, *The True Believer* (New York: Mentor Books, 1951).

5. Lester David, "Our Son Was Different," in Evelyn N. Bachelor et al., eds., *Teen Conflicts: Readings in Family Life and Sex Education* (Berkeley, Calif.: Diablo Press, 1968), 56–73.

6. Levy, *Maternal Overprotection* p. 222.

7. Arnold W. Green, "The Middle-Class Male Child and Neurosis," *American Sociological Review* 11 (February 1946): 31–41.

8. "Mom Is the Villain," *Time*, May 21, 1965, p. 83.

9. "Rehabilitation: Return from the Womb," *Time*, May 17, 1963, p. 93.

10. Based on a report in J. Louise Despert, M.D., *Children of Divorce* (Garden City, N.Y.: Doubleday, 1962), 160–166.

11. Pseudonyms are used in this case history to protect the identity of the individuals, who came to the personal attention of this writer.

12. Martha Lear, *The Child-Worshipers* (New York: Crown Publishers, 1963).

NOTES TO CHAPTER 6

1. This expression is borrowed from Eric Hoffer, *The True Believer* (New York: Mentor Books, 1951), who has used the concept in a broader sociological-historical manner, not necessarily in the specific context of Momism.

2. Abraham H. Maslow, *Motivation and Personality* (New York: Harper, 1954).

3. *The Greatest Is Love, an Illustrated Edition of the New Testament* (South Holland, Ill.: World Home Bible League, 1971), p. c.

4. Edward A. Strecker, *Their Mothers' Sons* (Philadelphia: Lippincott, 1951), p. 117.

5. Hoffer, *The True Believer*, p. 22.

6. Carl R. Rogers, *On Becoming a Person* (Boston: Houghton Mifflin, 1961), pp. 163–198.

7. "Maman's Boy," *Time*, November 19, 1965, pp. 46–47.

8. Patricia Cayo Sexton, *The Feminized Male* (New York: Random House, 1969), p. 4.

9. Robert J. Stoller, *Sex and Gender* (New York: Science House, 1968).

10. "Girlish Boys," *Time*, November 26, 1973, pp. 133–134.

11. Richard Green, M.D., *Sexual Identity Conflict in Children and Adults* (New York: Basic Books, 1974), p. 212.

12. Two typical studies are Nora Sayre, "Mothers of Addiction," *New Statesman*, May 7, 1965, p. 716, and John Schwartzman, "The Addict, Abstinence and the Family," *American Journal of Psychiatry* 132 (February 1975): 154–157.

13. David Laskowitz, "The Adolescent Drug Addict: An Adlerian View," *Journal of Individual Psychology* 17 (May 1961): 68–79.

14. Interview in "American Teens Lead World in Drug Abuse," *Arizona Republic*, November 26, 1969, p. 14.

15. Paul M. Pantleo and George W. Kelling, "Quantifiable Aspects of Human Figure Drawings by Male Narcotics Addicts: Replications and Extensions," *Perceptual and Motor Skills* 34 (June 1972): 791–798.

16. Stanley Einstein, "The Future Time Perspective of the Adolescent Narcotic Addict," in Ernest Harms, ed., *Drug Addiction in Youth* (New York: Pergamon Press, 1965), p. 96.

17. Strecker, *Their Mothers' Sons*, p. 122.

18. Hans Sebald, "The Pursuit of 'Instantness' in Technocratic Society and Youth's Psychedelic Drug Use," *Adolescence* 7 (Fall 1972): 343–350.

19. Betty Friedan, *The Feminine Mystique* (New York: Dell, 1971), pp. 271–272.

20. Bruno Bettelheim, "Student Revolt, the Hard Core," in *Vital Speeches of the Day* (1968–1969), 35: 406.

21. Strecker, *Their Mothers' Sons*, p. 6.

22. David M. Levy *Maternal Overprotection* (New York: Columbia University Press, 1943).

23. Hervey Checkley, *The Mask of Sanity* (St. Louis: Mosby, 1964).

24. Robert Knight, "The Psychoanalytic Treatment in a Sanatorium of Chronic Addiction to Alcohol," *Journal of the American Medical Association* 3 (1938): 1443–1448.

25. Arthur P. Noyes and Lawrence C. Kolb, *Modern Clinical Psychiatry* (Philadelphia: Saunders, 1963).

26. Eugene M. Fodor, "Moral Development and Parent Behavior Antecedents in Adolescent Psychopaths," *Journal of General Psychology* 122 (March 1973): 37–43.

27. Harold M. Skeels, "Adult Status of Children with Contrasting Early Life Experiences," *Monographs of the Society for Research in Child Development* 31, no. 105 (1966): 1–65.
28. Joseph H. Golner, "Learning Problems and Identity Problems of Latency-Age Boys," *Social Casework* 45 (November 1964): 534–539.
29. Garven Hudgins, "Cheating: Grave Pressure," AP Education Service (February 1969).
30. Karen Horney, *Neurosis and Human Growth* (New York: Norton, 1950).
31. Strecker, *Their Mothers' Sons*, p. 111.
32. Ibid., pp. 111–112.
33. See Martin Symonds, "Parents of Schizophrenic Children," *Journal of the American Academy of Psychoanalysis* 1 (1973): 171–178; Elliot G. Mishler and Nancy E. Waxler, "Family Processes and Schizophrenia," *Psychiatry and Social Science Bookshelf* 1 (September 15, 1966): 9; David Marcus, M.D., et al., "A Clinical Approach to the Understanding of Normal and Pathologic Adolescence," *Archives of General Psychiatry* 15 (December 1966): 569–576; James C. Coleman, *Abnormal Behavior and Modern Life* (Chicago: Scott, Foresman, 1964), pp. 255, 293, 296, 367; and Theodore Lidz, "Interview," in Robert Boyers and Robert Orrill, eds., *R. D. Laing and Anti-Psychiatry* (New York: Harper & Row, 1971).
34. Marcus et al., "A Clinical Approach," p. 575. Theodore Lidz et al., *Schizophrenia and the Family* (New York: International Universities Press, 1965).
35. Herbert Hendin, *Suicide and Scandinavia* (New York: Grune and Stratton, 1964).
36. A. A. Stone, "A Syndrome of Serious Suicidal Interest," *Archives of Genetic Psychiatry* 3 (1960): 331–339.
37. AP Report, New Orleans, September 4, 1965.

Notes to Chapter 7

1. Margaret Mead, "What Is Happening to the American Family?" *Journal of Social Casework* 28 (November 1947): 323–330.
2. William Ryan, in his probing *Blaming the Victim* (New York: Random House, 1971), cautions of this tendency. While not applying it to Momism directly, he talks about "blaming the victims" as they are involved in poverty, crime, unemployment, illegitimacy, and other acute social problems.

Notes

3. Bruno Bettelheim, "The Problem of Generations," *Daedalus* 91 (Winter 1962): 84.

4. Gary Mitchell et al., "Lesson from a Primate: Males Can Raise Babies," *Psychology Today* 7 (April 1974): 63–68.

5. AP Report, Enfield, Conn., May 10, 1974.

6. See especially the works of Abraham H. Maslow, *Motivation and Personality* (New York: Harper, 1954), Carl R. Rogers, *On Becoming a Person* (Boston: Houghton Mifflin, 1961), and Jerome Kagan, *Understanding Children* (New York: Harcourt Brace Jovanovich, 1971).

7. Robert W. Resnick, "Chicken Soup Is Poison," *Voices: The Art and Science of Psychotherapy* 6 (Fall 1970): 75–78.

8. Ibid., p. 76. The reader who would like to explore Gestalt therapy more fully is advised to consult Frederick S. Perls, Ralph F. Hefferline, and Paul Goodman, *Gestalt Therapy: Excitement and Growth in the Human Personality* (New York: Julian Press, 1958).

9. Edward A. Strecker, *Their Mothers' Sons* (Philadelphia: Lippincott, 1951), pp. 126–127.

10. William Glasser, *Reality Therapy* (New York: Harper & Row, 1965).

11. Theodore Lidz, "Interview," in Robert Boyers and Robert Orrill, eds., *R. D. Laing and Anti-Psychiatry* (New York: Harper & Row, 1971), p. 172. The reader who is interested in following up the idea of family-centered therapy is directed to one of the most prominent works in that area, Virginia Satir's *Conjoint Family Therapy* (Palo Alto, Calif.: Science & Behavior Books, 1964).

12. Patricia Cayo Sexton, *The Feminized Male* (New York: Random House, 1969), pp. 167–179.

13. See Constantina Safilios-Rothschild, *Women and Social Policy* (Englewood Cliffs, N.J.: Prentice-Hall, 1974), pp. 18–20; Alice S. Rossi, "Equality between the Sexes: An Immodest Proposal," *Daedalus* 93 (Spring 1964): 607–652. Margaret O'Brien Steinfels, *Who's Minding the Children? The History and Politics of Day Care in America* (New York: Simon & Schuster, 1973).

14. Marian R. Yarrow et al., "Childbearing in Families of Working and Nonworking Women," *Sociometry* 25 (June 1962): 122–140.

15. Lois M. Stolz, "Effects of Maternal Employment on

Children: Evidence from Research," *Child Development* 31 (1960) : 749–782.
16. Evaluation and summary of these studies are presented in F. Ivan Nye and Lois W. Hoffman, *The Employed Mother in America* (Chicago: Rand McNally, 1963), pp. 384–385.
17. Safilios-Rothschild, *Women and Social Policy*, p. 18.
18. Rossi, "Equality between the Sexes," pp. 631–632.
19. See a balanced and highly informed discussion of the commune situation by Sonya Rudikoff: "O Pioneers! Reflections on the Whole Earth People," *Commentary* 54 (July 1972) : 62–74.
20. Bernice T. Eiduson, Jerome Cohen, and Jeannette Alexander, "Alternatives in Child Rearing in the 1970s," *American Journal of Orthopsychiatry* 43 (October 1973) : 720–729.
21. Alvin Toffler, *Future Shock* (New York: Random House, 1971).
22. B. F. Skinner, *Walden Two* (New York: Macmillan, 1962).
23. Robert Rimmer, *The Harrad Experiment* (New York: Bantam Books, 1967).
24. George Orwell, *1984* (New York: New American Library, 1949).
25. Barrington Moore, "Thoughts on the Future of the Family," in Maurice R. Stein et al., eds., *Identity and Anxiety* (Glencoe, Ill.: The Free Press, 1960), pp. 393–394.
26. Joseph Goldstein, Anna Freud, and Albert J. Solnit, *Beyond the Best Interests of the Child* (New York: The Free Press, 1974). Other champions for the rights of the child are John Holt, *Escape from Childhood* (New York: Ballantine, 1975), and Richard Farson, *Birthrights* (New York: Macmillan, 1974).
27. H. Foster and D. J. Freed, "Child Custody," *New York University Law Review*, vol. 423 (1964).
28. "Children's liberation," along with the liberation of other oppressed groups, is a more or less international trend. The United States does not rank first in the vanguard of liberation-minded nations. Scandinavian countries and West Germany, for example, have followed "sensitive" laws for many years. West Germany further upgraded her custody laws in 1974 by radically limiting the power of the biological par-

Notes

ents. Accordingly, parents now must "consider the desire and the needs of children capable of insight, and discuss with them parental measures." The goal is mutual agreement. In cases of significant disagreement (as in educational or vocational questions), official counsel must be consulted. Also, in divorce cases the preference of the child for one or the other parent will now be taken into consideration. *Kulturbrief* 3 (December 1973): 25.

29. "Do Children Need 'Sex Roles'?" *Newsweek,* June 10, 1974, pp. 79–80.

30. Roger W. McIntire, "Parenthood Training or Mandatory Birth Control: Take Your Choice," *Psychology Today* 7 (October 1973): 34–143.

31. *Los Angeles Times* Service, June 24, 1964, and AP Report, Atlantic City, N.J., February 13, 1967.

32. See details on these aspects in Jessie Bernard, *The Future of Motherhood* (New York: Dial Press, 1974; Kingsley Davis, "Population Policy: Will Current Programs Succeed?" *Science* 158 (November 10, 1967): 738; "Meetings: Behavioral Sciences and Family Planning," *Science* 158 (November 3, 1967): 677–682.

33. Vincent M. Rue, "A U.S. Department of Marriage and the Family," *Journal of Marriage and the Family* 35 (November 1973): 689–698.

34. Safilios-Rothschild, *Women and Social Policy*, pp. 20–23.

35. Sexton, *The Feminized Male*, p. 29.

36. Ibid., p. 135.

37. Betty Friedan, *The Feminine Mystique* (New York: Dell, 1963), p. 356.

38. Myron Brenton, *The American Male* (New York: Coward-McCann, 1966); Warren Farrell, *The Liberated Man: Beyond Masculinity* (New York: Random House, 1974); Joseph Pleck and Jack Sawyer, *Men and Masculinity* (Englewood Cliffs, N.J.: Prentice-Hall, 1974); Jack Nichols, *Men's Liberation: A New Definition of Masculinity* (New York: Penguin Books, 1975).

39. Institute of Life Insurance, *Attitudes toward Selected Issues* (New York, 1974), p. 6.

Name Index

Aldous, Joan, 295
Alexander, Jeannette, 303
Alkire, Armand, 294
Altus, William D., 295
Anderson, Lorna M., 294
Angrilli, Albert, 296
Angyal, Andras, 299
Ardrey, Robert, 169

Bach, George, 293
Bachelor, Evelyn N., 299
Bales, Robert F., 292
Barclay, A. G., 297
Beach, F. A., 296
Beck, Aaron T., 294
Berenstain, Jan, 95, 296
Berenstain, Stan, 95, 296
Bernard, Jessie, 304
Bettelheim, Bruno, 198, 247, 300, 302
Bieber, Irving, 297
Bieri, James, 297
Biller, Henry B., 294, 297
Boslooper, Thomas D., 298

Boyers, Robert, 300, 302
Bremer, G., 293
Brenton, Myron, 99, 280, 281, 297, 304
Brill, Norman Q., 294
Brindley, C., 298
Brodsky, Archie, 291
Burton, Roger, 295

Carlsmith, L., 297
Checkley, Hervey, 300
Cohen, Jerome, 303
Cohen, Sidney, 191
Coleman, James C., 301
Cooper, David, 23, 292
Cusumano, D., 297

DaSilva, G., 294
David, Lester, 299
Davis, Kingsley, 273, 304
Degado, Ralph A., 293
De Rosis, Helen, 37, 293
Despert, J. Louise, 295, 299
De Vos, George, 291

DuHamel, Thomas R., 297

Eiduson, Bernice T., 303
Einstein, Stanley, 300
Erikson, Erik H., 50, 293

Farber, Bernard, 292
Farrell, Warren, 304
Farson, Richard, 303
Feinman, Saul, 297
Fisk, Fern, 297
Fodor, Eugene M., 210, 300
Foster, H., 267, 303
Freed, D. J., 267, 303
Freud, Anna, 266, 267, 303
Friedan, Betty, x, 8, 9, 30,
    120, 276, 290, 300, 304
Fromm, Erich, 176, 299
Fromme, Donald K., 294

Garai, Josef E., 296
Gesell, Arnold, 36, 292
Ginott, Haim, 37, 292
Glass, H. Bentley, 272
Glasser, William, 256, 302
Goldberg, Susan, 296
Goldstein, Joseph, 266, 267,
    303
Golner, Joseph H., 301
Goode, William J., 20, 292
Goodman, Paul, 302
Gray, Susan W., 297
Green, Arnold W., 65, 66, 67,
    69, 71, 115, 145, 295
    299
Green, Richard, 188, 300

Hall, G. Stanley, 109, 298
Hampson, J. L., 296
Hardesty, F. P., 296

Harms, Ernest, 300
Hartley, Ruth E., 296, 297
Hayes, Marcia, 298
Hefferline, Ralph F., 302
Heilbrum, Alfred B., Jr., 294
Hendin, Herbert, 228, 229,
    301
Hetherington, E. Mavis, 298
Hilgard, Josephine R., 297
Hill, O. W., 294
Hoffer, Eric, 178, 299
Hoffman, Lois W., 298, 303
Holt, John, 303
Horney, Karen, 222, 301
Howard, Sidney C., 8, 9, 74,
    291, 295
Hudgins, Garven, 301
Hyde, Janet, 296

Ilg, Frances L., 292

Jourard, Sidney M., 295

Kagan, Jerome, 296, 302
Kardiner, Abraham, 295
Kelling, George W., 300
Knight, Robert, 210, 300
Kolb, Lawrence C., 300

Lakoff, Robin, 297
Laskowitz, David, 190, 300
Lasowick, Lionel M., 297
Lear, Martha, 166, 299
LeMasters, E. E., 19
Lerner, Max, 32, 292
Levin, H., 295
Levy, David M., 130, 206,
    290, 294, 298, 299, 300
Lewis, Michael, 296
Lidz, Theodore, 259, 301, 302

Liston, Edward H., Jr., 294
Lynn, David B., 294, 297

McCord, Joan, 295
McCord, William, 295
McGinn, Noel F., 291, 293
McIntire, Roger W., 272, 304
Maccoby, E. E., 295, 297
Malinowski, Bronislaw, 56, 293
Marcus, David, 301
Maslow, Abraham H., 171, 299, 302
Mead, Margaret, 23, 246, 292, 301
Miles, Catherine C., 94, 296
Miller, B., 295
Miller, Walter B., 43, 293
Mishler, Elliot G., 294, 301
Mitchell, Gary, 302
Money, John, 296
Moore, Barrington, 24, 265, 266, 292, 303
Mussen, Paul H., 296, 297, 298

Nelson, E. A., 297
Newman, Martha F., 297
Nichols, Jack, 304
Nolte, Dorothy Law, 289
Noyes, Arthur P., 300
Nye, F. Ivan, 303

Orrill, Robert, 301, 302
Orwell, George, 265, 303

Pantleo, Paul M., 300
Parsons, Talcott, 31, 292
Payne, Donald E., 297
Peele, Stanton, 291
Perls, Frederick S., 255, 302

Peterson, Donald, 298
Pleck, Joseph, 304
Price, J. S., 294
Propper, Alice M., 295

Resnick, Robert W., 254, 302
Rimmer, Robert, 265, 303
Rogers, Carl R., 178, 299, 302
Rollin, Betty, 29, 47, 123, 292, 293
Rosenberg, Benjamin, 296
Rossi, Alice S., 1, 295, 302, 303
Roth, Philip, 2, 291
Rudikoff, Sonya, 303
Rue, Vincent M., 273, 304
Ruether, Rosemary R., 296
Rutherford, Eldred, 296, 298
Ryan, William, 301

Safilios-Rothschild, Constantina, 274, 302, 303, 304
Santrock, J. W., 293
Satir, Virginia, 302
Sawyer, Jack, 304
Sayre, Nora, 300
Scheinfeld, Amram, 296
Schuman, Anthony J., 294
Schwartzman, John, 189, 300
Sears, Pauline S., 294
Sears, R. R., 295
Sebald, Hans, 295, 296, 298, 300
Sexton, Patricia Cayo, 182, 260, 275, 276, 299, 302, 304
Siegelman, Marvin, 298
Skeels, Harold M., 215, 301
Skinner, B. F., 265, 303

Solnit, Albert J., 266, 267, 303
Sorokin, Pitirim, 31, 292
Spock, Benjamin, 36, 37, 88, 129, 293, 298
Staines, Graham, 293
Stein, Maurice R., 292, 303
Steinfels, Margaret O'Brien, 302
Stevens, Evelyn P., 293
Stoller, Robert J., 186, 294, 297, 300
Stolz, Lois M., 294, 302
Stone, A. A., 301
Storr, Anthony, 298
Strecker, Edward A., 41, 176, 177, 194, 206, 226, 255, 291, 299, 300, 301, 302

Symonds, Martin, 301

Terman, Lewis M., 94, 296
Thurber, Emily, 295
Toffler, Alvin, 31, 265, 292, 303

Watson, John B., 36, 292
Waxler, Nancy E., 294, 301
Whiting, John, 295
Whyte, William H., Jr., 54, 293
Wiesner, Jerome B., 239
Wright, Derek, 298
Wylie, Howard E., 293
Wylie, Philip, 2, 8, 9, 291

Yarrow, Marian R., 302

Subject Index

Acting out, 135
Addiction, 188–95
  human-figure-drawing
    test and, 191–92
  mother affinity and,
    190–95
  mother-supported, 135,
    147, 189
  mother's dependency
    neurosis as, 5
  prostitution and, 192
  psychopathy and, 209–10
  rehabilitation, 193
Adolescence
  discovery of Momism
    during, 70
  etiology in modern
    family, 24
  father absence during,
    60–61
  rite of passage and,
    81–82, 276–77
Adolescent psychopath, 210
  case study of Paul, 210–14
Aggression, 132–33, 152

Alcoholism, 194–95, 210
  case of Walter, 256
  psychopathic, 210
Anomie, 86, 95
Anxiety. *See* Neurotic anxiety
Armed forces, 236
Authoritarian personality,
  153, 224, 225
Authoritarianism
  child rearing and, 66–71,
    113–15
  boy's neurosis and, 66–71
  Dadism and, 115
Authority
  in black family, 61
  rational vs. irrational, 24

Bar mitzvah, 79
Beauty pageants and
  motherhood, 73–74
Black family, 61
Blaming the victim, 246–47

Charismatic leader, 171

Child. *See also* Child rearing
  as "conspicuous consump-
    tion," 38–40
  custody, 267–68
  discipline, 55–57
  divorce of parents and, 44
  family's personality
    function and, 33–34
  father-child interactions,
    53–62
  isolated, 215, 216, 226
  learning self-worth, 252
  "license," 272–73
  only, 44, 62–63
  perception of parents,
    76–77
  as "project," 30, 35–38
  "tax," 273
Child-care centers, 261–63,
    270, 274
Child rearing. *See also*
    Gender identity;
    Motherhood;
    Parenthood
  college education and,
    63–65
  father remoteness and,
    53–62
  in German family, 282
  intellectualized, 44,
    63–71
  masculinity vs.
    femininity, 87–114
  Mom's neurosis and, 50,
    215
  Momistic style of, 34–40
  mother-dominated, 55
  in nuclear family, 22–28
  parental interaction and,
    281–82

  psychological vs.
    biological parenthood,
    265–68
  and punishment, 129, 151
  Soviet experiment in, 282
  success motivation and,
    5, 30, 35, 39–40, 44, 51,
    64, 68, 72–74, 166, 286
  woman's liberation and,
    28–31
College education and
    motherhood, 63
College students, 196–98,
    207–8
Community standards and
    Momism, 72–77
Conditional love technique,
    9–10, 12, 50, 69–71,
    118, 120, 128–29, 148,
    151, 155, 156, 166,
    173, 188, 221, 230, 243
Consequence of Momism,
    11–13, 169–237
  AWOL servicemen, 236
  authoritarian personality,
    153, 224, 225
  boy-girl differences, 227
  combinations of, 235–36
  dependency syndrome,
    5–7, 11
  diagnosis of, 12–13, 70,
    237, 239
  difference between Mom
    and mother, 236–37
  duration of, 236
  escape from freedom,
    172, 176
  fright of solitude, 172–73
  inferiority complex, 218
  lack of autonomy, 5–7,

172–78, 220, 227
lack of self-actualization,
171–72, 178
lacking "authentic"
personality, 178–79
limitations of, 237
"love" needs of boy,
173–74, 218, 222
marital problems, 155–56
mental problems, 170,
204–28
the Momistic character,
233
most typical, 235
other-directedness, 5–7,
179
positive functions, 233
psychosomatic, 148–49
role of pimp, 192
silent or Silent Disease,
170, 186, 193, 194, 231–
37, 242 (*see also* Silent
Majority)
twilight zone between
morality and legality,
233
by types of Moms,
224–26
Corporal punishment, 35, 69,
71, 129
Cultural images
encouraging Momism,
279–80
Feminine Mystique, 8,
120, 121, 280
masculinity and
femininity, 278–84
Motherhood Myth, 8–9,
29–30, 242, 280
Cure of Momism. *See* Therapy

Custody, of children, 58,
267–68

Dadism, 86, 114–22, 275
compared to Momism,
121–22
girls' adjustment to boys,
117
Dating, 117, 140, 157–58, 166
Daughter, Mom-avoiding
script, 258–59
Defense mechanisms, 221
Delinquency, 102, 231–32, 277
psychopathic, 210
Depression, of boys, 59
Divorce
children and, 57–58,
75–77
effects on daughters,
116–17
effects on sons, 58–62
search for identity and,
33
Draftees, 226, 234
Drug problems, 170, 188–204,
214. *See also*
Addiction; Alcoholism;
Psychedelic drugs
the case of Francis, 199–
204
overpermissive mother
and, 191

Education
cheating in high school,
221
future of, 285
for parenthood, 270–73
the philosophy of
instantness and, 195–98

Education (*continued*)
  psychedelia and, 196–98
  sex, 261
  sex biases in, 111, 275
  special, 216
Ego, 130, 141, 150, 206
  boundaries, 118, 217
  crisis in Western World,
    32
  strength of mother, 62
Emotional symbiosis, 134, 136
Equalitarianism, 248

Familism, 26
Family
  communal or counter-
    cultural alternatives,
    263–65
  historical changes, 20–40
  Kibbutz system, 268
  laws, 267
  loss of functions, 31
  nuclear, 22–28, 246, 287
  personality function,
    31–34
  psychological vs.
    biological parenthood,
    265–68, 284
  schizogenic, 227
  traditional, 20–22, 25
Family Institute of Chicago,
    189
Father
  boy's masculinity and,
    97–98, 102, 107–14
  changing role of, 245–51
  –child studies, 112
  –daughter relationship,
    86, 113, 114–22
  femininity of daughter

and, 113–22
son's homosexuality and,
    138, 184–85
masculinity of, 60, 138
Mom-resistant script for,
    249–51
as negative model to girl,
    257–58
organization man, 53–55,
    67
parental function,
    246–51
primate experiment,
    248–49
remote from child-
    rearing, 13–14, 43, 53–
    62, 138, 184–85
weak, 138–40, 159,
    187, 217
Father-absence
  addiction of son and, 192
  effects on daughters,
    116–17
  effects on sons, 58–62,
    97–108, 111, 246
  middle vs. lower class, 60
  transsexualism and, 187
Female dominance, 111
Feminine Mystique, 8, 120,
    121, 280
Femininity
  characteristics of girls,
    58, 115
  Dadism and girls, 114–21
  daughter of Mom and,
    15, 117
Femininity game, 118–19

Gender identity
  boys, 152

girls, 114–22
    measurement of, 93–95
Gender Identity Research
    Treatment Program,
    188
Gender roles, 278–84. *See also*
    Gender identity; Sex
    roles
    changes of, 258
Gestalt therapy, 110, 255
Guilt leverage, 147–49

Hedonism, 141–42
Homosexuality, 170, 183–86,
    188, 192, 218
    case study of Jed, 138–41
Human liberation, 275
Hypochondriasis, maternal,
    132

Id, 32, 141–42
Identification
    mother-daughter, 112
    process, 66
Identity
    American search for, 32–
        33
    divorce and, 33
    female, 118
    Mom's search for, 34–35,
        40, 47
    rite of passage, 77–82
    sex identification, 89–91,
        93–114
Identity foreclosure, 117–19
    consequences of, 219
    case study of Tony, 219
Immaturity, 5–7, 144, 226, 232
Infantilization, 104, 131, 135,
    169, 173, 177, 183, 190,

196, 205–8
Initiation rite, 78
Instantness, philosophy of,
    170, 195–98

Job absenteeism, 143

Kindergarten, 96, 111

Love myth, 118
Lower class
    boy's rite of passage, 81
    child rearing, 65–71
    definition, 43
    family, 60–63, 64, 75
    father absence, 60–61
    parenthood, 72, 74
Lower East Side Narcotic
    Center, New York,
    189, 193

Machismo, 53
Male supremacy, 115
Marital problems, 144
Masculinity
    boy's identification
        process, 108–11
    characteristics of boys,
        58
    divorce of father and
        boy's, 59
    mother's femininity and
        boy's, 97–98
    mother's role conflicts
        and, 98
    rite of passage, 80
    role of, 85–114
Matricentric family, 61
Mental problems, 170, 204–
    28. *See also* Neurosis;

Mental problems (*continued*)
Psychopathy;
Schizophrenia
Middle class
and Momism, 41–84
definition, 41–43
father's organization-
man syndrome, 53–55
limitations of Momism,
51
Mom
"ailing," 147
child-worshiping, 165–67
comparison of types,
141–42, 167, 225–26
complementary mate
selection, 59, 139–40,
152, 154–55, 159, 162,
211, 217
degrading masculinity,
217, 219
domineering, 59, 117,
150–59, 217, 225, 235
case study of Irene,
156–59
case study of Peter,
153–56, 235
etiology of, 34, 103, 112,
124–27, 139, 257–58
feelings of relative
deprivation, 50
hostile, 151–52, 217, 219
and her "love," 10, 125,
126, 142, 143, 145–46,
193, 203–4, 205, 206,
227
"martyr," 146–50, 159,
207, 225
overindulgent, 141–46,
188, 210–11

overpermissiveness, 144–
46
overprotective, 59, 130–
41, 188, 190, 210, 215,
225, 254
possessive, 188
pseudointellectual, 162–65
"star," 159–62
types and consequences,
224–26
as victim of system,
246–47
Momism. *See also*
Consequence of
Momism; Mom;
Motherhood
affecting boys, 3, 14–15,
85–122
childhood symptoms, 6–7
Christianity and, 173–75
core feature, 127
definition, 1–7, 127
difference between Mom
and mother, 6, 50
father's role, 13–14
femininity of daughter
and, 15, 112
future of, 269, 284–88
historical development,
19–40
increasing, 285–86
Japanese, 11
Mexican, 11, 51–53
mother-daughter case,
156–59
neurosis of, 4–7
neurosis of boy and,
65–71
pressure to cheat in
school, 221

role of father, 53–62
shift from middle to
working class, 285–87
suppression of
masculinity, 110–11
systemic nature of,
246–47, 269–70
techniques of, 9–11, 30,
35–40 (*see also*
Conditional love)
technocracy and, 286–87
types and techniques,
123–68
upper class, 51
urban-industrial
conditions and, 16–17,
25, 285
Monomania, 222
Mother. *See also* Mom;
Motherhood
divorced, 44, 75–77
employment, 261–63
immaturity, 55–56
femininity of, 97
Mom-free script, 242–45
need for love, 55–56
neurotic, 4–7
neurotic conflict, 68, 98
relationship with
daughter, 15, 112
relationship with son,
14–15, 34, 85–122
schizogenic, 226
traditional role, 20–22
Motherhood
as compensation, 49–50
"career," 68, 72, 86
cultural taboo against
criticism, 7, 193
intellectualized, 63–71

lower class and father
absence, 60–63
middle class and father
absence, 60–61
success syndrome and, 5,
30, 35, 39–40, 44, 51, 64
68, 72–74, 166, 286
traditional, 63
Motherhood myth, 8–9,
29–30, 242, 280

Narcissistic attitudes, 206,
235, 255, 256
National Institute of Mental
Health, 191, 228
Neighbors, sensitivity to,
71–77
Neurosis
adolescent and adult,
70–71
authoritarianism and,
115
conditional love and, 145–
46
Dadism and, 120
defense mechanisms, 221
definition, 4
difference between
psychopathy and, 209
father-absent boys and,
59
forms of, 225
middle-class boy, 65–71
perpetuation of, 156
psychosomatic extension,
220
in sequence, 4–7
"situation" vs.
"character" neurosis,
220

Neurotic
anxiety, 173, 219–26
conflicts, 223, 224
dependency, 5, 187, 205–7
mother-child interaction,
4–7, 190
need for love and
affection, 10, 12, 69–
71, 222
power striving, 222
submissiveness, 223
withdrawal, 223

Oedipus complex, 57
Oswald, Lee Harvey, 183
Overmasculinity, 111

Parasitism, Momistic, 134
Parent. *See* Father; Mother;
Motherhood
Parental employment, 273–75
Parenthood
lower-class, 65
proficiency, 64–65
psychological vs.
biological, 265–68, 284
Peers, role of, 185, 187, 261
Prevention of Momism, 239–
88
birth control, 272–73
"child license," 272
"child tax," 273
curbing unfit and
unwanted parenthood,
270–73
daughter script, 257–59
"Department of Marriage
and the Family," 273
family interaction, 259–
69, 271
family therapy, 259

father script, 245–51,
274–75
mother script, 242–45
rite of passage for
adolescents, 276–77
son's script, 251–57
summary points, 283–84
Projection, 158
Protestant ethic, 39, 42
Pseudostupidity, 214–16
case study of Carl, 216
Psychedelic drugs, 195–204
the case of Francis,
199–204
and educational
philosophy, 196–98
and philosophy of
instantness, 195–98
Psychopathy, 143, 208–14
adolescent, 210
case of Paul, 210–14
etiology of, 210
hedonism, 211
Psychosis and father-absent
boys, 59
Puberty rite, 78
Punishment, 129, 151

Reaction formation, 126
Reality therapy, 256
Religion, 88, 171,
173–76, 234
Retardation, 137–38, 164–65,
214–17, 219
pseudo–, 214–16
Rite of passage, 44, 77–83

Sadism, 180–82, 235
Scandinavia
Momism in, 229–31
suicide study in, 228–31

Subject Index

Schizophrenia, 187, 226–28
Self–actualization
American women
and, 44–45
divorce and, 33
Momistic victims
and, 171–72
mothers' drive toward, 40
Self-fulfilling prophecy, 218
Self-worth
basis of, 221, 252
of Momistic children, 5,
233, 252
rejection of, 222
Sex biases
careers and, 275–76
cultural images and, 283
education and, 275–76
encouraging Momism,
276, 277–78
theology and, 88
Sex roles.
See also
Gender identity;
Gender roles
differential learning
process, 105–6
femininity, 114–22
inborn vs. learned, 107–8
learning of, 100, 103–14
masculinity and femi-
ninity, 87–114
models, 66
modifications of tradi-
tional, 86
rite of passage and, 77–78
theology and, 88
Sexual deviation, 169, 183–88,
210, 213
Siblings, 62, 154–55, 157
Silent majority, 231–37

case study of Kenneth,
234
Sirhan Sirhan, 183
Sissy, 139, 232
Social roles, 90–91
Social worker or caseworker,
189, 190, 214, 219, 233,
273
Societal pathologies, 172, 179–
80
Sociopath, 208. See also
Psychopath
Sports
aggression and, 261
Momism-curbing, 260–61
Sterilization, 137
Suicide
boys' childhood charac-
teristics, 187
case study, 143–44
as consequence of
Momism, 170, 228–31
male/female rate, 39–40
in Scandinavia, 228–31
in the U.S., 231
Superego, 32, 142, 146
Surgeon General of the Army
and Navy, 206
Symbiosis, mother-son, 227

Teenage subculture, 81–82
Teachers, 219, 275
Therapy, 134, 140, 207, 219,
228, 252–57
Transference, 135
Transsexuality
childhood characteristics,
186–88
effects of parents on, 59–
60
Trobriand Islanders, 56–57

317

Truancy, 143, 211–12
True Believer
  armed forces and, 176–78
  Christianity and, 173–75
  case of Vasseur, 180–82
  Communism and, 175, 176
  as consequence of
    Momism, 153, 169–83,
    232
  Nazism and, 175, 181–82
  occult and, 175
  racism and, 175
  totalitarian movements
    and, 175–76

Unisex, 89, 96
U.S. Office of Child
  Development, 288

Vasseur, the case of, 180–82
Vicarious living, 136, 152–53

Woman's liberation
  anti-liberation women,
    48–49
  backlash against, 95–96
  blue-collar mothers and,
    286
  child-care projects and,
    94–95
  differential male/female
    support, 48
  femininity and, 119
  half-way emancipated
    women, 43, 44–53, 87
  middle-class mothers and,
    45–46, 51
  Momism and, 46–53
  motherhood and, 28–30,
    39
  sex-role changes and, 86,
    102